Word Made Skin

KARMEN MACKENDRICK

Word Made Skin
Figuring Language at the Surface of Flesh

Fordham University Press
New York | 2004

Library of Congress Cataloging-in-Publication Data

MacKendrick, Karmen, 1962–
    Word made skin: figuring language at the surface of flesh/Karmen MacKendrick.
        p. cm.
    Includes bibliographical references and index.
    ISBN 0-8232-2406-6 (hardcover) — ISBN 0-8232-2407-4 (pbk.)
    1. Body, human (Philosophy) 2. Language and languages—Philosophy. I. Title.
B105.B64M33 2004
128'.6—dc22

                                                                2004018985

Printed in the United States of America
07 06 05 04   5 4 3 2 1
First edition

Contents

Acknowledgments

As always, the flaws in this book are my own doing, while what may be good here has come to me with help. Several people have provided invaluable aid and ideas. Richard Armstrong, ages ago, gave me suggestions for sources on scars. Matty Jankowski and Lisa Bell-Jankowski at the New York Body Archive were exceptionally helpful in gathering sources, images, and ideas for the Sacred Heart chapter. My research session at the archive was my first meeting with them, and I remain impressed by the amount of work they were willing to put into it as well as by the resources they've gathered. James DiGiovanna reminded me of critical passages in Nietzsche that were especially useful in the chapter on John, where discussion with Bruce Milem was also invaluable as a source of both references and ideas. Marcos Bisticas-Cocoves is a one-man research library, especially for questions of language, and has been infinitely patient with my inquiries. Carol Siegel was particularly helpful for her thoughts on the fold, but also for her enthusiasm about the project in general. In that regard I owe as well a special debt of gratitude to Virginia Burrus and Jennifer Glancy, whose faith in my work is so profound as to be contagious when I most need it. Both have also been endlessly helpful with their suggestions for further resources.

I have always been fortunate in my editors, and never more so than in Helen Tartar, whose combination of intelligence, patience, and tact is genuinely remarkable. The other participants in the editorial process, my outside readers Crispin Sartwell and Anne O'Byrne, provided very valuable feedback, and my thanks are owed to them as well.

I have had the opportunity to present many parts of this work to various groups. The Research and Development Committee at Le Moyne College funded a course reduction for me so that I could devote a bit more work to the chapter on touch for its initial presentation at the Uncommon Senses conference at Concordia University. The invitation to participate in New York University's conference Taking Off the Shroud: 200 Years of Gender in the Body of Jesus provided me a fabulous setting for developing the Sacred Heart chapter. The conference Contemporary Continental Philosophy of Religion at St. Martin's College in Lancaster, U.K., not only gave me a chance to present the work on John's gospel but also to publish a shorter version of chapter I in a collection gathered from among the papers given there (*Explorations in Contemporary Continental Philosophy of Religion*, ed. Deane-Peter Baker and Patrick Maxwell [Amsterdam: Rodopi, 2003]). Mario Saenz, in his capacity as director of Le Moyne's Honors program, gave me a chance to present "Ash Wednesday" to a startlingly interested crowd.

Finally, I am grateful to Alan Griffin for his stubborn supportiveness, moral and otherwise.

Introduction

Stretch your legs, go ahead and put your feet on a cushion, on two
cushions, on the arms of the sofa, on the wings of the chair, on the coffee
table, on the desk, on the piano, on the globe. Take your shoes off first. If
you want to, put your feet up; if not, put them back. Now don't stand
there, with your shoes in one hand and the book in the other.

—Italo Calvino, *If on a Winter's Night a Traveler*

Today, as persistently for many decades, two themes prominently recurrent in both Continental and analytic philosophy—indeed in theory
throughout the humanities—are body (often "the" body) and language. Each
is strange enough on its own. I have written before of bodies and of words,
and these in conjunction with pleasures and desires, and limits kept and broken. But I have found myself increasingly preoccupied, as well, with how
(indeed whether) these two might be written together. What senses might we
possibly make of them; what are their modes of repulsion and resistance, of
mutuality and attraction? Such an undertaking strikes me as particularly
intriguing since, in my experience, language and body never quite *come*
together; or, where it seems as if they might, most certainly they do not stay.

My books, I often suspect (knowing that they are not properly philosophical and indeed tend to be difficult to discipline) are in fact letters in

I

the absence of lovers—written, that is, not during spells of isolation but in the knowledge of their unspecificity of address. "Reading is the loneliest thing we do," remarked a listener at a conference where I read a version of Chapter 3, on touch. "Except writing," I replied, and the laughter in the room was, it seemed to me, more recognition than derision. We are, Jean-Luc Nancy says, "abandoned to writing."[1] Words reach out. Hands pick up books; eyes or fingertips scan text. Where, if at all, do words and bodies touch?

I have come increasingly to suspect, as well, that I say the same thing whenever I write. What I say when I write has to do with pleasures, though perhaps that is not quite the right word; it has to do with desires, though that term is almost too mild. It has to do with intensities and with limits. It has to do with bodies and with words. One of these days, I sometimes think, I may perhaps figure out what it is I've been trying to say, or to whom.

Until then, I go on writing. In all that follows, I have tried to sort out my singular obsession in terms of word and flesh. After a few remarks on methods and on my sources, I shall hint at a discussion of the mutual con-stitutiveness of self, desire, and limit. "Hint," rather than properly discuss, because in fact this discussion is one that unfolds throughout the course of the book, returning explicitly in the conclusion. In the chapters between I shall set forth a set of stories and of figures of speech that trace the dual paths of bodies and words: the story of the risen body in the fourth gospel of the New Testament and the figure of touch; T. S. Eliot's poem "Ash Wednesday" and the figure of the fold; visions and images of the Sacred Heart and the figure of the cut. The possibility of thinking together body and language (I wish that I had some clearer way to state this connection, but I have never found one) is framed for me by my ongo-ing interest in questions of desire and limit, questions that outline the paths to be followed here.

This tracing begins for me in the situatedness of my own language. Apparently students today are taught, somewhere in their secondary edu-cation, to eliminate the first person singular from all of their writing. Mine are forever asking timidly if they may, in fact, refer to themselves, saying "I." (As the alternative is almost always an agonizingly convoluted use of the passive voice, I tend to say "Yes," and sometimes even "Please.") This refusal of the "I" seems to be the one element that student minds retain in a stylistic ideal that is for the most part very unsuccessfully impressed upon them, an ideal of impersonal clarity and objectivity. I would never say that clarity is not a virtue, though it is one too little regarded in my own disciplines. But I would argue with the notion that clarity has a singular form, a form as "objective" as possible, a form that refuses to draw the slightest attention to itself. We as readers are supposed to see *clear* through such language to a meaning devoid of sensuousness, touched by an author without the slightest observable characteristic.

This is not what I want when I write.

I want my prose to reach toward—as Paul Celan said of his poetry, toward "an approachable you, perhaps."[2] Celan says of poetry, as I say of writing, that it is lonely.[3] The approach is endless; the possibility of touch is there, but not, I shall argue, the possibility of grasping.

I am fully wary and entirely skeptical of returning to some illusion of authorial and authoritative presence in a text defined only by my own intentions. (Moreover, I have been delighted more than once by readers who make of my work far more intelligent ideas than I could possibly have put there.) But I want my readers' minds to move with the words I make, and I want, sometimes at least, to bring pleasure in the reading. I want to *arouse* thought in the readers' diverse and to me unspecific selves just as much as I want to create certain more specifiable psychocorporeal movements of response by the letters I write to those I desire. I, defiantly and singularly first person even as I disappear into my text, nonetheless stay with that text. Lonely it may be, but we reach toward a set of approachable *yous*. The use of "I" is to mark a point in the movement of communication, one point in the communicative space, a point itself set into motion by the communicative act. I want it to matter that it is *this* voice; I want these words to sound in my voice. To those who know me, of course, that voice will come more richly laden with associations, but where the voice is all I have—and especially where the voice at the distance of text is all I have—I want it still to provoke response; I cannot imagine that "what" I say is really distinct from the ways that I have to say it. The stern warnings of my students' earlier teachers suggest that mine is not a universal desire, but I find it improbable that it should be mine alone.

Of course, in order to write this way I imagine the words in my own voice. It is always surprising to hear one's own words in other's voices;

sometimes one has a powerful urge to correct the rhythms and stresses of the words, to say, with Eliot's Prufrock, "That is not what I meant, at all." Language's physicality can impose itself, like meaning, only to a limited extent; it touches the reader or listener, but it does not take hold, it does not force. The ideal reader moves with the words she draws forth. To communicate in this way is not for me, as writer, to shine light upon a meaning wholly distinct from myself, but to make of the space between myself and others something mobile, seductive, crossable (though it will never stay crossed; spaces shift, too). Communication draws us and sets us outside ourselves, but this drawing cannot occur unless we begin as, and return to, those selves—changed by the acts and passions of crossing. And so to speak of language and body is also to speak of ourselves, with the strong suspicion that we are not there where we had expected to find us. This is the final thing that I have tried to do here—to show how thinking desire and limit in the relation of body and language must affect how we think, and think of, our own selves.

Serious Superficiality

Women are considered deep—why? Because one can never discover any bottom to them. Women are not even shallow.

—Friedrich Nietzsche, *The Gay Science*

My questions about body and language, and about the possible ways to approach and write about those questions, are caught up, it seems to me, in the very nature of the philosophical pursuit—perhaps even in our very understanding of philosophy. In some ways, I think, they are superficial questions in a discipline that has long been in love with depth. The figures with which I work here—the touch, the fold, and the cut—are all figures of surfaces.

Philosophy, etymologically the love of wisdom, is traditionally conceived as the *search for* the wisdom that one loves. Just what either search or love entails here, to be sure, has remained vague. Luce Irigaray wonders what might happen "if the meaning of the word *philosophy* remained plural: the love of wisdom and the wisdom of love. This possible interpretation would imply that philosophy joins together, more than it has done in the West, the body, the heart, and the mind."[4] Generally, however, wisdom has been considered to have *something* to do with Truth, perhaps to be a matter of knowing Truth when one encounters it. And Truth, classically, has to do with essentials, with the essence of matters and not with the accidental or frivolous.

In this classical conception philosophy has, as Gilles Deleuze suggests, a single question: "What is?" asked of various subjects, in regard to various objects, but always seeking, Socratically, essence over example.[5] As Plato presents him to us, Socrates does not want to know *Which man is pious?* but *What is piety itself?*,[6] he is less concerned with *Which city-state is just?* than with the very nature of justice itself;[7] he does not seem to care that Alcibiades loves him but is deeply concerned with getting at the essence of love itself.[8] For Plato, if not so clearly for Socrates, essential nature entails participation in an eternally true Form, an abstraction somehow more real than any of its material instantiations.

Plato's pupil Aristotle moves from the ambiguities of form to the formative principle of essence, sorting out "the primary constituents of things" and determining generalities: "Whatever has generality of being would serve best as a principle, so that the first and most general kinds would be principles."[9] Aristotelian "essence," later understood as the *quiddity* or "whatness" of things, is only a bit more clear than Platonic "form." But the concerns remain universal—that is, philosophy remains concerned with universals—as Western philosophy grows and branches from its dual Platonic and Aristotelian root systems. What is the essence, what is the form; what is the genus, the most general category: *What is?*

For centuries, it seems, these fascinating if mythical eternal universals underlay philosophy's question, *What is?* (From Heraclitus onward there are exceptions, of course, various turns away from the straight path to truth—negative theology and assorted postmodernisms being conspicuous among them, loving the very absence of answers.) But by the nineteenth century, after systematicity's great last gasp in Kantian critique, the work of Friedrich Nietzsche has decisively changed the questions on us. From "What is?," the question that searches for essence, we move to asking "Which one?" The faith in universal and eternal truth is shaken here. But more: even our faith in singularity is shaken. We no longer find *one* essence behind multiple instantiations. Multiplicity sneaks back into philosophical prominence, and with it *fragmentation,* as Nietzsche and philosophers after him affirm broken-ness rather than a seamless oneness.

In his work on Nietzsche, Deleuze sees the question *Which one?* as return-ing always to the "same" answer, the will to power. So it might seem that we are back to unity and universals after all. But Deleuze adds, "[Nietzsche's] Dionysus is the god of transformations, the unity of multiplicity, the unity that affirms multiplicity and is affirmed of it.... This is why Dionysus keeps tantalizingly quiet: to gain time to hide himself, to take another form and to change forces."[10] Generally, philosophers emphasize the *unitive* half of this mutual affirmation. After all, as Plotinus pointed out in the third century, "Not a one, a thing is not"—or, in a less delightful if somewhat more clear translation, "It is by virtue of unity that beings are beings."[11] But taking transformation seriously, we see that the question is one of perspec-tive, and so it isn't *one* question at all. Perspectives have a way of multiply-ing, after all. *Which one?* is a question about the asker (Which one asks?), but also about the one to whom the question is asked (Which one is called upon to answer?), a question about a series of questions (Which one of these is asked?). And it is a question about *which one* is meant from among the indef-initely multipliable relations of wills and forces within, between, across the question, the questioner, the one called upon to speak. *Which one?* is a singu-lar question: it opens immediately onto plurality.

With this open question we are not back to pointing out, to the osten-sive definitions that Socrates successfully surpassed. Contrary to what might be our initial impulse, we do not point and say, "this one"; *this* changes, too, and "one" becomes considerably complicated. We must cross the Socratic search with the pre-Socratic, Hericlitean emphasis on change. And with multiplicity and fragmentation, with perspectivalism and its tendency to shift, we also move from our faith in the static eternal *Being* of the Forms to a focus on *becoming* and change. Philosophy might well begin to seem hope-less at this point. What good is it to love wisdom if Truth is never found, if by the time we think we've found it the truth is somewhere else, or is many other places as well as that in which we seek it? Part of the answer must be that the love, and the pleasure attendant upon it, attach now to the search itself; the process becomes its own object. The pleasurable pursuit of phi-losophy becomes a pleasure *in* pursuit, a desire always just beyond the limit of the given.

Bodies and words move, together and apart. This movement of change and becoming leaves some trace of its changing, some scar of its path. Even this is not simple; we don't find a single line to trace in any explanation, any idea, any truth. The Nietzschean emphasis on genealogy tells us that any concept or idea or truth can be traced along multiple lines of descent, of cultural and historical meaning. "Truth" becomes not one essence but an indefinitely multipliable splitting and rejoining. (Nietzsche's genealogy is, of course, an ancestor to Foucault's archaeology.) Our search for wisdom, our philosophy, it seems, becomes the record of this fragmentation. What, if anything, still holds its questions together? Or is it only that they are all the same question, the same question denying any sameness at all, *Which one?*

These are my suspicions: that the question "What is" is a *prehensile* question, a question seeking to *grasp*. It is a comprehensive question; it covers every case of its given term. It is a question of comprehension: it seeks to grasp the meaning of its given term. It is a question that would hold knowledge secure; it *understands* and it *overcomes*;[12] it takes hold and it masters. "Which one?" does not. It *touches*—tracing out an often-broken path across a surface. It *folds*—back upon itself to multiply the questions, unfolding new questions with every seeming answer. It *cuts*—it intersects, it fragments, it opens possibilities. It does not grasp.

And I suspect that the trace of joint and fragmentation itself still bears exploration, that it joins some of the most important of philosophy's scattered themes—brings body together with language without ever fusing or uniting the two. More precisely, I suspect that we may thematize that which is both fragmentation and joining, schism and suture. And that we may best do so in a philosophy of touches and folds and scars, surfaces marked without depths revealed; a philosophy of the touch that does not grasp, the fold that does not close up, the cut that reveals the complexities of surface, cutting across questioner, listener, question; a philosophy of surfaces and multiplicities, of openings, of the constitutive incision.

Surfaces have gotten a bad name, I think, as "superficial" comes to mean hasty and disregardable, lacking an awareness of nuance and complexity. The superficial is not without its eminent philosophical support: "Since everything lies open to view," declares Ludwig Wittgenstein, "there is nothing to explain. For what is hidden, for example, is of no interest to us."[13] Yet he too condemns the superficial in its more common sense: "Some philosophers (or whatever you like to call them) suffer from what may be called 'loss of problems.' Then everything seems quite simple to them, no deep problems seem to exist any more, the world becomes broad and flat and loses all depth, and what they write becomes immeasurably shallow and trivial."[14] This triviality suggests that such philosophers are overlooking the sheer complexity of surface: What is on the surface may still come as a surprise to us. Thus Kandinsky writes of Rembrandt: "I felt that his pictures 'last a long time,' and explained it to myself that I had first to exhaust *one* part continuously and then the *other*."[15] Later he uses different techniques to achieve his own surface profundity: "I wished to bury in each part [of my paintings] an 'infinite' number of initially hidden colors. They had to remain completely *hidden* at first ... and only as time went on to show themselves, at first unclearly and tentatively, to the studiously attentive viewer, then resound more and more."[16] Just as our hands, when we encounter a desirable object, take their time, become extraordinarily alert and attuned to the extent and permutation of surface, so, too, our thought, when we think of surface, can take its time, moving over the same territory to discover new characteristics, touch differently. We cannot dwell *in* surface as if it were the Heideggerian depths of Being, but it is nonetheless worth dwelling *upon*, worth lingering over.

In the contemplation of surfaces, the series of seams and folds between language and body has long both drawn and frustrated my own thought (in which frustration I doubt I am anywhere near to being alone). "The body is a text," we all hear, so often that some of us have begun to doubt it; "the text is a body," we rarely hear, unless we read Barthes (who in any event regards this relation, though favorably, as perverted).[17] Words call to the flesh, but the flesh, as Maurice Merleau-Ponty so elegantly points out, calls at least for speaking as well, for speaking words as much as for contact of skin with skin: "if my words have a meaning, it is not *because* they present the systematic organization the linguist will disclose; it is because that organization, like the look, refers back to itself: the operative Word is the obscure region whence comes the instituted light, as the muted reflection of the body upon itself is what we call natural light."[18] Merleau-Ponty's language here evokes the ungrasped surface, the surface we touch "when the silent vision falls into speech, and when the speech in turn, opening up a field of the namable and the sayable, inscribes itself in that field, in its place, according to its truth."[19]

Yet on the whole the two, the flesh and the word, have remained disjoint explorations. Out of phenomenology develops a respect for the body, a nonreductive recognition of its senses and capabilities. Out of structuralism, as from all the literary traditions, comes a love of language, on the centrality of which the otherwise hostile sects of Western philosophy can still agree. The need to cut across the division between language and body, though—to see where one touches the limit of the other, to see them mutually enfolded—is rarely gratified. Rarely is not never, of course. Nietzsche argues throughout his work for the corporeality of language and thought alike. More explicitly combining phenomenological and structural traditions, the later work of Merleau-Ponty (particularly in *The Visible and the Invisible*) not only reconsiders vision in a world that is also deeply tactile and kinetic, but considers language in its sensuous richness.

It is here that we become less Wittgensteinian. Wittgenstein writes, "Whenever I say: here we are at the limits of language, that sounds as if some kind of self-denial were necessary; but on the contrary, we have reached complete satisfaction, since there are *no* questions left over." [20] On the contrary, dealing with surfaces we never do find the complete satisfaction of in-depth exploration; the surface is inexhaustible, the cuts and folds infinitely multipliable; there is always one more limit toward which word and flesh reach, at which they approach one another. There are infinite questions left over; to leave them unasked is to deny the pleasure inherent in seeking— the peculiar pleasure/pain of desire, where the questions of body and language may most readily, perhaps most interestingly, be asked.

Source Material: Theories of Desire

We weren't looking for origins, even lost or deleted ones, but setting out to catch things where they were at work, in the middle: breaking things open, breaking words open.

—Gilles Deleuze, "Letter to Serge Daney"

As I've suggested, this crossing between word and flesh is central not only in Merleau-Ponty's late work, where the structural begins to cut across the phenomenological, but also in Nietzschean theory, where language is deeply physical—where poetic rhythm is meant to ensnare the attention of the gods and the bodies of human listeners alike, books (and gods too) are valued only if they can dance, thought is known by its tempos and sinuosities[21]—and bodies, as Michel Foucault will later tell us, are (culturally) inscribed.

This last claim is now so commonplace that its force may be lost to our hearing. Foucault, like Deleuze, is an important and usually obvious source of the questions I undertake here. In his earlier works he is, among other possible designations, clearly a philosopher of discourse. (One fact not always noticed about Foucault is that before his fame as a philosopher of cultural inscription he is a meticulous archaeologist of description, of taxonomy and representation across disciplines.[22]) His concerns are historical—his archaeological method echoing and elaborating the complications of Nietzschean genealogy—but also epistemological and conspicuously linguistic. To be sure, discourse and language are not precisely identical:

> If I spoke of discourse, it was not to show that the mechanisms or processes of the language [*langue*] were entirely preserved in it; but rather to reveal, in the density of verbal performances, the diversity of the possible levels of analysis; to show that in addition to methods of linguistic structuration (or interpretation), one could draw up a specific description of statements, of their formation, and of the regularities proper to discourse.[23]

Though not the whole of discourse, language, as this statement reveals, is central; language plays its part, too, in power.

Analyzing histories of institutions of power, Foucault concerns himself with ways of speaking and modes of silencing: "In appearance, speech may well be of little account, but the prohibitions surrounding it soon reveal its links with desire and power. . . . Speech is not merely the medium which manifests—or dissembles—desire; it is also the object of desire."[24] Words do not merely express desire into the world, as if from the interior of an individual, but draw desire to themselves. In the exploration of desire and power, body and language are once again brought together: "Such discourse is both the silent language by which the mind speaks to itself in the truth proper to it, and the visible articulation in the movements of the body."[25] In fact, he makes this connection as early as *The Order of Things*, in whose foreword he writes, "What I wished to do was to present, side by side, a definite number of elements: the knowledge of living beings, the knowledge of the laws of language, and the knowledge of economic facts."[26] Continuing to draw language to body, by 1979 he can declare, "It is always the body which is at issue,"[27] and then turn to three volumes on the body in its erotic disciplines and pleasures, to innumerable interviews on politics, ethics, or cultural affairs—a turn always returning to the physical.

Yet Foucault, under Nietzsche's influence (as is Deleuze, to be sure, and we know too that Deleuze and Foucault are mutually influential), does not in the course of his work *exchange* the word for the body, discourse for physicality. The move from language to body is not an abandonment but an expansion of the former. Rather, his language, too, always reminds us of the body: it does so even early on; where in his interpretations of other thinkers he explores languages of sexuality, or of death and its avoidance;[28] his bodies are, even in silence, discursive.

For Foucault, discourse is an *event*, and we trace its surface:[29] Touching, folding, and cutting form the modes of surface contact. Across these senses, with these modes, we can mark the scar that makes the skin, the path traced by the sense of words. Two sets of themes come together here: a philosophy of surfaces and thus of a search for wisdom that does not seek to grasp; and a thinking of body and language as these intersect, mark, fold into one another. The former provides the (moving, impermanent, choreographic) structure for the latter.

In this marking, though Foucault remains a persistent influence, my methods will be multiple. Certainly Foucault is there, but so too is Deleuze, not merely as a Nietzschean but in a mode we might call the Deleuzean-Leibnizian, taking Deleuze's words on Leibniz for the strong reading that they are: "There are two poles, one toward which all principles are folding themselves together, the other toward which they are all unfolding, in the opposite way, in distinguishing their zones."[30] Other persistent influences cluster around the obsessive themes I've raised already. As I have indicated, this work manifests my continued interest in desire and its relation to limit. Here, specifically, I am concerned with desire as a question of those figures of speech. That is, I am concerned with desire as a question of reach and contact, overlap and intersection, not of grasp—desire as a question of distance and limit, with which it is always implicated.

In exploring this implication, we should be careful not to claim a causal relationship in either direction. Nor is the exploration I present here particularly complete; certainly I won't pretend to a survey of all such theories of desire. A brief overview, though, of a few of the most relevant among those whose theorists clearly have some interest in word and flesh may be of use, and may, as well, help to focus the argument of the present work: that word and flesh are with one another in a curious liminal relation of contact, implication, and incision, each in its own odd way a relation of desire and drawing, seduction and delight. Flesh is drawn to language, and words in return to flesh.

On the Limits of Desire

> There is always some limit which the individual accepts. He identifies this limit with himself. Horror seizes him at the thought that this limit may cease to be. But we are wrong to take this limit and the individual's acceptance of it seriously. The limit is only there to be overreached. Fear and horror are not the real and final reaction; on the contrary, they are a temptation to overstep the bounds.
>
> —Georges Bataille, *Erotism*

We ought properly to start with Plato—with whom, Deleuze and Guattari argue, theories of desire already began to go wrong: "To a certain degree, the traditional logic of desire is all wrong from the very outset: from the very first step that the Platonic logic of desire forces us to take, making us choose between *production* and *acquisition*. From the moment that we place desire on the side of acquisition, we make desire an idealistic ... conception, which causes us to look upon it primarily as a lack."[31] In fact, they argue that even theories such as Kant's, which allow desire some kind of productivity, go on to restrict that productivity to the realm of fantasy: "In point of fact, if desire is the lack of the real object, its very nature as a real entity depends upon an 'essence of lack that produces the fantasized object.'"[32] They elaborate: "In a word, when the theoretician reduces desiring-production to a production of fantasy, he is content to exploit to the fullest the idealist principle that defines desire as a lack, rather than a process of production."[33]

It is risky to attribute *a* theory of desire to Plato, who articulates so many in such varying voices (indeed, desire seems even for him rather more a matter of "Which one?" than of "What is?"). But at least two of the speakers in the *Symposium*,[34] arguably the two most vivid and memorable speakers, give accounts of desire (here in the form of love) as a kind of lack. Aristophanes sets forth a vivid myth of three primary types of humans—male/male, female/female, and female/male—whose original fused bodies are sliced in half by envious gods. Hence humans as we are now are universally incomplete. Each seeks her or his missing other half, seeks, in that other, self-completion. Thus, says Aristophanes, the reluctance and pain of lovers upon parting: in corporeal contact they come closest to the fusion they lost before becoming themselves.[35] What we seek in the other is the other part of ourselves: it is the self that is lacking. But, crucially, the self completed would be another being entirely: made complete, one is not oneself at all. Human flesh is constituted as lacking, and I would suggest that it lacks, is drawn by and into, not only other bodies, but dialogue—into language, too.

In the same dialogue, Socrates, who attributes his account of love to the goddess or prophetess Diotima, is more specific in his—or is it her?—designation of desire as lack. Speaking first in his own voice, Socrates engages Agathon in dialogue:

> And now ... bearing in mind what Love is the love of, tell me this. Does he long for what he is in love with, or not?
>
> Of course he longs for it.
>
> And does he long for whatever it is he longs for, and is he in love with it, when he's got it, or when he hasn't?
>
> When he hasn't got it, probably.
>
> Then isn't it probable ... or rather isn't it certain that everything longs for what it lacks, and that nothing longs for what it doesn't lack?[36]

Clearly, insofar as love is a form of desire, we find here the theory of desire as lack that Deleuze and Guattari will so vigorously bemoan. When Diotima begins to speak, however, she complicates this image of love as lack. Love, she says, is between beautiful and ugly, between good and bad, not precisely conceivable as either having *or* lacking.[37] Born out of poverty and plenty, Love is "never altogether in or out of need."[38] The aim of love's desire is not simple possession of the desirable object—rather, she says, "To love is to bring forth upon the beautiful, both in body and in soul,"[39] an early hint of our considerations here, as "begetting upon the soul" is the creation of thought, thought manifest in words. She goes on to explain the ground of this desire: "And why all this longing for propagation? Because this is the one deathless and eternal element in our mortality."[40] Our desire for otherness, for what must be other because we can only wish for what we neither are nor have, is at the same time our desire for ourselves—just as it was for Aristophanes, despite the divergence of the myths. More precisely, we wish to make our own what we are not, but also to make ourselves where we are not, to displace ourselves into the future. Such desire climbs from the base level of physicality to the highest abstraction, from the single beautiful body to the form of Beauty itself.[41] Desire is lack, but lack is a potent force in its own right.

Desire, here, moves beyond the sensuous corporeality it nonetheless requires.[42] This quality of desire as going beyond, even in lack, retains its importance for millennia, reappearing most vividly and altering, perhaps, most interestingly in the nineteenth century with Hegel. Word and the corporeal world would seem to be opposed here—Hegel writes, "Language is the disappearance of the sensuous world in its immediate presence, the suppression of this world."[43] But this relation of disappearance and suppression is linked precisely to desire. Hegel's theory of desire—especially as read through Kojève, who shifts Hegel's emphasis onto the question of human desire—is also a theory of disappearance: more precisely, of annihilation or negation. And our very selves are made in this disappearance of the immediate world, at least if, as Kojève has it, "Man becomes conscious of himself at the moment when—for the 'first' time—he says 'I.' To understand man by understanding his 'origin' is, therefore, to understand the origin of the I revealed [indeed, I would add, constituted] by speech."[44] To make myself, to reveal constitutively my own selfhood, is at the same time to invoke the disappearance of the world, there where I say constitutively, as if divinely, *I am.* I am this which is not the (rest of the) world. This is the wisdom of desire, close, I suspect, to what Irigaray (also making the connection to divinity) calls the wisdom of love: "Philosophy and theology will find in this wisdom of love a possible reconciliation. The divine there assumes an important place as the becoming of the human itself which, through love, transubstantiates body and spirit. And, with them, the spaces where they dwell, that they build."[45]

And this which is not the world, this negation of the world, is desire too: "It is in and by—or better still, as—'his' Desire that man is formed and is revealed—to himself and to others—as an I, as the I that is essentially different from, and radically opposed to, the non-I. The (human) I is the I of a Desire or of Desire."[46]

The simplest (admittedly oversimple) instance of desire as annihilation or negation is that of hunger for food. If I desire an apple or, more realistically, a box of Godiva chocolates, I certainly do not wish simply to admire the object from a distance, nor even to know it in the manner that Hegel calls "contemplation." That is, I don't simply want to know *about* it, not even all about it. I want to eat it, to consume it, to make it no longer different from me—not by becoming it, but by enlarging (sometimes all too literally) myself. More generally, desire, because it implies what is not present just as clearly as it did for Socrates (I cannot want food when I am satiated), negates. It goes beyond the world which is given, and does so by means of action. Human desire, however, is far more complex. Kojève argues that it is more symbolic—human beings, alone, can desire "a non-natural object, … something that goes beyond the given reality."[47] Ultimately, the only candidate for such an honor is desire itself, desire being precisely that which goes beyond the given reality. My desire, as Lacan will later have it, is the desire of the other. Flesh and word, as I shall try to indicate, have for one another this kind of seductive otherness; the desire of and for the other is at the same time, in the Platonic (and, as we shall see, Freudian) manner, a desire for an impossible self.

For Hegel, selfhood emerges in the struggle by which I seek the desire of the other while withholding my own—impossibly, of course, since my seeking manifests desire already. Only when we acknowledge our mutual lack of self-sufficiency, acknowledge that we desire mutually the very desire that only another can give us, can we become selves, can each of us, in embodied and intelligible speech, say "I."

For Hegel, then, desire demands limit, *because* it exists as the urge to exceed limit. Paradoxically, the desirous self wants to encompass within its limits the desire of another—which could not remain other within these limits.[48] Ultimately, desire plays off the distinction between finitude and infinity, between the delimited and the unlimited, as the desire of finite beings to go beyond limits (the very limits that constitute them, of which point we, with Bataille, shall soon make even more).

Without limitation, there would be no desire, only a being in the state of perfect satisfaction—"*wanting* nothing, *desiring* nothing . . . *satisfied* by what he is."[49] This is a godlike state, perhaps, but for a God wholly divergent from the insatiable deity of desire we shall read, in the next chapter, through the gospel attributed to John.[50]

The possibility of perfect satisfaction is a peculiar one and seems to neglect the renewability of desire. (As a colleague of mine memorably pointed out, if you were ever perfectly satisfied by something, you'd never want it again.) In fact, for most of us, at least, there is something peculiarly dissatisfying in the very notion of a satiation so complete that desire would be forever annihilated by it. This renewable, indeed often self-restoring quality of desire is central to what is perhaps the most familiar and arguably the most influential Western theory of desire, that of Freud, for whom desire primordially arises in flesh but repeats itself, in what he believes to be the way of all memory, as words.

Here, too, self comes about in difference and in desire, though for Freud these moments are more closely linked, with the ego emerging into the infantile consciousness at just the moment when an unsatisfied impulse lingers. When, for instance, the infant's caregiver does not appear with nourishment as the infant hungers, the infant senses a world beyond its control—hence beyond its self, the boundaries of its body. This powerless otherness, the recognition of not-me, of that which is absent from me, cuts the shape of me out of the fabric of the world: the I is made as the realization of boundaries, the limits of my skin and of my power.

If, then, desire seeks satisfaction, the ultimate aim of desire must be to return to the plenary gratification prior to the self—and so the *self's* desire must always be unsatisfied, satisfaction being simultaneous with loss of self. Besides, stimuli from within the self, such as the contractions of the stomach, and from without, such as the aroma of cinnamon rolls, constantly rearouse even gratified desires. Desire here is linked to lack in two distinct, though not unrelated, ways: it comes about first as the subject is born from the realization of its own lack (the lack of completeness and of the ability to satisfy itself), its finitude. And it seeks what the desiring subject does not have.

This rather Platonic point may not yet be clear, and becomes so, if at all, only in Freud's distinction between the aim and object of desire. The *aim* of desire is the cessation of some unpleasant sensation of tension. But the *object* of desire, the source somehow of that release, must be what the subject lacks, whether that object is ingestible, insertable, penetrable, or otherwise gratifying. So desire—always ultimately and impossibly for the lack of subjectivity, for the "pure" flesh and language from which the subject emerges—directs itself for its partial, possible satisfactions at what the subject lacks.

It would appear that, though both Freud and Hegel theorize desire as lack, they see its annihilating impulse differently: for Hegel, it is directed at the object (taken into the enlargement of the self); for Freud, at the subject (annihilated in the unitive gratification at the heart of all life-drives). The disparity in that which is to be annihilated may, however, be only apparent. Hegel's annihilating desire, if we follow either Bataille's suspicions or the vaguely Neoplatonic sense of unity that Hegel himself so often echoes, will ultimately undo the self. If indeed "The 'I' is the I of desire" and if desire annihilates, then the I is the I of annihilation; if, as Lacan will suspect, the genitive is reversible, then the self is likewise annihilated. That is, I desire Desire, and desire in whatever case is annihilating: I desire annihilation. At a minimum, the I is transformed, its present state annihilated, by its own enlargement.

For Freud, we might expect preservation of self in the elimination of desire; preservation of equanimity and serenity at least, and a moment's peace for the poor, multiply besieged ego that bears this sense of selfhood.[51] But, as Freud realizes, in a suspicion that must have alarmed him, the susceptibility of desire to arousal from both outward and inner stimuli means that there is only one option for perfect peace, and that is death. If Eros, as he claims, aims toward unity but also toward "discharge," desire's own elimination, it is far more in sync with Thanatos, the impulse toward death, than we like to believe. And in this strange coinciding, the death drive seeks an ante-natal, or at any rate ante-ego, state. That is, in this urge no longer to desire, desire seeks return to the "oceanic,"[52] to the boundlessness of infancy, prior to any dissatisfaction—or self. Such is, in fact, Rilke's elegiac conception of the strangeness of death: "Seltsam, die Wünsche nicht weiterzuwünschen"[53]—how strange to desire desires no longer; how strange not to be dissatisfied, how strange not to be alive.

Thus, though we might crudely say that for Hegel desire seeks to assimilate and for Freud it seeks to eliminate, in both cases it pushes destructively against the boundaries of the finite self that is the condition of its possibility: what is assimilated is otherness, such that there is same; what is eliminated is otherness, such that there is same. But self requires otherness, and where perfect sameness is, there self is not. While otherness is most conspicuous in the separation of the same type—other bodies, other minds—I suspect, too, that body and language are other to one another, drawing desire, setting limits, and never coinciding.

Hegel's version of desire seems to define desire as lack more clearly than Freud's does. But Freud, too, recognizing the *object* of desire, sees that object as external; desire's discharge demands what the desiring subject lacks, demands an other. That desire, being about limits, must also be about otherness is central to the largely Freudian but more overtly linguistic and structural psychoanalysis of Lacan.

Lacan lacks Freud's emphasis on the somatic. Indeed, as he in some regards replaces it with an emphasis on language, he might appear to be the other half of a psychoanalytic pair, with the desire between body and language demanding a synthesis of the two. But in fact neither sorts matters out quite so neatly.

For Lacan as for Freud, desire arises in an originary experience that is at once lack and separation, absence and the seed of identity. The infant has no desires as such but only needs—basic, simple, and (if renewable) nonetheless temporarily satiable. Need is not linked to language; it expresses itself, as Luce Irigaray puts it, in "somatic pain, . . . screams and demands."[54] The body, not yet reaching toward, implicated within, nor entered into language, is not yet self.

The sense of self for Lacan derives from that which is outside self, first through the famous mirror stage, in which a child (mis)recognizes her own image—that is, takes it for herself, which seems sensible enough, save that it is, in fact, only an image of her, and a too neatly unified image at that. Lacan insists upon disruption in subjectivity; as Stephen Moore points out, "Lacan holds Freud to his unsettling early vision of the human subject as split or profoundly disunified, even to the point of accusing the later Freud of backing away from his early insights." He quotes Lacan's *Écrits:* "The radical heteronomy that Freud's discovery shows gaping within man . . . can never again be covered over without whatever is used to hide it being profoundly dishonest."[55] Indeed, even the mirror image gives us a less unitary self than one might at first suspect: what is identified as the self is only an image, outside the body that the self will come to identify as its own; already, at minimum, a doubling.

If the imagistic sense of self falsely covers over the fissures of selfhood, the next stage of selfhood, the entry into language, is unavoidably fragmentary. Like Kojève, Lacan has a strongly structuralist sense of language as that into which one enters, not that (a skill set, for example) which one might possess. Language exceeds any one who speaks it; as John Leslie writes, "The rhetoric of Lacan's seminar put into practical form the principle ... that language has the capacity to say more than what it says. Language, in short, speaks through human beings, as much as they speak it."[56] Though exceeding those who speak it, language still cannot capture the fullness that psychoanalysis supposes to precede the subject. Like the subject, it takes its meaning from difference, from absence, from what *is not* in a given place. And so the subject, made by seeing itself on the outside and by saying "I" in words, is always divided, always differentiated, and always in some peculiar sense elsewhere—and always, returning us to Plato's Aristophanes, in search of an impossible return to a never-present wholeness.

Divided and, desiring, incomplete. For Freud, gratification is inevitably partial because drives are both partial and renewable. For Lacan, satisfactions are metonymic, incomplete, always striving toward a wholeness that is incompatible with the very existence of the desiring subject.

Deleuze's theory of desire, elucidated in collaboration with Guattari, could not, at first glance, be more opposed. While it would be somewhere between dangerous and absurd to identify a central thesis in *Anti-Oedipus,* surely one important claim is precisely that desire is *not* lack, but productivity. The error leading us to identify desire as lack is our sense that the desirous subject and the desirable object pre-exist, possessing and receiving, respectively, the force of desire. As Deleuze remarks in a later interview, discussing *Anti-Oedipus:*

> Desire is ... not internal to a subject, any more than it tends towards
> an object: it is strictly immanent to a plane which it does not pre-exist,
> to a plane which must be constructed. ... There is only desire insofar

as there is deployment of a particular field, propagation of particular fluxes, emission of particular particles. Far from presupposing a subject, desire cannot be attained except at the point where someone is deprived of the power of saying "I." Far from directing itself towards an object, desire can only be reached at the point where someone no longer searches for or grasps an object any more than he grasps himself as a subject. The objection is then made that such a desire is totally indeterminate, and that it is even more imbued with lack. But who has you believe that by losing the co-ordinates of subject and object you lack something?[57]

Desire, in this theory, is constructive: it does not lack, and it is not lack. Yet here too, Deleuze and Guattari's important insight notwithstanding, it *is* linked to lack, to deprivation—the subject herself is lacking, absent (unable to say that self-constituting "I") at the very point where desire *is,* equally unable to differentiate the object. To lose, even if we only lose coordinates, *is* to lack, but we must understand this without conceiving lack as powerlessness or even negativity. Desire here belongs to no one; indeed, it demands dispossession. Lack is *shifted:* "Desire does not lack anything; it does not lack its object. It is, rather, the *subject* that is missing in desire, or desire that lacks a fixed subject; there is no fixed subject unless there is repression. Desire and its object are one and the same thing."[58] The subject, who is lacking, is drawn by that desire/desirable object outside herself, but the desire is that drawing power, not the lack within the one drawn. This makes sense, after all, in terms of lack, too: the ultimate emptiness of the vacuum draws forcefully into itself.[59] Indeed, we retain our selves, our "fixed subjectivity" only where we deny desire, only where we refuse to be taken outside ourselves. There is, despite the overt hostility to psychoanalysis, an intriguing resonance with Freud here. The subject is made by the refusal of the outside (which is, of course, nonetheless essential to its constitution); and the subject's relation to desire is one of lack—but desire now is positivity, force, and power, while the subject retains absence. The subject is repression's insistence upon finitude, cut into the flux and flow of desire. The subject says, stubbornly, "I," as if the word could surround and contain the ego within the body.

Desire, as Deleuze and Guattari are well aware, is paradoxical. The subject is indeed missing in desire, is indeed lacking. But this emptiness is at the same time an emptying out of overfullness, self reaching beyond self. This lack is as potent a power as could be conceived: if anything is stronger than hunger, in any of its innumerable mutations, certainly I have never found it, and I suspect the same of all those I read here. I would argue chiefly for the *power* of desire, against the view of desire as a kind of mere emptiness—unless we concede emptiness's seductive force. But this picture must be complicated, as in fact most of these theories already, if indirectly, suggest. The complication comes about in the realization that a simple opposition—lack *versus* power—is too simple; that lack is not powerlessness at all. We are drawn to, and by, and just beyond our own limits. We will persistently try to speak bodies and flesh out words, as if by doing so we could both find and lose ourselves.

It is psychoanalysis, both (though not alike) Freudian and Lacanian, that Deleuze and Guattari take on, as a sort of negative forebear to their own ideas. However, the more direct ancestry of this theory of positive, productive desire is Nietzschean. Nietzsche's "will to power," though notoriously indefinable (appropriately enough for an author insistent on flux and the impossibility of the fixed), is certainly not altogether unlike desire. Nietzsche insists upon the positivity of this force, its creative urgency which cannot be unlinked from its destructiveness—creation will make room for itself.

Nietzsche also links desire directly and necessarily to limit, though with some intriguing differences in their mutual constitution. The will to power is, fundamentally, the will to overcome—that is, necessarily, to cross some limit. (The twentieth-century philosopher most directly identified with the idea of transgression, Bataille, is, after all, deeply Nietzschean, though under Kojève's influence as well.) Poorly interpreted, as it often is, the will to power, the force of desire, thus appears as an unconditional and situationally insensitive urge to dominate and conquer. But several points in Nietzsche's work speak against such a reading. Most obviously, the "self," constituted by relations of forces (interactions of wills to power) as much as any other "thing" in the world,[60] includes, insofar as it lives, the desire above all for *self*-overcoming. It is our own limits we most seek to break, but "our own" is infinitely complicated by the breaking of limits.

And this breaking cannot occur without regard for its context, as that context is itself an element of the limit setting. Nietzsche writes in *Twilight of the Idols,* "In the Dionysian state . . . the entire emotional system is alerted and intensified: so that it discharges all its powers of representation, imitation, transfiguration, transmutation. . . . The essential thing remains the facility of the metamorphosis, the incapacity *not* to react."[61]

Desire is constituted by limit but is itself power, a transformative power that makes the world in its image: "In this condition one enriches everything out of one's own abundance: what one sees, what one desires, one sees swollen, pressing, strong, overladen with energy. The man in this condition transforms things until they mirror his power—until they are reflections of his perfection."[62] What is more, transformation is its own urge and delight; the will seeks out what resists it. Desire forms, seeks limits, breaks them, forms anew. There is, as Bataille later realizes, a contradiction within the subject, which pushes beyond itself to a destruction it cannot will, to the loss of any sense of will as its own: the necessary consequence of rupturing limits. That the I of language is never entirely one's own we have known for quite some time; that the I of flesh is also not quite one's own we are learning to imagine.

In recognizing this paradox as Nietzschean, Bataille also attributes to Nietzsche the expression of a sense of desire at its purest and most intense: "An extreme, unconditional human yearning was expressed for the first time by Nietzsche *independently of moral goals or of serving God.* Nietzsche can't really define it, but it motivates him and it's what he unreservedly makes his own."[63]

Bataille, following upon Nietzsche's sense of the subject as complex and impermanent, is well attuned both to the power of desire to undo subjectivity and to the complicity of the subject in that power. Here the impossibility of desire becomes apparent. He repeatedly expresses the self-exceeding urge: "The sovereign desire of beings is what is beyond being."[64] There is unquestionably a sense of lack in desire—lack as absence, but also as woundedness and the consequent disruption of identity and integrity.[65] We may desire in lack, but we also desire what lacks; "what *attracts* isn't immediately being but a wound, a break."[66] And yet in this double emptiness and openness we find ourselves again:

> The beloved turns aside—is different from me.
>
> But without this difference, this abyss—*my recognition of this beloved would have been in vain.* Identity still remains in effect. Only when our

response to desire remains incomprehensible is that response true. A response that is understood destroys desire. These limits define desire (define us). We are to the degree that we risk ourselves.[67]

Here the themes of desire, lack, subjectivity, and limit intersect. If desire is lack, it is also productive; lack itself constitutes the subject, a being who *is* only by virtue of limits that desire will push toward rupture. And in thinking these themes I find I can also think flesh together with word.

Bataille's understanding of desire and of "communication" as a mutual laceration is the theory underlying the pair of chapters on the cut, the sixth and seventh chapters that follow. Behind the second and third, on touch, is the work of Jean-Luc Nancy; and behind the fourth and fifth, on the fold, is Deleuze, to some extent in his work with Guattari but more in his historical, in this case Leibnizian, mode. I must admit, to be fair to these figures, that theirs has been an inspirational and background sort of influence; I am not explaining their theories but beginning with them.

I have already set forth some of the relevant Bataillean theory. Nancy is perhaps more obviously a thinker of absence, abandonment, and spacing than of tactility. But a brief, crucial passage in the essay "Of Divine Places" reminds us of the proximity of these themes: "There is the god who approaches man to the extent of touching him, and the god who retreats from man to the extent of abandoning him infinitely. The two are the same."[68] The sense of absence and withdrawal makes no sense without touch. Indeed, Nancy's gracefully elusive philosophical work suggests, as Jacques Derrida points out, thought modeled on tactility, with its mobile quality and its feel for the ungraspable. The subject, for him, appears in spaces—communitarian spaces of "compearance" or postlapsarian secular spaces, but always *with*. That is, there is no self-sufficiency, no self without the need for that which it is not. At the limit of the self, the skin as much as the ego (Nancy is, as we shall see in Chapter 2, much intrigued by skin), is the desire to reach toward, and the drawing of a reaching desire. Derrida notes the tactile—and tactful—character of Nancy's thought in an essay entitled "Le Toucher," an exploration of the mysteries of space and touch in Nancy's thought; there is a complexity of thought in Nancy's work upon which we shall barely touch here.

Deleuze's own thought is not, of course, quite separable from withness either, nor from his thinking-with Guattari. Thus, in his marvelous dual consideration of Leibniz and baroque arts (his thinking-with Leibniz), Deleuze remains drawn to the productive power of desire. Here he explores a particular mode of complexity, entailing infinite divisibility, motility, and inclusion without interiority. Thinking the fold, the "final cause" of which is inclusion,[69] Deleuze nonetheless invokes Nietzsche as much as Aristotle: "Folding-unfolding no longer simply means tension-release, contraction-dilation, but enveloping-developing, involution-evolution. . . . The simplest way of stating the point is by saying that to unfold is to increase, to grow, whereas to fold is to diminish, to reduce, 'to withdraw into the recesses of a world.'"[70] Will expands and contracts, actively and reactively; *there is* folding and unfolding.

To think these is, as I shall suggest throughout the text and argue in the conclusion, to think a mutual pairing of desire and limit. And thus to think, not in the depths, but at the edges, on the skin, at the surface of the page on which we write. We explore surfaces because they are, precisely, limits; because limit is implicit in desire; because surface itself is seductive,[71] impelling us to touch, to enfold, to open.

My choice of initial story for this exploration owes itself to Jean-Luc Nancy's insightful "Corpus," in which human bodies are linked in mimetic complexity to the body of the incarnate and crucified God,[72] to Christianity and its peculiar and perverse histories. And so I shall begin with the body of the Word, the Body of Christ, in one particular depiction, in one of the places where these are most conspicuously brought together, the Gospel of John. From this strange story of the Body of the Word, other bodies unfold and regather, the questions of words stretched and scrawled across them. Some of this unfolding reveals the unexpected. The path between may indeed be a broken, certainly a bent one, but the line is there, inviting us to trace it. Thus:

Word Made Flesh

The text "Corpus" is exscripted, to speak with Nancy, written out, that is, in a way that distances it from the breath and the tongue. It is already divided, shared. Here is my body, take it and eat, even in my absence, especially in my absence, in remembrance of me it seems to say. Is there not a whiff of the incarnation here?

—Gary Shapiro, "Jean-Luc Nancy and the Corpus of Philosophy"

En archē, it begins; *in the beginning; ēn ho logos, kai ho logos ēn pros ton theon, kai theos ēn ho logos.* . . . As Jerome translates it in the fourth century, *in principio erat Verbum, et Verbum erat apud Deum et Deus erat Verbum,* rendering the polysemous *Logos* more nearly *Word,* as we have it: *In the beginning was the Word, and the Word was with God, and the Word was God.* And so we find ourselves in the delightfully peculiar fourth gospel, attributed to the name of John.

We may be tempted by long familiarity into an insufficient attentiveness to the deep strangeness of this claim—and the Word *was* God. Word of God, Word about God—those seem (comparatively) unproblematic. But even granting that the "lack of a definite article with 'God' in Greek signifies predication rather than identification,"[1] surely Godness is a peculiar quality to predicate of a Word, even where the Word itself does bear that definite article. I hope to draw attention to the claim's strangeness without

25

making arguments for any dogma. Suffice it to say that something interesting, and odd, and important to the history of our thinking about words is going on here. Nor is dogmatic devotion needed to see the importance of Christianity for our sense of bodies, though this importance is most often negatively portrayed. That is, when we think of the Christian attitude toward the body, we are most likely to think along the Pauline and Augustinian axis that warns us against the worldly temptations posed by the flesh and its pleasures. But this somatophobic tradition, if dominant, scarcely exhausts the interpretations of the flesh in Christianity. I shall argue for a reading of that importance, that centrality of the flesh, which takes the Incarnation with serious pleasure, which responds to an embodied God with an appropriately intense desire.

John's gospel is a key site of the Christian emphasis on the flesh. The author or authors of John may well have been writing against the docetic heresy, which endeavored to work around the paradoxicality of the Incarnation by declaring that it was in spirit alone that Christ was God, the flesh being mere appearance if indeed it was anything at all. This sentiment, however heretical, is not unpopular; a corporeal divinity is at best a perplexity and most likely an embarrassment philosophically—especially as Christianity is increasingly Hellenized. John's carnal emphasis recurs in the great attention drawn both to somatic acts such as eating[2] and, more dramatically still, to Christ's body after the resurrection. Interestingly, Christian orthodoxy has held stubbornly to the paradoxes of the Incarnation, declaring heretical all sorts of efforts to uncouple Word from flesh—not merely docetism, but all manner of variants on Manichean or Catharist dualisms which would divorce fleshly matter from immaterial divine spirit, even in the body that is, or at least is occupied by, Christ.

That the very Greek gospel of John would begin with the Word is unsurprising. This Word, which is implicitly both God and God's speaking, both being and creative power, is John's first take on the Trinity's second person. But it is hardly the last, and for our purposes two others—Light and Flesh—are important. These will in turn complicate this Verbal beginning.

I want to begin by noting the use of aural and luminous as well as tactile imagery for the person of Christ in this gospel, then go on to explore the puzzles presented by the different means by which each of those who perceive the resurrected body of Christ does so. I shall suggest a

Nietzschean reading, in which Christ's will is responsive to the combination of desire and faith in those who encounter him in this story, and shall argue that, rather than a promise of endurance, the transfigurative element of the story is a transformation in what passes. Touch functions in John as an image of the experientially powerful, which is neither lasting nor graspable.

In the beginning, Christ is Word, but almost immediately he is Light (1:4–9). As the Word is spoken in primordial silence (and thus inaudibly, too, or at any rate unaudited, as there is no one to hear it), so too the Light shines in darkness. Darkness fails to comprehend Light (*et lux in tenebris lucet et tenebrae eam non conprehenderunt*; Vulgate 1:5), either to understand it or to overcome it.

I shall explore below some of the metaphorical resonances of the Light, but first we must note that just as Word is also Light, so, too, is it Flesh: "And the Word became flesh and made his dwelling among us" (1:14). Interestingly, and at first surprisingly, this Flesh seems to be *essential* to the glory of Word and of Light. It is only *here*—after this Incarnation—that "We saw his glory, the glory as of the Father's only Son" (1:14). Without ears to hear it, the Word remains unheard;[3] and it seems that light too must become flesh as the very condition of its recognizability, its visibility, its shining (it "enlightens everyone," ambiguously perhaps, at 1:9). Darkness does not understand light, but flesh (which is thus not, as the Manicheans might have it, darkness only) makes possible the shining of light, the sounding of the word, in the world.

These three, then, are interleaved, infolded, neither distinct nor identical. The Word will be incarnate as flesh; without incarnation, it remains inaudible, spoken to no one. The light becomes flesh, too; without this becoming, it remains invisible, its shining indistinguishable from darkness. Flesh is not simply that which blocks the light but that which makes possible the very fact of illumination, as both medium and object of luminosity. Flesh, which is both Light and Word, is also the medium of *touch*, which enfolds and cuts across a nearly bewildering array of meanings. And so this spiritual son, who is also God, is given to the material world through a polysensuous presentation: sound, sight, surface. While even here Flesh may sometimes seem to be presented in opposition to Spirit, as in 6:63 ("It is the spirit that gives life, while the flesh is of no avail"), the distinction may not be between the body and the soul[4]—rather, it is more likely an emphasis on the supernatural status of Christ even as body.[5]

As promised, I shall note, though briefly, some of the many senses of Light in this gospel. In fact, much of the imagery of John is imagery of visibility, of seeing (here, as so often elsewhere, equated with knowledge) even where it is not specifically of luminosity.[6]

First, Light is goodness opposed to the evil of dark: "The light came into the world, but people preferred darkness to light, because their works were evil. For everyone who does wicked things hates the light" (3:19–20). This goodness is identified with truth: "Whoever lives the truth comes to the light" (3:21). Those who are good have nothing to fear from truth. Those who are evil, like animals who dwell in the dark, are confused, threatened, and even endangered by the Luminosity to which they are as unsuited as unaccustomed.

The association of Light with Truth is so strong that there is something odd about the very idea of falsity in illumination. It is not unheard of, to be sure; Origen in *First Principles* writes:

> Our soul is either "enlighted with" Christ, "the true light" (Jn 1:9) which never goes out, or, if it does not have that light which is eternal, it is doubtless illumined by a temporal and extinguishable light, i.e., by him who "disguises himself as an angel of light" (2 Cor 11:14) and fills the hearts of the sinners with a false light so that what is really passing and subject to decay might seem good and valuable.[7]

Yet here again, despite the unusual sense that light may be false, we find truth linked to goodness. The false light (that borne by Lucifer, perhaps) misleads us about the nature of the good, but it remains the proper function of light to illuminate goodness for us.

Elsewhere, this goodness seems to be life: "Whoever follows me will not walk in darkness, but will have the light of life" (8:12). This Light is persuasive but not irresistible, and some refuse it just as they refuse to hear the divine voice: "Moreover, the Father who sent me has testified on my behalf. But you have never heard his voice nor seen his form, and you do not have his word remaining in you, because you do not believe the one whom he has sent" (5:37). Light shines and is seen, or not seen, or both alternately: "A little while and you will no longer see me, and again a little while later and you will see me" (16:16). Sometimes it is seen miraculously, as by the blind man whose sight is restored—by touch. In this miraculous instance, Christ, declaring himself once more "the light of the world" (9:5), mixes his saliva with dirt to make mud, "and smeared the clay on his eyes, and said to him, 'Go wash in the Pool of Siloam. . . . So he went and washed, and came back able to see" (9:6–7).

As we can already see, Christ works synaesthetically, works as and by many senses in one. In chapter 12, we find two-thirds of a Trinitarian synaesthesia. Where the Father is voice ("Then a voice came from heaven"; 12:28), the Son comes as light ("The light will be among you only a little while"; 12:35). And, as we shall see later, while seeing is often believing and even knowing, so too are hearing and, more dramatically still, the touch that may let us see. And if, indeed, the breath Christ directs upon his disciples in chapter 20 is identified with the Holy Spirit, then this abstract, unanthropomorphic third of the Trinity is given lightly yet in the most tangible of ways, given and known as the lightest possible touch, the movement of air by a body.

To hearing first, however. The Word must, of course, exceed sensory metaphors, yet it cannot be irrelevant that it appears as both sound and light, potentially corresponding to the word spoken and written. Both turn out to be significant in John, and I shall of course argue for the importance of the tactile Word as well. It is in its aural form that language is most often miraculous here. Not the sight of God, but the sound of that voice will (in the ultimate miraculous gesture) raise the dead: "The dead will hear the voice of the Son of God, and those who hear will live" (5:25); "a time is coming when all who are in the tombs will hear his voice and come out" (5:28).[8] Most dramatically, Christ's voice calls forth Lazarus. Noting that God as father always hears him (11:40), Christ calls in turn to Lazarus, "'Lazarus, come out!' The dead man came out, tied hand and foot with burial bands" (11:43–44).

Though the sound of the voice is miraculous and may be associated with life even more strongly than light is, the equation of spoken word with truth is not so invariant as that of truth with light. While light is never presented in John as false or as evil, spoken words are less determined. True hearing knows truth; the inability to recognize truth is identified with the inability (or—and, I would argue, interchangeably—the refusal) to hear it. "Whoever belongs to God hears the words of God; for this reason you do not listen, because you do not belong to God" (8:47). Those who do hear—genuinely and in their own right—seem to be persuaded; "Many more began to believe in him because of his word, and they said to the [Samaritan] woman, 'We no longer believe because of your word; for we have heard for ourselves'" (4:41–43).[9] I shall suggest below that truth is drawn by desire; the Word is made to speak by those who are eager to hear it.

Even Pilate, a rather more ambiguous figure than we might expect, is uncertain of truth when he speaks and hears: "Everyone who belongs to the truth listens to me," Christ declares, but Pilate responds famously, "What is truth?" (18:37–38). Yet when he declares Christ *rex Iudaeorum*, he holds fast to this truth: *quod scripsi, scripsi*, he declares (Vulgate 19:22); what I have written, I have written (19:22). What he has written will remain, will hold true. And yet what we are inclined to understand as fixity, the Word set down and held, may ultimately be subordinate to the fleeting and mortal sense of touch. The *living* Word cannot be static, and Pilate's conviction that what he has written *is* written holds to a static sense of eternity. Eternity in John seems more compatible with the Plotinian eternity of vibrance and return, of a "fullness of life"[10] that is sufficient to the Neoplatonic overflow of emanation.

Even after Christ's death and foretold resurrection, we find both sight and sound as routes to truth. But in these later passages the third persuasive sense, touch, appears in its most intriguing aspects. There is little touch earlier in this gospel: as we have noted, Christ touches the eyes of a blind man and restores his sight. Mary washes Christ's feet with her hair, and he later washes his disciple's feet (presumably though not explicitly with his hands). John leans (rather provocatively, I have always thought) against Jesus at the Last Supper, asking questions. But these early invocations of the tangible are relatively few. It is death, oddly, or rather the intersection of death with life, that unfolds a richer sense of a tangible, tactile Incarnation.

At his crucifixion, Christ is nailed to the cross and pierced in his side (19:34)—but unbroken (19:33), as if to keep our attention on the complexities of the torn surface and not on the invisibility of fractured bones. He is entombed, and then the strangeness really begins.

As I earlier remarked, both sight and sound serve others in their recognition of truth, and this is the case too in the truth of Christ risen. Each modality appears singly as well as synaesthetically. The first to see the tomb empty is Mary Magdalene. Alarmed rather than reassured, she informs two of the disciples, Simon Peter and John, who rush to see for themselves.

These two do not even need to see Christ walking about, as they later will; *not* seeing him in the tomb—that is, finding the tomb empty—is a sufficient appeal to their faith, or at least to John's. "He saw and believed," we are told (20:8); it is not clear whether the same holds for Simon Peter. However, given the special status of both disciples—Simon Peter will be the rock upon which the church is built,[11] while John has the role of beloved of Christ—it may well be that theirs is already a superior faith, an unusual relation to Christ even among the disciples.

Just as she is the discoverer of the empty tomb, so too the first person to *see* Christ risen will be Mary Magdalene. But it is not sight that convinces her. At first, she takes this strange man for the gardener: "She thought it was the gardener, and said to him, 'Sir, if you have carried him away, tell me where you laid him, and I will take him'" (20:15). And so a direct sighting is no more convincing to her than was the sight of the empty tomb. Her recognition, instead, is aural: "Jesus said to her, 'Mary.' She turned and said to him in Hebrew, 'Rabbouni'" (20:16).

At the sound of his voice, she recognizes him, she knows. But she cannot touch him; he orders her *mē mou haptou. Noli me tangere,* Jerome has it; "Touch me not," says the King James, while the New American gives "Stop holding on to me"—and the reason Christ gives for this is odd: "for I have not yet ascended to my father" (20:17). This demands some thought. The ascension and the resurrection may be one and the same,[12] but their joint temporality is still unclear.

The puzzle of translation, the movement between *touch* and *hold,* is intriguing, reflecting some ambiguity in the Greek *haptou,* which may mean either hold (even cling) or touch (and was even used by Plato for "perceive," suggesting that Platonic forms are indeed stable, that we can hold forever onto our perceptions of them).[13] It suggests that what is forbidden is not only the tangible but the prehensible; it warns against a touch that would grasp rather than brush across the surface. Certainly Christ is not to be grasped, but just as certainly this will remain true after his ascent. Intellectually, it is hardly strange to suggest that god cannot be fully grasped, cannot be rationally comprehended. Yet he is, also, not to be *touched,* and this is odd on many grounds.

To begin with, we might expect, given his recent return to the world of matter, to the carnality of spirit, that Christ would warn Mary that he is not yet fully *descended from* the Father. Not yet material again, he could not yet be the object of touch. Yet this is not what he says. "I am not yet ascended" suggests a most peculiar state of body, neither here nor there, visible and audible but intangible, still in the *process* of resurrection, as if the ethereally refined matter of Christ's spirit were still, with the stiff painfulness of the ultimate Morning, reassembling (with) his body. Or, more elegantly, it suggests a true indissociability of body and spirit, a truly spiritualized body, which has not yet overcome death fully, though it is on its way. Still, it is most puzzling that resurrection should be such a temporal process, a process still in progress when Mary sees and hears her teacher. After presenting one more puzzle, I shall suggest some answers to this difficulty which strike me as more promising than the assumption that resurrection proper simply takes a few days.

After this first sighting and first hearing, the puzzles only multiply. Christ's next appearance occurs after he has left Mary Magdalene. To make this appearance, he walks through the wall of the building that houses his disciples. This seems consistent with his intangibility; neither Mary Magdalene nor the wall can touch him.

Dramatically entering the building, he may be untouchable, but he is clearly visible, and those disciples who are present know him on sight. Of course, their sight has been prepared by hearing; Mary Magdalene, acting on Christ's orders, has told them of her encounter (20:18). Christ seems by this point to be ascending toward tangibility, as he is able not only to speak to the assembled as well as to be seen by them, but also, as we have noted, to breathe upon them, thus imparting to them the Holy Spirit (20:22).

Thus far we find, then, three modes of conviction and persuasion. Simon Peter and John, called to the empty tomb by a fearful Mary Magdalene, are brought to believe that Christ has risen by the absence of a sight: that is, by seeing that his body is not in the tomb. Whereas their faith is strong enough, Mary's is still a somewhat shaky belief: when she encounters the man she believes to be the gardener, she asks where Christ's body has been *taken*. And so the second, and more effective, mode of persuasion is aural: she believes when he speaks.

The third mode is directly rather than indirectly visual, yet it too gestures toward the sight or site of an absence. It must be persuasive that Christ walks in despite the locked door, yet what that sight gives us, or rather gives to his disciples, is as much the absence of tangibility as the presence of vision. And it is surely indicative that the vision that ultimately persuades the assembled is that of Christ's *wounds:* "Jesus came and stood in their midst and said, 'Peace be with you!' When he had said this, he showed them his hands and his side. The disciples rejoiced when they saw the Lord" (20:19–20). That these wounds indicate a certain *absence* (after all, they are holes in the flesh), as well as a great corporeal peculiarity, becomes still more evident as the tale continues.

There are only eleven assembled for this convincing appearance, and when the twelfth disciple appears he will prove to be stubbornly dubious. He insists not only upon sight, but upon the touch that Christ has forbidden others: "[Thomas] said . . . 'Unless I see the mark of the nails in his hands and put my finger where the nails were, and put my hand into his side, I will not believe it'" (20:25). Events unfold accordingly. After a period of eight days, Christ comes in through the wall again, but this time to a full assembly. Thomas, among the assembled, remains unpersuaded by this sight; accordingly, Christ tells him, "Put your finger here and see my hands, and bring your hand and put it into my side, and do not be unbelieving, but believe" (20:27). Upon which evidence Thomas is finally persuaded, finally believes.

But note again how strange is this mode of persuasion. Thomas does not simply touch Christ's body. Rather, he extends his hand *into* the wounds in that body, the gaps, the fissures, the spaces of absence around which that body is risen. It is not even clear if he makes contact with Christ's flesh at all. As if this were not odd enough, we remind ourselves that this is the *risen* body—surely, we think, a body that could rise from the dead could also heal? Why, that is, do these wounds remain at all, and why is it only there that Thomas finds his truth?

Before taking up this new set of puzzles, perhaps we should quickly review the peculiarities of the body that unfold in chapter 20 of John's gospel (that is, postresurrection). First, there is the puzzle of ascent and descent, in which we find tangible materiality quite unexpectedly linked to ascension: *touch me not, for I am not yet ascended to the Father.* Then there is the sheer multiplicity of persuasive modes, which is odd because it suggests that *vision,* philosophy's preeminent sensory modality, is not always adequate evidence, even when it has faith on its side, and even when what gives itself to be seen is the Light, the very means and medium of vision. There is the curious persistence of those wounds, which we might reasonably expect to have healed. There is the tension between an intangible Christ who can walk through walls and the tangible Christ who can breathe on his disciples and invite the touch of the doubting Thomas. And there is that permission to touch itself, odd not only because it directs itself to what is fragmented and torn, but because it is permission at all, given to Thomas and not to Mary Magdalene.

Various explanations of this set of puzzlements, of course, are possible. One seems neither Judeo-Christian nor properly Platonic, though it is an entertaining thought: perhaps body and soul alike are assemblages of atoms, and the process of reassemblage is a slow one. Thus Mary Magdalene is forbidden to touch Christ because he is not yet ascended; that is, drawn back into the atomic coherence of life. By the time Thomas touches him, Christ is fully accessible to the touch.

Aside from the improbability of such an atomistic argument appearing in such a text—which does not trouble me too greatly; after all, I shall soon be anachronistic enough in my own reading—this explanation fails to address all of our puzzles. It does make sense of two of them: why Christ is intangible because he is not ascended (assuming some identity or interplay of ascension with the proper assembly of bits into living form), though we might more often think of materiality as descent; and why he is off limits to Mary Magdalene's touch and not to Thomas's. But it doesn't tell us how, immediately prior to that tangibility, he steps into a room without opening the door. Nor, though this is less of a puzzle, does it tell us why so many different sensory encounters with Christ are presented. Finally, it does not tell us why this body fails to heal.

In seeking a way to bring these apparently contradictory passages together, we might suggest that this delay in tangibility is due to a mending of the body. This doesn't really work either, though, because, as we have seen, resurrection is not a *healing* process. This is evidenced by Thomas's touch. He touches, not Christ healed, but the very absence of healing, the wounds in the hands and side of the risen body. The resurrected body seems to be not less, but more material, more marked by its encounters with other matter, with the spear and nails that have torn it open. Why is this risen, divine body still injured?

The role of these wounds is critical. Ascension to the Father seems to be a matter of becoming more fully of the earth; ascent and descent seem indistinguishable. What happens to Christ ascendant isn't his increasing removal from the world but his increasing materiality. In fact, it is an intensification of the most material of traces, the marks of the intersection of matter (spear, nail) with matter (flesh). A miraculously healed Christ would not, we realize, have persuaded *any* of the disciples, except perhaps the first two. Yet they, too, we note, are persuaded by an *absence*.

Of course, we might just see an unresolved contradiction here, as different traditions work out their dominance in Christian history. Carolyn Walker Bynum, in her marvelous work *The Resurrection of the Body in Western Christianity*, presents this historical puzzle clearly. "There is a full range of interpretations of Jesus's resurrection in the Gospels and Paul, and if Christians chose eating the honeycomb rather than the *noli me tangere*, that choice requires explanation.... Why did powerful voices among the Christians of the later second century reject more spiritual or Gnostic interpretations of the resurrected body?"[14] Unquestionably there are traditions in conflict even within the gospel of John. But Mary Magdalene and Thomas come very close together in the text; can this be a simple oversight, an unawareness of the contradiction, or are they in some way reconcilable?

Freedom, Desire, Will

The water imagery in John is a river of desire, then; it issues from the Fourth Evangelist, although it cannot be said to have originated with him.

Stephen Moore, *Poststructuralism and the New Testament*

A reading that emphasizes the "fullness of life" and the *intensity* of living in eternity seems more fully able to embrace these contradictions. Under such a reading—again, of the sort most generally though not unequivocally identified with Neoplatonism—the distinction between ascent and descent is ultimately without weight; emanation and return are not stages in a temporal process—or, more precisely, they are stages only in a temporal process, and a recurrent process at that. But what time gives us as processual and cyclical, the perspective of eternity *presents*—it is, and that is all. Christ is fully ascended when he is fully descended, he *is*, at his utmost.[15] The departure is the coming back; the emanation is the return.[16]

This is, at least to me, more satisfying than the previous options, but it still doesn't tell us why resurrection would be a process that takes a certain amount of time, even if only from the perspective of time. (That is, from the view of eternity, no time at all is taken.) And it is even less clear why Christ can walk through walls just before Thomas touches him. Perhaps the resurrection, the ascension, takes time in time precisely to emphasize, to intensify, the temporality of Christ, while outside of time it is always already, purely eternal. As Christ ascends and descends, those most material marks, the wounds in his hands and his side, become most evident. They too are glorified; Christ remains wounded, but his wounds don't fester any more than they heal. Thus materiality is most strongly indicated just where its effects are most strongly negated: he does not heal; he does not rot. He is most and least material, and spirit and matter seem in the end not to be opposed at all.

The puzzles of multiple modes of presentation and sometimes-permitted touch remain. Here too another reading is possible, a reading drawing together freedom and desire. Of all those who know Christ, we realize, Thomas is the most skeptical; his name is to this day easily paired with doubt itself. He alone *needs* to touch Christ, just as Mary Magdalene gets what she needs when he speaks to her, just as the other disciples get what they need when they see him enter their building. And here I would like to make things stranger still. Suppose, I would like to suggest, that the medieval Franciscans were to this extent right, and the way to knowledge of God is not intellect (or, complicating matters, not intellect alone) but will, will drawn by love. Will here belongs not to reason, but to a desire indistinguishable from need. To complicate this, let me suggest as well that in John what the disciples and Mary Magdalene manifest is a *desire to know* Christ, rather than a disconnection of desirous will and knowing. These they no more separate than they might disconnect flesh and the Word.

But will, as just about any philosopher can tell you, is hard to understand. William of Ockham, for example, puzzles over the seemingly obvious notion that "every act of will can be bad," yet "to love God is an act that is only virtuous and nothing but virtuous"—a puzzle worsened by the fact that only willed acts count as either virtuous or vicious.[17] That is, if loving God is virtuous, then we must love by an act of will; yet if this love is by will, then it ought to be possible for it to be vicious. Yet it is inconceivable that the love of God can be a vice, and so we find ourselves in a logical impossibility. Are love and will really so incompatible with reason?

Certainly they often seem to be. In this, as in other regards, human will even alone is plenty puzzling, but we must note that especially the will of God has always presented Christianity with any number of theological conundrums, and undertaking a solution to them, the reader will be relieved to know, is well beyond my present intent.[18]

I am more interested here not in the effects but in the manner of this will's working—and the correspondingly peculiar nature, as I shall later argue, of its freedom. That human will is free is a notion many Christian thinkers have held dear, despite the occasional existence of determinist or predestinarian sects. For St. Augustine, freedom is so precious a good that it explains away the problem of evil: we are given the freedom to choose and to act upon our choices, and if sometimes we choose evil over good, this remains a lesser evil than the deprivation of our freedom would be. For some thinkers, free will is so great—and so uniquely human—a good that the very angels envy us for it.[19] Freedom presumes some lack of constraint upon the will; God's will presumably lacks constraint altogether. But just what does this absence of constraint really mean? What, that is, are the meanings we might give to freedom?

Customarily we conceive will in one of two ways: as a conscious, generally rational, deliberative faculty; or as "willfulness," irrational and impetuous force. In the first instance we fail to act in accordance with our own will when we are externally forced (say, pushed out a window), but we also act in some sense in-voluntarily when we are "weak-willed," when we give in to that urgent demand for a cigarette, or one more fudge brownie, or one more night away from that damned manuscript. In the second sense, we act most in accordance with our own will when we defy obstacles, objections, maybe even common sense. Thus Descartes can warn that we must always use reason to keep the will in check, assuming an obvious distinction between these faculties.[20]

In both senses, the will is inseparable from a sense of freedom, and freedom, in fact, from autonomy. The link between freedom and reason demanded by the first understanding of the will is an old one. It seems to me best, if quite diversely, formulated in Aristotle and Kant. For both, will is most important in connection with virtue. Aristotelian virtue is servant, of course, to happiness, to human *flourishing*, life at its utmost, meaning the life of rational contemplation.[21] Virtue is cultivated by habituation and reaches its pinnacle in the development of rationality. The virtuous soul is relatively unimpeded in its flourishing; thus, we are most free when will can be most directly put into act and when the enactment of the will is most nearly in accord with its own imperatives. Voluntarism is particularly linked to rational deliberation on the part of a free agent and implies the power to act: "We deliberate about what is up to us … about the actions we can do."[22]

Kantian autonomy is more complex, and wholly unconcerned with any recognizable sense of happiness.[23] (Indeed, though desire for Kant has to do with morality, pleasure and pain have to do with the quite different judgments of aesthetics.) Morality for Kant is wholly based in will, and will in reason. "Nothing can possibly be conceived in the world, or even out of it," Kant declares, "which can be called good without qualification, except a Good Will."[24] And will is wholly autonomous (in the literal sense of self-legislating) and wholly rational (indeed, "reason is imparted to us as a practical faculty, *i.e.* as one which is to have influence on the *will*,"[25] or, as Deleuze puts it in glossing Kant, "the moral law is the sole determining principle of the good will"[26]). All else is impulse and merits the sneers of the good. We manifest autonomy when we act on motives that are purely rational. Reason gives to the will the laws that it rightly obeys or wrongly breaks: "Our existence has a … far nobler end, for which, and not for happiness, reason is properly intended."[27]

Though neither Kant nor Aristotle does so, it is easy enough to give this link between freedom and reason a religious resonance: in our God-given reason is freedom from the temptations of the flesh. But what if this flesh, too, is modeled on God's? What if the flesh itself wills? Those of us familiar with the midnight urge for Ben and Jerry's can be fairly certain of the strength of such a willful, sarkic desire.[28]

Willful irrationality has not been a favorite of philosophers, among whom it seems in general to be relegated to the status of unfreedom, giving in rather than taking on. Most often, in this conception, freedom becomes defined almost wholly in relation to external impediment, and we act freely when no one and nothing prevents us from doing as we please. This, of course, gives rise to deeper arguments around psychological freedom or the lack thereof (we may do as we please, the question runs, but can we please as we please?). Yet perhaps it is precisely in giving, if not giving in, that will is most nearly divine in its freedom.

This is not to imply a slackness or weakness of the will. It is rather to give the will a Nietzschean spin, to suggest that the will is most free when it works in accordance with the irrational laws of the body,[29] and this particularly where the body is not reduced to the mechanistic.

Freedom here is work under the law of the flesh itself. Heterodox as this undoubtedly sounds, I think that in fact we find in this willful freedom what is for some Christian (especially Thomistic) theologians a significant attribute of God, that of being "fully in act," where act is not processual (any more than are emanation and return, though Thomas would no doubt gravely dislike this parallel), but opposed instead to potentiality, to *potency*. We may already realize how oddly this sits with more conventional senses of free will. Of such senses, the Aristotelian formulation is both concise and representative: "For when acting is up to us, so is not acting."[30]

To say that God is in act is to imply that nothing of God's is undeveloped, is not yet; nothing of God's is only possible. Traditionally this emphasizes the immutability of God, the unchangingness of divine perfection. Yet this divine eternity gets most strange in connection with the incarnate member of the Trinity: Christ is human, too, and must act, as we do, in and through time. The peculiarity of Christ's *will*, however, retains in time some of the strangeness of a will at once so free that it is fully in act and at no time unfulfilled, yet utterly without other possibilities, the very existence of which we intuitively link to freedom.

My sense of the matter is this: that in the person of Christ as presented in the fourth gospel the puzzles of will and freedom are the very puzzles we have already found. Each disciple, and Mary Magdalene, too, gets exactly what she or he needs to compel belief, and to hold faith firm. Yet Christ's responses seem equally compelled, drawn by this very need. The will, says Ockham, *cannot* in fact obey the command not to love God—even if it is God who gives it—simply because this obedience is itself a manifestation of the love for God.[31] This loving will also obeys love; the love of God manifests not only the love of the human will for the divine but the remarkable love of the divine for the world; after all, it is John who tells us, "For God so loved the world that he gave his only Son" (3:16). Simon and John need little, perhaps nothing, because they already have everything; they believe and they know, having no need of a further proof that might transform that belief into understanding: Simon is of such sturdy faith that elsewhere, at least, he is identified as the rock,[32] his faith absolute; John is the beloved, his security unshakable. Mary needs the sound of Christ's voice, needs to hear the Word spoken, but in that speaking she knows Christ as her teacher. Thus she does not need to touch him, and though Christ will give her all that she needs, he will not exaggerate that need. And, acting in time, he cautions that his resurrection is temporal, though eternally accomplished, emphasizing for the reader the peculiarity of this double nature.

For nine of the other disciples, an inexplicable (an incomprehensible) vision, their teacher entering without need for a door, suffices for their faith. For Thomas, the most doubtful, the strongest sense is yet required, and Christ, having cautioned Mary Magdalene not to touch him, allows Thomas to touch him—but, we notice, to touch specifically his wounds. From *touch me not* to *touch me here, where I am not.* Each of the faithful is drawn into a curious combination of presence and absence: the sight of an empty tomb, the speaker who speaks to forbid tactile contact, the visible man who nonetheless passes through walls, the touch that touches only what is torn away already. No one *comprehends* Christ, no one has *proof*; each has exactly enough to sustain faith. Knowledge of the divine is faith alone; not grasp, but touch.

Transfigurations of Faith

The mystery of incarnation: a body of ideas, precepts, experiences made concrete, become flesh; the story of a life and of a death compressed into one memorable picture capable of evoking an immediate emotional response. In such an image, the word, the concept is made palpable and becomes a physical presence.

—Martin Esslin, *Artaud*

And faith here has an odd sense, transfigurative or transformative, a redemptive sense best understood in conjunction with *desire*, the desire to know, understood in near-Deleuzean terms, not along the Platonic model of lack but as its own form of fullness. Again, if we conceive of desire simply as lack, then we can understand further that when we obtain and incorporate (assimilate, annihilate) that thing, desire, satisfied, ceases. Even hunger, of course, is scarcely so simple; we always get hungry again. (There are even appetizers, designed to whet the desire for food even as they fulfill it.) Yet we tend to think that if we still desire, it must be because we are unsatisfied. In John, the desire to *know* is at once satisfied and sustained, and precisely in this the world is transformed, made, as Nietzsche surprisingly says, "blessed": "Blessedness is not promised, it is not tied to any conditions: it is the *only* reality—the rest is signs for speaking of it . . . "[33]

We should pause to look more carefully at this image of desire without lack in a world of blessedness without reserve. Echoing Nietzsche's dismissive condemnation of the "priestly class," Deleuze writes, "Desire: who, except priests, would want to call it 'lack'? Nietzsche called it 'Will to Power.' There are other names for it. For example, 'grace.' Desiring is not at all easy, but this is precisely because it gives, instead of lacks."[34]

This notion of sustainable, satisfied, and yet insatiable desiring has its place in Christianity, as well. The notion of *epektasis* elucidated by Gregory of Nyssa suggests that we yearn eternally toward knowing and being-with God, but not because our yearning is ever unsatisfied. Rather, the satisfaction feeds the striving.[35] God is infinite: there is always more. Perhaps the "dissatisfaction" or incompleteness of each mode of knowing Christ's body in John is in fact a metaphorization of this infinity, a sense that no matter what one gets, no matter how delighted and secure one may be in one's faith, there is always more. The pleasures of desire are perfectly sustainable.

The world in which an embodied God is risen from the dead is far more mysterious, and more delightfully enticing, than it was before his death. "Knowing" that Christ is risen—that is, having enough to sustain this faith—transforms the world. Here the *opposition* between lack and desire is clear: it seems that those who most desire to know Christ risen are also the easiest to persuade. The greatest desire requires the least to fulfill it.

The more desire, the less other than desire is required. Desire emerges not as an annihilating but rather as a creative force. In a vaguely Deleuzean move well before Deleuze, Pseudo-Dionysius credits Creation to God's desire, an other-directed Eros. Presumably God lacks nothing—but desires everything. In this context we may recall the Deleuzean emphasis on the creative power of desire as "strictly immanent to a plane which it does not pre-exist."[36] It is not that desire exists, and *then* creates, but that it is created with creation. Here, too, we may see in Deleuzean desire a model of divine creation: Perhaps creation is the Dionysian outpouring of Eros. Perhaps God is God, as some Neoplatonists argue, by virtue of separation from the world God creates. But this separation, as much as the reunitive urge, can be seen as an act of Eros, of desire. Desire (even where it is constitutive of identity) relies, as we have seen, upon difference, and if Eros is creative, perhaps divine Eros creates first by making desire itself possible, by manifesting creatively the desire for desire. Stephen Moore also reads the gospel of John as a story of desire, though he focuses upon earlier imagery (4:10): "What Jesus longs for from this woman ... is that *she* long for the living water that *he* longs to give *her*. Jesus thirsts to arouse *her* thirst. His desire is to be the desire of this woman, to have her recognize in him that which she herself lacks."[37] Pseudo-Dionysius meets not only Deleuze but Lacan, and desire in action continues to create.

Desire, in keeping with this creative model, draws as much as being drawn. Gregory writes, "The souls, therefore, draw to themselves a desire for their immortal bridegroom and follow the Lord God."[38] Faith, too, easily satisfied, desires everything—it transfigures the world and desires that transfiguration, rather than simply being, as Bruce Milem puts it, "an unfounded cognitive commitment."[39] Gregory links faith to *epektasis:* "Since comprehension of His transcendent nature cannot be fathomed by human reasoning and intelligence, faith takes its place and fosters it (*epekteinousa*)."[40]

As I have already indicated, desire in the gospel of John is linked to knowledge—the will to know God in the person of Christ. But just as desire for reverses its customary sense to become *at the same time* creation of, so too knowing God reverses into God's knowing us.[41] "The eye in which I see God," writes Meister Eckhart, "is the same eye in which God sees me."[42] The hand Thomas puts into the side of the risen body of God is the hand God reaches into the transfigured world. Explaining the identity of the touching and abandoning gods, Nancy writes, "The god who touches man touches him so as to leave him to himself, not so as to take hold of him and detain him."[43] *Do not hold on to me* is a request the divine is prepared to respect as well as to make. The knower becomes known, and is transformed with the world by a knowledge as strange as desire. Our desire is intellectual as well as somatic; our words tell us what we will as much as what we know; our senses tell us what our language cannot comprehend.

This interpretation necessarily means reading the resurrection as a gift of something other than individual sempiternity. Nietzsche in *The Anti-Christ* (somewhat misleadingly titled in translation, as he is full of praise for Christ while nonetheless thoroughly anti-Christian) argues vehemently against the value of the resurrection. Christ, on Nietzsche's reading, serves not as dogmatist but as exemplar; someone whose "religion" is lived blessedness rather than doctrine (of this, more below). Peculiarly, Nietzsche sees the resurrection as *destructive* of the very notion of a redemptive *life:* "From now on there is introduced into the type of the redeemer ... the doctrine of his death as a sacrificial death, the doctrine of the Resurrection with which the entire concept 'blessedness,' the whole and sole reality of the Evangel, is juggled away—for the benefit of a state *after* death."[44] Like much that is malicious in Christianity, this turn is attributed to Paul. In Nietzsche's reading of the Pauline shift in emphasis, we find him (Nietzsche, that is, not Paul) at least potentially aware that the pre- and post-resurrection Christs need not be understood in opposition:

> The type of the redeemer, the doctrine, the practice, the death, the meaning of the death, even the sequel to the death—nothing was left untouched, nothing was left bearing even the remotest resemblance to reality. Paul simply shifted the center of gravity of that entire existence *beyond* this existence—in the *lie* of the "resurrected" Jesus. In fact he could make no use at all of the redeemer's life—he needed the death on the Cross *and* something in addition.[45]

Later Nietzsche adds of that "something": "The great lie of personal immortality destroys all rationality, all naturalness of instinct—all that is salutary, all that is life-furthering, all that holds a guarantee of the future in the instincts henceforth excites mistrust."[46]

If in fact the resurrection is read as a guarantee of "personal immortality," of perpetual endurance, then the blessedness of living as we know it is put into doubt. But if the resurrection is read instead as a transfiguration of the temporality of living, such that time and eternity no longer stand in opposition but are emphasized at once, then the blessedness of life is emphasized, too. Just as Paul may be faulted for making no use of the redeemer's life, so, too, may Nietzsche for making no use of his death. That is: perhaps the *sequence* life-death-life, by its very unexpectedness, takes us out of sequentiality as we understand it, suggests not events that follow one another but an irruption into time of life outside of time—the fullness of eternity, the overflow of *living* into the space of death. Again, we are dealing with a metaphorization: in time we understand in sequence what eternity gives us, not as always the same, but as every transfiguration at once. Words and the movements of bodies, the Word and the Flesh, must occupy time, but they may show us a way out of it.

As I shall suggest in the next chapter, the sense best suited to the temporal exploration of nonlinear temporality is that of touch. Despite all the visual and luminal imagery of the early chapters of John, despite the miraculous healing and creative power of speech, the lingering mysteries as well as the strongest answers are presented through touch.

As I shall also argue there, touch, most conspicuously of all the senses, is always double. While it is often possible to label active and passive participants in tactile contact, it is no less true that to touch, even to touch an inanimate object, is always to be touched in return. Merleau-Ponty writes, "between my movements and what I touch, there must exist some relationship by principle, some kinship. . . . This can happen only if my hand, while it is felt from within, is also accessible from without, itself tangible, . . . if it takes its place among the things it touches, is in a sense one of them, opens finally upon a tangible being of which it is also a part."[47] The inevitable response of touched flesh (because even stillness, whether anticipatory or hostile or deeply attentive, is a response) makes this truth still more evident: If my left hand can touch my right hand while it in turn contacts some tangible thing, can touch it touching, "why, when touching the hand of another, would I not touch in it the same power to espouse the things that I have touched in my own?"[48] When we touch flesh, the touch is more than simply *double;* it renders useless the tidiness of our two-part distinctions, notably the opposition between act and passion. Touch is a double action, and so, too, not touching is up to neither Christ nor Mary Magdalene, but to that which is between them: the touch me and believe is up to neither Christ nor Thomas, but to that which calls across them. Both and neither: Nancy writes, "It is by touching the other that the body is a body, absolutely separated and absolutely shared."[49] The puzzle of the Incarnation is that of separation and sharing, human with divine, God father with God son, human with the Son of Man. A touched God who is always in act is the God of the Passion, too.

Christ's is perfect responsive flesh, manifesting across all the senses the dual responsivity most characteristic of touch. The will this flesh manifests is divine and human at once. In it act and potency are indistinguishable; what *can be* given is also what is of necessity called forth; what can be known but never grasped is always already granted, faith sustained—without ever rooting itself in the solidity of proof. It sustains the drawing forth of desire and of faith; it rises and it descends.

Whatever sensory modality gives the flesh of Christ in these striking chapters nonetheless, somehow, participates in the peculiarities of touch. Christ's perfect freedom is manifest as perfect responsivity, and Nietzsche gets this much wrong: if, as he claims, Dionysus overcomes both the boundaries and the coherence of individuation,[50] if the Dionysian is the inability not to respond rather than the chill of rational or even imagistic distance, if "the will to power is manifested as a capacity for being affected,"[51] then we find in the gospel of John not Dionysus *versus* the Crucified,[52] but a paradoxical synthesis of the two, as of freedom and necessity, of will and obedience in call and response, of flesh and the word, of knowledge and incomprehensibility.

Nietzsche's reading of Christ (the "only Christian")[53] prior to the crucifixion does seem appropriate to the gospel of John. The *faith* offered by the Incarnate God is not doctrinal, he argues: "Such a faith does not … defend itself—it has no idea to what extent it could one day cause dissention. It does not prove itself—either by miracles or by rewards and promises, and certainly not 'by the Scriptures': it is every moment its own miracle, its own reward, its own proof, its own 'kingdom of God.' Neither does this faith formulate itself—it lives, it resists formulas."[54]

Faith and not proof; a way of living so fully alive as to be its own reward. *This* world, Nietzsche argues, is transfigured in this original Christianity, rendered blessed.[55] "Every kind of distancing relationship between God and man is abolished,"[56] he writes. There is no distance between the body and the soul, between this world and the next, between profane and sacred— between the flesh and the word. The wounds themselves are ultimately material and wholly transfigurative, the mark of death transfigured by the impossible fact of living.

Christ, in this reading, has no "power" of resistance. "Neither by words nor in his heart," Nietzsche says, "does he resist the man who does him evil."[57] And this nonresistance is transfiguration, too. It is the awareness of the entire world as blessed, desirable, desire itself. Nietzsche will allow holiness to the figure of Christ on the cross, if not afterward. He analyzes the dialogue between Christ and one of the thieves crucified next to him, the thief who, in his last moments, is also aware of the blessedness of the world: "'That was verily a *divine* man, a child of God!'—says the thief. 'If thou feelest this'—answers the redeemer—'*thou art in Paradise,* thou art a child of God.' *Not* to defend oneself, *not* to grow angry, *not* to make responsible . . . But not to resist even the evil man—to *love* him . . . "[58]

To love: to be wholly attuned to, to respond precisely to need, to give what is needed without overwhelming the gracefulness of desire. The will of John's Christ is a will so perfectly attuned to this blessed world that deliberation makes no sense. The will of God the Father creates the world in an overflow of desire; the will of God the Son redeems the world in a return of desire. And, if we are good Trinitarians, we find once more that the emanation is the return, and the Holy Spirit proceeds from the Father and the Son.

Both the visuality of light and the aurality of speech appeal to well-developed senses of the Word—the former read, the latter heard. But where the Word becomes flesh and dwells among us, we face a third and less expected modality, that of touch. Perhaps, in fact, *Word* is the difference between body and flesh, between will-less corpse and the responsivity of flesh in motion. Flesh is body that hears and reads the call to touch.

Finally, and paradoxically, it is touch, the most transient of senses, that stays. Though light is both life and truth, it too begins in the Word (God, after all, *says* "Let there be light"), a word that both makes and mends, a word divinely creative and miraculously healing. But also a desiring and creative word that touches and draws touch, a vision that reminds us of Christ's hands on the beggar's eyes, a vision reminding us of the "inscription of the touching in the visible, of the seeing in the tangible,"[59] a Word reverberant in receptive ears. Skin, says Nancy, has neither inside nor outside, "it is the skin, all the various types of skin, here and there open and turned into membranes mucous, poured out inside of itself, or rather without either an inside or an outside." Then: "But the skin is always exhibition, exposition, and the minutest look is a touching that brushes against it, and exposes it once more."[60] Touch, which cannot stay at all, which passes over and cannot grasp, is what stays with us, reminding us that we cannot, not quite, comprehend. The meaning of the Word is not eternal in the static, still sense, but in the sense that each of those touched by it in this gospel feels the strength of faith rather than proof, the memory of contact rather than the grasp of vision. It is an eternity in time of blessed transformation—as if it were a touch that could last without grasping.

Touch

Bodies are first to be touched.

—Jean-Luc Nancy, *"Corpus"*

Here we may begin in a manner distinctly nonscriptural. I travel, rather more often than I would really prefer, by Greyhound bus. On one such occasion, in the seat beside me a large woman with vividly pink fingernails and a bright orange shawl stroked, it seemed compulsively, a small and rather unattractive toy gorilla. Drawn at first by her vivid colors, I soon became intrigued by her fondling of this toy. I confess that for a few minutes I wondered if perhaps she suffered from a diminished mental capacity or exceptionally severe travel anxiety, but there was no other evidence suggesting either interpretation. And so I assumed, instead, that the gorilla was a gift from someone she loved—someone who loved her as well, I hoped. The repetitious pattern of her bright-nailed fingers on the toy animal was a scaled-down version of the lover's caress. By this I do not mean that she exactly projected onto the toy her lover's body, nor that there was anything particularly lascivious in her conduct with it—that would have been disturbing even by bus-trip standards—but that something in the nature of the amorous or erotic touch was transferred to this one remaining object. I started to wonder just what that something was—why did it make such immediate sense to see this ugly toy as a gift of love?

Lonely myself, I tried to find support for my back and space for my knees, and I began to write a letter. Perhaps inspired by my seatmate, I wrote to someone I loved. "I love you," I wrote, and felt, being in the midst of rather a bad case of it, that I could never write it enough; I miss you, I need you, I am on the bus and the woman next to me is occupying half my seat and stroking a toy gorilla. It was not a very impressive letter, and in the end I was wise or cautious enough to leave it unsent, but I think its qualities as typical in the language of love remain.

Subject verb object, yet less variant still: I verb you, love want need miss over and over and over. Adore desire crave and demand. Note this list of particular and peculiar verbs, so urgent in their transitivity, as if they would suffice to transport us one to another, as if they could overcome that irrevocable and not merely grammatical distance between subject and object. It is no wonder that love drives even the most verbally inept among us to try our hands at, or almost as humiliatingly to struggle against, poetry. Poetry of all language's forms most manifests these ridiculous needs, this caressing repetition, this frustrated fragmentation, this attention to the feel of the voice in the mouth and its sound in the ear. It is of all of these that I would speak here. Communicative urgency, rhythmic (and other) repetition (with the changes these repetitions bring to our sense of temporality), broken insufficiency, and kinetic mobility characterize the tactile in both language and flesh. And tactility marks, as I have already suggested, one of the points of contact between the flesh and the word—as seems appropriate for the sense of which contact is the medium.

In what follows, then, I want to explore the tactility of language as both word and touch manifest and demand repetition, as both hint toward a peculiar synaesthesia, as both remind us of the importance of limit for expression and desire alike, and finally as both evidence communication not merely in the mundane but also in the abstract philosophical senses, the communication of the tangible yet ungraspable, the knowledge of desire which never gives us facts.

I should hasten to reassure the reader that I am not going to set forth here any more details of my own correspondence. That much I shall spare us both. I shall, however, intersperse throughout this discussion the language of other and better writers to speak, at first by speaking in particular of amorous discourse, of what it might mean to conceive of words as touch. Amorous or erotic discourse is an obvious place to start this exploration, because it provides us such a vivid instance (being an extreme case), for language and for touch both. And it is an obvious successor to the discussion of John, both because it so perfectly intermixes the sacred with the profane and because John reads so nicely as a parable of insatiable desire. Eroticism in both secular and religious language marks a maximum of intensity and urgency combined with insufficiency, and as is true in so many different kinds of instances, what is the case throughout their range for both language and touch becomes especially clear at maximal or limit points. That is, the extreme magnifies and so makes more visible the "normal." Looking at both ostensibly secular and overtly sacred amorous discourses, we find poetic language not only in what we think of as poems, but also in the forms of love letters and of prayers.

Not only do both these (related) forms of discourse manifest tactility, but I would even argue that they both *demand* the tactile. Again, this is to some extent the demand of all writing. "Writing," as Constance Classen points out, "is tactile as well as visual, requiring the touch of one's hand. Speech is not only auditory, but also kinaesthetic."[1] A mass-market guide called *How to Write Love Letters* (I couldn't resist it) urges the would-be correspondent to take advantage of the tactile and kinaesthetic elements of writing (not, admittedly, phrasing it in those terms): to choose heavy paper and smoothly flowing inks, to make the letters a tactile pleasure, and to show in them the touch of the hand, which is at such a remove when our words come laser-printed.[2] And Jean-Luc Nancy argues that perhaps "one has to understand reading as something other than decipherment. Rather, as touching, as being touched. Writing, reading: matters of tact."[3]

And we must indeed be tactful. Besides the difficulty of speaking such language, one encounters as well the difficulty of speaking *about* such language. The language of love is so generally, and so profoundly, insufficient that even to speak of it is always in some measure an embarrassment, at least for those of us who pretend to be intellectuals—those of us who are devoted to the use of words. Secular desire shares this embarrassment with the whole of religious expression, where we so often find ourselves carefully qualifying our expressions lest our fervor be misread. Still, if it is of touch one would speak, one must touch upon these subjects (touchy subjects, I am tempted to say)—ideally, of course, with a certain delicacy. *I was touched by your words*, we say, but what do we mean when we say it? *Reach out and touch someone*, the old New York Telephone ads urged, but how were our voices to do so? Perhaps we should make our telephonic conversations more poetic, in accordance with Celan's sense of a lonely, outward-reaching poem.[4] Reach out toward someone—even to touch is never wholly to take hold. Perhaps this is why tactile language keeps repeating.

Repetition

Touch makes it possible to wait, to gather strength, so that the other will return to caress and reshape, from within and from without, a flesh that is given back to itself in the gesture of love.

—Luce Irigaray, *An Ethics of Sexual Difference*

Roland Barthes quotes Novalis as saying, "Love is mute ... only poetry makes it speak."[5] As I have already hinted, poetry is of all language the most carefully and consciously attuned to repetition, and "Repetition, as Gertrude Stein notes, is the language of sexual love."[6] "You say I am repeating," writes T. S. Eliot in "East Coker," "something I have said before. I shall say it again / Shall I say it again?"[7] In no overt fashion a love poem, "East Coker" nonetheless shows us what poetry has in common with both the astonishingly elegant flights and the painfully cheesy inadequacies of language faced with Eros. We end up repeating what we (and others) have said before, always seeking the words that might at long last prove adequate—and always suspecting that they will not, always ending with a question: *Shall I say it again?* And repetition, repetition consequent upon and intertwined with incompletion, is characteristic too of the sense of touch. To touch (I shall say it again) is not to grasp; the knowledge given us by touch is always partial, and passes over, and returns. It always leaves more to be desired.

It is not only worldly forms of love that manifest themselves in repetitive discourse. We have seen poetry here already; the opening prologue of John's gospel "is poetic in structure, with short phrases linked by 'staircase parallelism,' in which the last word of one phrase becomes the first word of the next."[8] The last becomes first, and poetic repetition takes form. That desire pervades the embodiment of the Word in this gospel is a claim I have already argued. The ways in which desire manifests itself in both word and body, between language and flesh, are often tactile ways, and indeed desire seems to bring tactile traits into our other senses, as I shall argue later.

We have already seen that, if the love letter is one form of amorous discourse, another is the prayer. The litany is prayer as repetition, recurrent phrases linking pious intentions.[9] The very existence of standard prayers emphasizes the value of repetition; though we have in all probability long since ceased to attend to their meanings, their rote and rhythmic repetition may induce in us a state that, if not exactly trancelike, is at a meditative remove from mundane distractions. The use of prayer beads, such as rosaries, adds a physically tactile repetition to the meditative processes.

In such repetition, *rhythm*, repeating *patterns* of temporality, is important. Rhythm, Nietzsche claims, has as its original and chief function not the aiding of memory but the entrapment of divinity:

> When one lets rhythm permeate speech . . . the utility in question was *superstitious.* Rhythm was meant to impress the gods more deeply with a human petition. . . . A rhythmical prayer was supposed to get closer to the ears of the gods. Above all, men desired the utility of the elemental and overpowering effect that we experience in ourselves as we listen to music: rhythm is a compulsion; it engenders an unconquerable urge to yield and join in; not only our feet follow the beat but the soul does, too. . . . one tried to *compel* the gods by using rhythm and to force their hand: poetry was thrown at them like a magical snare.[10]

So too does rhythm ensnare more secular desire. Jeanette Winterson writes in *Written on the Body,* "Your morse code interferes with my heart beat. I had a steady heart before I met you. . . . Now you alter its pace with your own rhythm, you play upon me, drumming me taut."[11]

We seek to ensnare, but not to grasp and hold still—rather, to enter into the very movements of another. After all, when we write of or in corporeal forms of love, we want the pressure and vibration of our words to *repeat* in our lovers' bodies. And as much as we would touch with our writing, so too we would write with our touch. To quote Winterson again, because she is so very good at saying these things: "Articulacy of fingers . . . signing on the body body longing. Who taught you to write in blood on my back? Who taught you to use your hands as branding irons? You have scored your name into my shoulders, referenced me with your mark. The pads of your fingers have become printing blocks, you tap a message onto my skin, tap meaning into my heart."[12]

Repetition—of rhythm, in grammatical parallelism, or of select charged words—is one of language's key tactile elements. Touch of all our senses is most aligned with repetition. I have suggested that language in some senses demands tactility. So too touch, especially touch at its most aware, touch at its most alert and intense, virtually demands repetition, and to understand tactilely is almost certainly to understand by repetition, to run our hands over or to feel our skin in contact. Not only moving, but moving *back*, going over, questioning and returning. Not only saying, but always saying it again. Sight is famously static. Though of course we know that the eyes do move, the usual sense of vision is that once we have seen a thing we can fix it there and move on. Celan's poem "Night" writes this fixity:

> Exchange of eyes, finite, at the wrong time:
> image-constant,
> lignified
> the retina—:
> the sign of eternity.[13]

The gaze, finite and time-fixed (hence potentially at a time which is wrong, like that of the disciples whose hour is not yet), is nonetheless the sign of a static eternity (image-constant), an image fixed on the retina. Interestingly, touch has been used in terms of the absence of knowing, of a reaching-toward which characterizes our relation to a time-not-yet:

> "Delight in blindness," as Nietzsche said, giving this title to aphorism 287 in *The Gay Science:* "'My thoughts,' said the wanderer to his shadow, 'should show me where I am: not reveal to me where I am going. I love ignorance of the future and do not want to succumb to impatience or to savoring beforehand what is promised.'" (Bataille uses a stronger translation—"ignorance *that touches on* the future"— which indicates how one must "feel one's way" through the labyrinth and also that the relationship to the future does not enter into a theoretical, optical perspective, cannot be taken as a horizon.)[14]

Touch, though, draws us toward synaesthesia. Thus, interestingly, the eroticized gaze becomes more synaesthetically tactile; it slides, it lingers, it repeats its movements. This is especially apparent where that gaze is undesired: think of the "elevator eyes"—the up and down movement of the gaze along another's body—of certain particularly rude men.[15] But it is apparent in situations of greater mutuality too. Celan writes in "Corona":

> My eye moves down to the sex of my loved one:
> we look at each other,
> we exchange dark words,
> we love each other like poppy and recollection,
> we sleep like wine in the conches,
> like the sea in the moon's blood ray.
>
> We stand by the window embracing, and people look up from the street.[16]

Here where eyes *move*, the exchange is made not in image but in words. Memory and the forgetfulness evoked by the opiate of the poppy hint at time's recurrence and loss, its rhythmic flux. Eroticized sight participates in an incompletion and repetition not otherwise characteristically visual. When we *speak* visually of love, we move slowly and repeatedly over the body. Andrew Marvell, in a poem known to every high-school student of literature, mocks this movement elegantly as he addresses "his coy mistress":

> An hundred years should go to praise
> Thine eyes, and on thy forehead gaze;
> Two hundred to adore each breast,
> But thirty thousand to the rest
> An age at least to every part,
> And the last age should show your heart.

The structures of our words repeat aurally even as our eyes move over visually, combining motion in vision with repetition in sound and form. Reminding us again of the parallelism between love letter and prayer, St. Augustine's outbursts to God in his *Confessions* are as dramatic as any more profanely passionate missive:

> Late have I loved you, beauty so old and so new: late have I loved you. And see, you were within and I was in the external world and sought you there. . . . You were with me, and I was not with you. The lovely things

kept me far from you, though if they did not have their existence in you, they had no existence at all. You called and cried out loud and shattered my deafness. You were radiant and resplendent, you put to flight my blindness. You were fragrant, and I drew in my breath and now pant after you. I tasted you, and I feel but hunger and thirst for you. You touched me, and I am set on fire to attain the peace which is yours.[17]

Here we begin in but swiftly depart from the visual, as the structure of the sentences recurs and flows on, and we find ourselves finally back in touch. Augustine in impassioned form frequently performs these sweeps across the senses; one further instance is irresistible:

But when I love you, what do I love? It is not physical beauty nor temporal glory nor the brightness of light dear to earthly eyes, nor the sweet melodies of all kinds of songs, nor the gentle odour of flowers and ointments and perfumes, nor manna or honey, nor limbs welcoming the embraces of the flesh; it is not these I love when I love my God. Yet there is a light I love, and a food, and a kind of embrace when I love my God—a light, voice, odour, food, embrace of my inner man, where my soul is floodlit by light which space cannot contain, where there is sound that time cannot seize, where there is a perfume which no breeze disperses, where there is a taste for food no amount of eating can lessen, and where there is a bond of union that no satiety can part. That is what I love when I love my God.[18]

Touch, I want to say, is the most nearly multiple of our single senses.

Synaesthesia

The light illuminated the four corners of the floor and the four corners of the ceiling in an octave of praise. As Picasso painted she sang in eight points of light.

—Jeanette Winterson, *Art and Lies*

A visual-tactile synaesthesia is not unintelligible (and indeed, a work like Merleau-Ponty's *The Visible and the Invisible* makes such synthesis not only persuasive but lovely), but vision is not the sense most obviously linked to tactility in language. Rather, it seems most evident that to think of the touch of words must be to attend to their sound. There is, of course, a literal tactility to spoken language in particular, a set of physical sensations that means we are speaking, and while the tactility of fingers on a keyboard is a limited pleasure, there is an undeniable physicality in the rhythm of a pen on a page. Hearing too—as we hear not only when we listen but even inwardly as we read—has its tactile quality. We listen to and we listen for movement, for rhythm and flow. As the words-as-sound slide by, we hear sibilant and glottal stop, the buzz of the voiced consonant and the recurrences of assonance and rhyme. Nor is this tactility restricted to the listener or reader. The stretch and contraction of the vocal folds of the larynx, the movement and pressure of the breath in the throat, the tensions of the lips, attune our skin to sound. Skin touches, words move, we speak. Writing we attend not merely to the designation but as well to the sound of the words, feeling them as they form.

Again, we speak and we write *as if*—as if we could transfer this movement to the reader. We want our letters to be a pleasure to read, to speak; we want our words to touch where our skin cannot, to evoke our very specific touch in its absence; we want our prayers to touch the very limit of the profane, to touch upon the world beyond that in which we speak them. Bataille has argued that the sacred is *about* limits—and indeed to touch the limit is sacrality itself. "We *touch* the origin,"[19] Nancy writes, apropos of Bataille; we never grasp it. He adds: "Perhaps everything happens between loss and appropriation"[20]—in the realm of touch, which cannot hold on. If the divine may be linked with that which infinitely draws our desire, then we find again the interconnectedness of desire and limit, desire drawn by what it must reach out to touch.

Sound is more generally mobile than sight. But it moves along the line of time, and, while we may recur to tone or phrase, there is little in hearing to *demand* such recurrence—little, unless that tone or phrase somehow *touches* us. Literature's most famously recurrent sound bite may be the "little phrase" from the Vinteuil sonata in Proust's *Remembrance of Things Past*. This phrase, which has lingered in Swann's mind and so excites him when he hears it played again at the home where he is a guest,[21] is introduced *as a tactile experience*. Madame Verdurin, the hostess, has encouraged Swann a bit lasciviously to stroke the bronze mouldings on the chairs he has admired. He is perhaps surprised to find them rather pleasant—"Swann had begun, out of politeness, to finger the bronzes, and did not like to stop."[22] He is drawn away, however, to listen to the sonata, and this by a peculiar description: "Come along; you can caress them later. Now it's you who are going to be caressed, caressed aurally. You'll like that, I think. Here's the young gentleman who will take charge of that."[23] And so the pianist is introduced, and indeed the little phrase caresses Swann aurally, repeating itself in his memory, entangling itself with his loves.

Taste and scent may linger, and in re-encounter they are known to provoke deep memory. After all, the lengthy *Remembrance* is famously provoked by the taste of a tea-dipped madeleine: "Whence could it have come to me, this all-powerful joy? I sensed that it was connected with the taste of the tea and the cake, but that it infinitely transcended those savors."[24] But they too move within the arrow of time. It will take touch to hint to us that time perhaps is not straight. Kathy Acker says, "I am thinking that the more I write, the less convinced I am that writing, be it about time, is time. Is change, rhythm. Those movements of time. Need writing be only one kind of time, linear time, that form called history? Need writing end?"[25] Interestingly, despite her doubts, I think that she makes the case for a writing that *is* both time and about time, but precisely not about historical time; rather, it is about rhythmic time, precisely insofar as rhythm is not merely change but necessarily repetition. Without recurrence no rhythms can ever be marked.

Again, repetition lurks in all of language, where its peculiar effects have been explored by any number of philosophers and literary theorists. But the language of Eros is of all speaking and writing most conspicuously repetitive—most overtly demanding of repetition. (Perhaps this is because, as Nancy notes, "repetition is the condition of affirmation"[26]—and Yes I said Yes I will Yes.) As erotic language is repetitious not only in structure but in sound and recurrent rhythm, poetic image and alliteration, so too does touch in desire repeat, recurring to the same surface with delight or astonishment, whether taking comfort in the deep familiarity of a well-known body or recurring incredulously to a pleasure always new, as if one certainly could not have remembered it rightly, not even in the instant since one felt it last. This uncertainty, though it may be an unanticipated feature of repetition, is consistent in body and word where each confronts Eros. It returns us to the divide between touch and grasp. *Do not hold on to me:* an imperative of meaning too.

Moving to the Limit

> Hence the necessity of converting reflexive language. It must be directed
> not toward any inner confirmation—not toward a kind of central,
> unshakable certitude—but toward an outer bound where it must
> continually contest itself.
>
> —Michel Foucault, *Thought from the Outside*

"To touch," writes Derrida, "is to touch a border, however deeply one may penetrate, and it is thus to touch by approaching indefinitely the inaccessible of whatever remains beyond the border, on the other side."[27] In all probability, the most conspicuously repetitive element of erotic discourse is the lovers' constitutive avowal, as that of prayer is the magnitude of the divine beloved and the unworthiness of the loving human (and, correlatively, of inadequate human language). Barthes argues that here we run up against the limits of language. In fact, for him, amorous discourse, in its very impossibility, works language against language, against our false hope of endlessly stable and fully contained meaning. Like the sacred, this language is in some strange sense *about* limits. Love, he argues, "has of course a complicity with my language (which maintains it), but it cannot be *lodged* in my writing."[28] Like touch, complicitous with language, it cannot *stay* in the text. It acts through:

> *I-love-you* is active. It affirms itself as force—against other forces.
> Which ones? The thousand forces of the world, which are, all of
> them, disparaging forces ... Or again: against language. Just as the
> *amen* is at the limit of language, without collusion with its system,
> stripping it of its "reactive mantle," so the proffering of love ...
> stands at the limit of syntax, welcomes tautology ... rejects the ser-
> vility of the Sentence (it is merely a holophrase). As proffering, *I-love-
> you* is not a sign, but plays against the signs.[29]

Note the parallel Barthes draws between the *I-love-you* of the secular erotic and the *amen* of the amorously sacred. Note how full of movement this observation is: play with, against, into; force and activity. The tactility of language is in some measure the motility of language; its recognition means recognizing fluidity. In fact, exploring touch in general we note how often and how intensely, if scarcely surprisingly, the tactile is linked to the motor, tactility to motility and kinaesthesis. A philosophical discussion of touch tends, with seeming inevitability, toward a discussion of palpation and manipulation, of stroke and caress. But still further, to a discussion of walking, dancing, to the movements of the muscles. Movement is allied with repetition: to stay is not to repeat. We move; we move on, and we return.

Motion is as crucial as contact. Proximity and distance, to gesture toward a later chapter here, infold and unfold in the same space. Nancy writes:

> From one singular to another, there is contiguity but not continuity. There is proximity, but only to the extent that extreme closeness emphasizes the distancing it opens up. All of being is in touch with all of being, but the law of touching is separation; moreover, it is the heterogeneity of surfaces that touch each other. *Contact* is beyond fullness and emptiness, beyond connection and disconnection.[30]

This passage brings touch into contact not only with the folds of proximity and distance, but with the openness of the cut (the final figure in the present work), via another text of Nancy's—his discussion of his heart transplant: "But still, the process of transplantation imposes the image of a passage through nothingness, of a sortie into a space emptied of all propriety and all intimacy, or—looking at it from quite the opposite point of view—of the intrusion into me of this space: tubes, pliers, sutures and catheters."[31] Neither one's own proper self (an impossibility, he notes)[32] nor proximate intimacy, the transplant is a chiasmic double-crossing of spaces in which he is deeply touched, in contact with his own exteriority; indeed, "the truth of the subject is its exteriority and its excessiveness, *its infinite exposition.*"[33] Like skin, the subject is exposed.

Classen notes that *touch* has a double meaning: "both to perceive by the sense of feeling and to bring into contact with something else."[34] Recognizing how fundamental this tactile sensibility is, she notes, "Touch appears to be the most basic and diffuse sense in English, providing terms applicable to all the senses. This may be because all the senses are experienced as being quasi-tactile in nature."[35] Indeed, she notes that the word *sense* derives "From the Latin *sensus*, meaning sense, feeling, based on the Indo-European root *sent-*, to go, find out."[36] To touch is fundamental to feeling, to sensing—and to sense is to go, to set in motion, to *bring into* contact. Touch moves; we may say equally that we are touched or moved by language. Moreover, we call the sense of touch "feeling," a term likewise applied to affect; those who feel more are more sense-itive. The body as *sense* is flesh, beyond mechanistic dualism. Nancy writes:

> regardless of the perspective used—dualism of body and soul, monism of the flesh, symbolic deciphering of bodies—the body remains the organon, the instrument of the incarnation, the mechanism or the work of a *sense* that never stops rushing into it, presenting itself to itself, making itself known as such and wanting to tell itself there. The body, *sense,*—in this double sense of the word that fascinated Hegel.[37]

In fact, it is rather difficult to conceive of an immobile touch. Even the sense of pressure or contact seems, somehow, to require movement. For instance, sometimes, before I sleep, one of my cats curls up against me, and I can feel the pressure of its body against my ribs. In the manner of sleeping cats, it doesn't move much. But I am not at all sure, if the cat and I did not both breathe, or if at any rate there weren't breathing, somewhere between us, I would continue to know that it was there. Undoubtedly I would feel warmth. But surely pressure is that slight resistance that meets me each time I inhale, or shift, or each time that the cat does the same. My own breathing may not be required, as my other cat curls up near my non-breathing feet, and I feel its presence too, but it too breathes and its small heart beats.

It is not merely that they feel warm against me. Temperature alone does not register as touch—my icy fingertips in the winter register the temperature well, but I would not say that they feel touched by the air. Yet my face feels touched by the wind, as my skin by the breath of someone close to me, a subtle touch at the very edge of contact, stirring the fine hairs at the back of my neck—as the air *moves* against me, with a softer pressure than would be required even for voice.

Perhaps the trait of our senses generally, that invariant (in this sense immobile) stimulation seems eventually to cease to register, is especially a trait of touch. Perhaps too this is the tactile trace in all our senses—that our sense organs and sensed objects alike must move in relation to one another. We move our eyes over surfaces, hear the sounds rippling across our tympani, taste what comes into contact with our taste buds, smell tiny particles that bump the linings of our noses. But, as Derrida points out, "Touch is the sense most affected by its object."[38] Whatever we touch, it touches us back. And if it does not, we have failed to touch it—as if our words did not reach the *you* they so ardently approached. And this too is tactility manifest in language: that at least sometimes we wish not merely to make an impact upon, but to communicate—to touch, connect, make contact. Tactility is inseparable from *withness*—even the "with" in which "the Word was with God" "connotes communication with another."[39]

We find that the terms in which approach-to-another is most urgent are also the most demanding of recurrence. "I love you" is famous for not staying said; it is an affirmation that must be repeated. Having said it once is seldom sufficient later on; if it ceases to be repeated, the beloved may well begin to wonder. In other circumstances the repetition of words and phrases will rapidly wear on us; we have all undergone the sorts of exhausting conversations in which the person with whom we are speaking feels compelled to reiterate what we have long since understood as well as we ever shall. On the other hand, the affectionate holophrase to which Barthes points grates upon the ear only where it is undesired, unreciprocated; then it becomes the worst of repetitive phrases—and in this too it is much like touch; there is little more annoying than the undesired caress or even contact (think of bodies packed too tightly into subway cars or local buses). But where they are desired, the very cessation of the repetition of phrase or touch would bring us some alarm.

Desire, like both word and touch, is never precisely locatable. It is, like the active force of which Barthes speaks, always *between*. It *draws*, as the particular need of each follower's faith drew Christ's response in the previous chapter, where the love that this faith manifests is a force sufficient to draw forth the response it requires in order to go on.

It is chiefly of the profane lover's discourse that Barthes speaks, but this reaching out is just as marked in the intense eroticism of Augustine's prayer; the *amen* is as much a limit as the *I-love-you*. As I have suggested, too, there is something particularly compelling in the tactility of this discourse, though the compulsion may be a dangerous one. Again, eroticism marks a limit-point for touch and for language alike. Slavoj Žižek writes, "The horrifying, lethal, and at the same time fascinating borderline that we approach when the reversal into bliss is imminent is what Lacan . . . endeavors to indicate by means of the Greek word *ate.* There is a fundamental ambiguity to this term. *Ate* simultaneously denotes a horrifying limit that cannot ever be reached—that is, the touch of which means death—and *the space beyond it.*"[40] The space beyond it is the loss, I suspect (it is scarcely an original suspicion) of self, of subjectivity—of the security of those boundaries which mean oneself. The space beyond is outside both self and, like the risen body, ordinary time. We cannot touch upon limits without sensing the possibility of their rupture.

Indeed, even the language of this holophrase is never quite one's own. Winterson writes, "Why is it that the most unoriginal thing we can say to one another is still the thing we long to hear? 'I love you' is always a quotation. You did not say it first and neither did I."[41] You did not say it first— but shall I say it again? We recur to recurrence, we move back over again.

Communication

> Touching the limit—which is the possibility of touch itself—the lovers, however, defer it: except in the case of a common suicide, an old desire that abolishes limit and touch at the same time.
>
> —Jean-Luc Nancy, "The Inoperative Community"

Neither you, nor I, language and touch *reach,* always between. One surface approaches another, touches perhaps if we are fortunate, never fuses.

Touch, being and belonging always between, is always double. Gabriel Josipovici tells of a friend who felt compelled, on a tour to Rome, to *touch* the famous ruins he encountered as well as to see them.

> But why, I asked him, had he not been content merely to see, why had he felt the need to *touch*? 'I really don't know,' he said, and then, 'I suppose touching something confirms its presence.'
>
> Its presence to you, but also your presence to it. The doubleness is crucial.[42]

The doubleness of touch is that of words as well. The crucial doubleness of discourse demands that we be present to one another, though we can never be fully so; especially when we write we are present in our own absence, there in our words. We speak to be heard, but also to hear in return; write to be read, but also as some tiny contribution to our own reading. Language, when it is not reduced to nonresponsive monologue or polemics, is call and response.

Our words reach out toward the touch of flesh: "Language is a skin," Barthes writes; "I rub my language against the other. It is as if I had words instead of fingers, or fingers at the tips of my words. My language trembles with desire."[43]

I have been speaking of eroticism as a limit case of language, suggesting that limits show us the center too. But in a broad sense all language is not only tactile, as I've already indicated, but in fact erotic in intent, with its limit cases only rendering that intention more evident. Eroticism, as Freud already notes, always reaches out, even forming the bonds of community[44]—of those who speak to one another. The breadth of this sense of eroticism, however, must be emphasized. I do not mean that we seek the specifically sexual arousal of every listener or reader who comes into contact with our words (surely an alarming possibility in many instances). Nor would I exaggerate the polymorphously perverse potential always inherent in tactility. But if we take seriously the unitive—in the Bataillean sense, the communicative—aspect of eros, we might also consider that we seek some small measure of that joining-together or moving-across-to in both our touch and our words. This is still more obvious if we combine the senses of touch: even if, speaking, I only lightly touch the back of your hand for emphasis, I imply this dual jointure: be *with* me on this, my fingertips say; attend to these words if to nothing else.

This is not to give in to the "illusion of expressivity" against which Barthes rightly warns us: "What obstructs amorous writing is the illusion of expressivity."[45] That is: when we communicate, it is not always to express. As Acker writes, "I'm not arguing that writing is wedded to nonsense and not to communication; obviously to use language is to enter the world; rather, I am hoping that communication need not be reduced to expression."[46] What is important is not that I express myself, but that something pass between us—ideally, as Derrida writes, a tactful something.[47]

When Georges Bataille writes of eroticism, he begins by discussing discontinuity, the absence of union or the uncloseability of the space-between. And he begins in a discussion of language: "this gulf exists, for instance, between you, listening to me, and me, speaking to you. We are attempting to communicate, but no communication between us can abolish our fundamental difference. If you die, it is not my death. You and I are *discontinuous* beings."[48]

When I speak to you, whoever I and you may be, I seldom speak poetically. Nonetheless, my words, like Celan's poems, reach—determinedly or hesitantly—toward some approachable you. Perhaps they may even touch that you. But only that: you may say that you grasp my meanings, but here at the distance of words I cannot quite grasp your grasping. Perhaps not even my own; Josipovici writes of touch, "That is surely the point. I do not have the subject in my hand. I do not hold it. But where then is it?"[49] I will never fully apprehend your comprehension or your lack thereof, and the more I want to load my words with meaning the more probable it becomes, I suspect, that some measure of what I offer will elude your grasp.

What I have said of eroticism in particular might be said more generally here: touch is the limit case of language. Conversely, the language of touch is a language about limits and a language always approaching limits. Josipovici writes:

> The dream of touch: that which joins me to the other by bringing both of us to life.
>
> But it remains a dream so long as one is not working. So long as one is not advancing towards the boundary. Which means so long as one is not prepared to cross the boundary. To return to the empty room. The silent mirror. The temptation, the melancholy of addiction.
>
> So long as one imagines that grasp, finally, can be substituted for touch.[50]

As we have already and often noted, grasp and touch are of course not substitutable. Grasp, says Classen, derives "from the Old English *grespan,* to grab."[51] There is, it seems to me, an impatience here as well as a decisiveness. By contrast, as Levinas suggests of the caress, what touch "seeks is not situated ... in the light of the graspable."[52] What we seek in touching, the desire implicit in the gesture of touch, is not an answer but a continuation. Touch is language without resolution, meaning without definition. Classen even suggests that touch-based terms for thought, as opposed to visually based terms, imply "a more active involvement," as opposed to the detachment and finality of visual terms.[53]

Though not detached, the unfinished modality of touch does not attach itself either. It implies neither grasp nor fusion, a mode neither of annihilation nor of consumption. Freudian eros demands union, as I've said, but we've known since Aristophanes told his story at the *Symposium* that union is an ungratifiable desire. Neither word nor skin joins by contact. Nancy writes, "Touching one another with their mutual weights, bodies do not become undone, nor do they dissolve into other bodies, nor do they fuse with a spirit—this is what makes them, properly speaking, bodies."[54] Even in language, even in spirit, we are never wholly disembodied. Eros is sustained, and indeed it is only made possible, by its necessary incompletion. Desire is annihilation, as the Hegelians have argued; but it is sustained, as they do not argue, by the impossibility of annihilation—by the very failure of annihilation or even possession. It is not only the object of desire that eludes control and destruction; it is, more strongly still, desire itself. And this is a desire easily linking worldly to theological senses of love. As Caroline Walker Bynum writes, "However much the theologians of the thirteenth century might define blessedness as the stilling of desire, spiritual writers came increasingly to treat love as a longing that cannot be satiated or filled, magnifying itself forever as each increase of joy further stimulates need."[55] The economy of desire is not, after all, simply that of consumption; if there is annihilation here, it is beyond the limits of the consuming, and speaking, subject. It may, in fact, be the annihilation of those limits, but it remains incomplete; we always find ourselves back within the boundaries of our own egos, yet this "within" is incomplete as well.

Limitation, of course, is frustration too. Derrida asks, "What is it to touch thus one's own limit? It is also not to touch, not to touch oneself enough, to touch oneself too much: impossible sublimity of tact, the diabolical machination of love when it dictates infinite renunciation."[56] Whether the eroticism with which we are concerned is corporeal or theological—or, in the tradition of the livelier mystics, both at once—we find it terribly difficult (next to impossible) to say just what we mean. Somehow, once more, our words are always inadequate. We ourselves, speaking, are inadequate; as Barthes writes just before he remarks upon the illusion of expressivity,

I cannot *write myself*. What, after all, is this "I" who would write himself? Even as he would enter into the writing, the writing would take the wind out of his sails, would render him null and void—futile, a gradual dilapidation would occur, in which the other's image, too, would be gradually involved . . . , a disgust whose conclusion could only be: *what's the use?*[57]

At the theological level, this sense of futility and inadequacy is equally vivid. It is given serious expression in the negative-theological injunction, where we are warned that to speak of God (reducing divinity to merely human terms) is to err, in logic at least, perhaps to the point of sin. This same inadequacy is wonderfully exhibited and parodied in Monty Python's *The Meaning of Life*, in a dutiful responsoria at a school chapel:

Let us praise God. O Lord, . . .
. . . ooh, You are so big, . . .
. . . so absolutely huge.
Gosh, we're all really impressed down here, I can tell You.
Forgive us, O Lord, for this, our dreadful toadying, and . . .
And barefaced flattery.
But You are so strong and, well, just so super.
Fantastic.
Amen.

This, at the extreme of the absurd, is both the frustration of prayer and the impetus to negative theology: speaking is ridiculous. As Wittgenstein notes, when we speak of religion (or, for that matter, of ethics), "What it says does not add to our knowledge in any sense. But it is a document of a tendency in the human mind which I personally cannot help respecting deeply and I would not for my life ridicule it."[58] What can one possibly say of what is said to exceed all saying? How is it that what is supposed to be the highest truth is least graspable; how can we even touch upon it? (And who would have thought that the rarifiedly philosophical realm of negative theology might find itself so closely linked to the seemingly solid positivity of the Incarnation?)

Touch, too, finds itself at once delighted and frustrated at this limit: it is never quite enough; it cannot finally grasp. Even those devout believers who are certain that what touches them is God cannot hold onto that touch. In the return to the self that would allow them to speak it is the loss of that unspeakable contact—the god who touches is the god who retreats. Humanity, like Christ not fully ascended, is ungraspable, cautions *do not hold on to me*. Human and divine, sacred and profane, subject and subject may touch, but do not hold on.

Touch itself, like speaking, like reading, like hearing and writing, touches upon limits—bringing edge to edge—and so threatens them. But if the limits themselves are broken, the boundaries crossed in the communicative instant, it is always only an instant, and it is to the isolation of our selves that we return. Touch cannot stay, and we must always wonder if the body we touch, touch but cannot consume, will be there to await the return of our anxious seeking sensing skin. We like to imagine that our words endure, but they do not. At most they repeat; they only follow one another, and so we must always be asking: *Shall I say it again?*

Touch, again, is implicitly contact—but not connective fusion. It is never quite unitive, never offers us the impossible finality of fused skin surfaces and selves. For Bataille, as I have also said, the reach across the abyss is at once sexual and theological. Selves in fusion, like saints with gods, are selves no longer. Touch may lift us out of the incessant and intolerable boredom of selfhood or it may seem to get to our depths—*you touched me deeply*, I might say—but it must finally *stay*, if it may be said to stay, at the surface, there, where our skins end—even if our skins themselves have been opened. Rather: it can only cross the surface, and go on, perhaps to return.

We must once more take care not to confuse the complexity of surface with other senses of the superficial. The full weight of my speaking may not burden you, but if you hear or read my words you have access to as many meanings as I. Hearing me, you keep my saying from the senseless abyss of private language. And though touch will never fuse our separate skins, when we rub off a few epidermal cells we can know, if only in the slide of the passing moment, that solitude is not the whole of the story: "But I cannot refer to the gulf which separates us without feeling that this is not the whole truth of the matter. It is a deep gulf, and I do not see how it can be done away with. None the less, we can experience its dizziness together. It can hypnotize us."[59] As Nancy puts it, "It is by touching the other that the body is a body, absolutely separated and shared."[60] There is an abyss, a space of separation, but we can experience it together.

In this rhythm—that is, this return of the "same" again, return to the original division of separation and sharing—is the touch of words. "From one to the other is the syncopated repetition of origins-of-the-world, which are at each time one or the other."[61] This is not a steady beat, but rhythm and repetition offer us nonlinear times, and so too they suggest times that do not proceed toward some fixed end. As Kathy Acker writes: "Language, if it is not propaganda or media blab, is the body."[62] A thought that turns us back to language at its furthest remove from "media blab," at the greatest distance from chatter, back to poetry, wherein, she says, "the world is the word. Words. Not that precisely. Precisely: the world and words fuck each other."[63]

Contact and elusion. Other words, other bodies touch us as transiently and yet as irreversibly as Nancy's God. Eroticism belongs to limits and to the impossibility of completion. Elisabeth Grosz writes, in "Refiguring Lesbian Desire," "The sites most intensely invested always occur at a conjunction . . . they are always surface effects between one thing and another—between a hand and a breast, a tongue and a cunt, a mouth and food, a nose and a rose."[64] But this is not only a somatic truth; it is the touch of our words as well. Contact between is not transfer across. Edmond Jabès writes, "We do not speak truly except at a distance, there is no word not cut away."[65]

Cut away, yet reaching toward, and, just sometimes, reaching. Once more: Eros is language at its limit, touch at its limit. But there is another sense of boundary here, as body and language, each reaching urgently toward one another, each running up against the impossibility of expressivity, also find one another at their *respective* limits—as if I had words at the tips of my fingers. That is: body is the limit of language, and language of body. "I am," says the incarnate Christ,[66] echoing the God of the Old Testament and declaring his own extratemporal status.[67] Here at the limit of language is an assertion no more a sentence than the holographic "I love you." Nancy writes:

> dictionary entries, entries into language, body registers, registers of bodies. . . . We need to recite, to blazon, body after body, place after place, entry by entry.
>
> All this would be possible only if we had access to bodies, only if they were not impenetrable, as physics defines them. Bodies impenetrable to language, and languages impenetrable to bodies, bodies

themselves, like this word "body," which already withholds itself and incorporates its own entry.

Two bodies cannot occupy the same space simultaneously. Not you and me at the same time in the space where I speak, in the place where you listen.[68]

This gap exists, is the space between the places we occupy. Touch is not fusion; hearing is not comprehension. Luce Irigaray warns us of what we miss in confusing these matters: "Too entrusted to a certain look or a certain listening-to in the service of representation, the relation with the other has forgotten what it owes to touching—among others visual and acoustic touching. Then the approach becomes seizure, capture, comprehension, all gestures of incorporation, introjection, apprehension in which the other as such vanishes."[69] Something always eludes us, draws us forth into another question, another touch, word to flesh to word again. "What does a word touch," Nancy asks, "if not a body? But there you have it: How can one get hold of the body? I am already speechless."[70] Touch does not take hold; tactility reminds us of the language that logic ignores: poetic, shifting, recurrent, desirous, and tantalizingly, seductively, elusively corporeal.

Unfolding "Ash Wednesday"

I thought of a maze of mazes, of a sinuous, ever growing maze which
would take in both past and future and would somehow involve the stars.

—Jorge Luis Borges, "The Garden of Forking Paths"

My first ideas do not always lead me in useful directions. Seeking a
figure of the fold, a story from which to unfold the theory, I
entered first into the image of the labyrinth. A well-placed conference
brought me to the labyrinth at St. Martin's in Lancaster (U.K.); the patience
of a friend willing to drive the French countryside brought me to the more
famous instance at Chartres, where the roped-off floor helped aid my resistance to making of myself the spectacle of a labyrinth-crawler, but could do
nothing for my obvious tourist status as I took fascinated photos. I read
Eliade on the subject (his comments evocative rather than extensive); I
reread Borges, with pleasure (deciding that any research that provides an
opportunity to read Borges cannot be wholly misconceived). I indulged
myself in the entertaining originals, in Apollodorus and Plutarch. And, in
the manner of many who enter labyrinths, I found myself wandering.
Eventually I made my way out, but found I was still rather close to where I
had begun—though the links between folding and turning, with their

implications for the strange directionality of the fold, were made for me there. The labyrinthine stories were complex, but their problem for this work was less their complexity than their sprawl. I needed a more contained image, a smaller work more tightly folded upon itself.

My mind still wandering around the idea of the labyrinth (or the idea itself, perhaps, still wandering the haphazard corridors of my brain), I was surprised to come upon a set of just-similar-enough images, in an unrelated rereading of T. S. Eliot's "Ash Wednesday." The poem was hardly new to me, but I had not remembered its being so full of folds. By the time I reached the phrase "At the first turning of the second stair" (which opens the poem's third section), I began to feel I had found what I needed, delighted in the image of the accordion-folds of stairs (Deleuze uses the image of a staircase in his work *The Fold*), twisted again to turn back upon themselves in what seemed a rising spiral, pausing every once in a while to take in the view from a landing window. Here was the labyrinth brought more clearly into words, and given an intriguing vertical dimension at the same time.

More exciting still, however, was the elusively unnamed, yet clearly Marian, figure in the fourth section of the poem, "wearing white light folded, sheathed about her, folded." With this figure, the labyrinth of words took on flesh, and the enfolding of body and word that I sought became much more clearly possible than the labyrinth alone had made it. If this woman is Mary, wrapped in the light, then that which she held within herself—the Light and the Word—is now enfolded about her.

In this chapter's effort to unfold "Ash Wednesday," I want to consider the images within the poem of twisting and turning, of horizontal crossing and vertical ascent, in terms both of Deleuze's discussion of event and inflection in *The Fold* and of Søren Kierkegaard's presentation of faith in *Fear and Trembling*. Like touch, the fold gives us a sense of knowing that is at once elusive and continuing. Intriguing gender issues emerge as the feminine figure in the poem appears to embody immanence and the apparently masculine narrator transcendence, but the theory from both Deleuze and Kierkegaard suggests strongly that both knowledge and faith belong to the former—and thus undermines the respective values usually given to these terms.

The enwrapping light plays a fascinatingly multiple role in "Ash Wednesday," bringing Mary into the fold of the Deleuzean discussion. Near the end of *The Fold*, after his examination of architecture, gardens, and, not incidentally, metaphysics, Deleuze turns his attention to an unexpected locus of folding: that of drapery in clothing, both as worn and (especially) in its painted and sculpted representations.

> The fold can be recognized first of all in the textile model of the kind implied by garments: fabric or clothing has to free its own folds from its usual subordination to the finite body it covers. If there is an inherently Baroque costume, it is broad, in distending waves, billowing, and flaring, surrounding the body with its independent folds, ever-multiplying, never betraying those of the body beneath. . . .
>
> We find it in painting, where the autonomy conquered through the folds of clothing that invade the entire surface becomes a simple, but sure, sign of a rupture with Renaissance space. . . . And when the folds of clothing spill out of painting, it is Bernini who endows them with sublime form in sculpture, when marble seizes and bears to infinity folds that cannot be explained by the body, but by a spiritual adventure that sets the body ablaze. His is not an art of structures but of textures.[1]

So the sculptural, and to some less tangible extent the painted, fold implies neither structures and depths of space nor the internality that these imply in turn. Rather, the art of folds is an art of textures, of touchable and complicated surfaces. Deleuze continues his discussion with exemplary images of drapes and folds in paintings and sculptures. His paradigmatic image is Bernini's Teresa, yet by his description I found myself reminded most immediately of the figure who is iconographically draped, cloaked or in flowing robes, the figure so close to the one Eliot sheathes in light—the figure of Mary, whose body in Christian myth gives birth to the flesh of God. After all, when in John the Word becomes flesh and takes up its dwelling among those of flesh (*pasa sarx*, all of flesh; all of humankind),[2] that flesh is born in the way of all flesh, out of the body of a woman (though as the story has it Mary is an exceptional instance, a woman of immaculate soul, herself conceived without any sin). The flesh of the God-bearing virgin surely offers material for contemplation, and despite Deleuze's talk of draperies freed from the formal constraints of the bodies they cover, we mustn't be fooled into thinking that we should consider Mary's (or anyone else's) draperies as if they were wholly freestanding. We are considering here not just the folds of the cloak but also the bodies beneath clothing's "independent folds"—not so independent at all, I suspect, if only in the fact that the body provides the excuse for the enfolding. The Light is not independent of the body that gave it birth. Bodies are folded up and folded about as well, not least by words.

And of course we cannot forget the mutually implicated folds of language. In fact, I would like here to twist the Deleuzean discussion a bit, to look at the ways in which words as well as figures wrap and fold. So my concern is not only with Mary's body hidden in the folds of surrounding illumination, but also with the folds of words, which can both hide bodies and show them to us, and, correspondingly and conversely, with the ways that words are wrapped up in bodies. And language, of course, has its own folds too.

The fascination of the reversal given to us by Eliot's poem—a poem full of reversals, of turnings—is in the light. The *Protevangelium of James*, one of the noncanonical gospels, identifies the Light with the infant Jesus in an intriguing account of his birth:

1. . . . And Joseph said unto her: Come hither and see. And the midwife went with him.
2. And they stood in the place of the cave: and behold a bright cloud overshadowing the cave. And the midwife said: My soul is magnified this day, because mine eyes have seen marvellous things: for salvation is born unto Israel. And immediately the cloud withdrew itself out of the cave, and a great light appeared in the cave so that our eyes could not endure it. And by little and little that light withdrew itself until the young child appeared: and it went and took the breast of its mother Mary.[3]

This light withdraws (as a "bright cloud"), expands into an unendurable great light, contracts again until it appears as the body of a child. For the illuminated mother, this light is not only her son, brightly about her in a manner at once revealing (illuminating) and protective, but also the Word wrapped around flesh, illuminating it. Here too Mary, who held the words of Christ in her heart, is revealed by what she holds within.

Ash Wednesday, of course, marks the beginning of the season of Lent, forty days of penitential preparation for the sadness of Holy Week, when the crucified Christ is commemorated, with the prize of Easter awaiting at the end. All of that seems to be the son's story, plotted in advance by the father. But the story enwrapped in "Ash Wednesday," the story at the heart of those twists and turns, seemed to me to be a mother's story as well, a story of a particularly feminine body. Virginia Burrus writes, in *The Sex Lives of Saints*, "Neither surface nor depth, neither revealed nor hidden, the feminine constitutes a folded and enfolding terrain—a thick surface—of heterogeneous eroticism that Irigaray has . . . described as 'far more diversified, more multiple in its differences, more complex, more subtle, than is commonly imagined.' It is also more secret, stubbornly evading linguistic transparency."[4] Even illuminated, Mary retains her secrets: that is, the Word that issues from her is never transparent.

This seems a proper point at which to turn more directly to "Ash Wednesday," in which the twists and turns, the multiplying folds and spirals of words may not be precisely baroque, but certainly exemplify the spiritual adventures of bodies: not only the complex dyad of the mother/son: flesh/word, but adventures of memory and forgetfulness, hope and despair, ascent and decline. I am certainly not going to be arrogant enough to attempt anything like a complete interpretation or reading of the poem as a whole, but rather intend to trace through it running themes of inflection and enfolding. From these, in turn, I would unfold, as in the meditation on touch, a sense of flesh and word drawn together in sustained desire.

Spiraling Out of Time

But time is not only linear. Unlike Ariadne, for we do not hold Theseus as our lover, let us, by changing the linearity of time, deconstruct the labyrinth.

—Kathy Acker, "The Words to Say It"

"Ash Wednesday" has a rather labyrinthine beginning. That is, it begins by twisting about upon itself, precisely by denying any impulse to such twists, returning repeatedly to this denial:

Because I do not hope to turn again
Because I do not hope
Because I do not hope to turn.

The hope to turn again, or re-turn, might seem to be, almost definitionally, a religious longing. But at the opening of "Ash Wednesday," the poet-narrator is determinedly in the state that Kierkegaard would call "resignation," for Kierkegaard a necessary prelude to faith but far from faith itself.[5] He has renounced desire, first through its objects ("this man's gift and that man's scope"), then through its worldly manifestations ("the infirm glory of the positive hour ... the one veritable transitory power"). He *cannot*, he says, "drink / There, where trees flower, and springs flow." The image of the living water will recur, but at this point we must suspect that he does not have faith in that water itself. Without faith or hope, he is deprived of two-thirds of the theological virtues, and closest he can come to love, the third, is this act of renunciation.[6]

In this state of resignation, time and place are strictly and unambiguously finite: "time is always time and place is always and only place." Stubbornly, he declares, "I rejoice that things are as they are and / I renounce the blessed face / And renounce the voice." The renunciation extends to the visible body and audible voice of the god who might be in the world, the incarnate god with a face. Hope is for elsewhere. And because he has renounced the presence of the divine in the world, the speaker constructs something, stubbornly, upon which to rejoice ("Consequently I rejoice, having to construct something / Upon which to rejoice").

But this is an austere and difficult rejoicing; it is a determination to renounce the world as if there were joy in that renunciation, but we find little. It is not active, desiring joy (or joyous desire) that the speaker expresses or even seeks, but release from the memory of sin: "And pray to God to have mercy on us / And I pray that I may forget." The air in this verse is "small and dry," as is the will—a will effortfully uncoupled from desire. And though there is a plea for Marian intercession at the end, it is a sad and minimal plea, without the annunciatory glory of the full "Hail Mary"—"pray for us sinners now and at the hour of our death / Pray for us now and at the hour of our death."

It is as if Eliot's narrator were working out of the tradition in which things of the world must be forgotten precisely so that the ever-present blessedness may be remembered. But he is a long way yet from reaching that remembrance. Forgetfulness is a surprisingly effortful task. Memory is still associated with recurrence, with the inability to release, with the heaviness of judgment.

We find an interesting twist upon this association in Deleuze, when he takes up the temporality of judgment. The ultimate unfreedom of damnation, he suggests, is not a once-and-for-all condemnation from above, but a constant expression of refusal:

> the damned ... does not pay retribution for a past action, but for the hate of God that constitutes the present amplitude of his soul and fills it in the present. He is not damned for a past action, but by a present action that he renews at every moment. This hate of God in which he finds a horrible pleasure is rebegun endlessly.... Judas is damned not because he betrayed God, but because, having betrayed God, he hates God all the more.[7]

Is it memory or forgetfulness we find in this refusal—forgetting of the open possibilities of redemption, or remembering the rage against the divine? Is this infinitely renewed refusal the inability to forget, to give up the grudge, against which the speaker of this first section prays?

In the second section, the active effort of forgetfulness becomes a mode of devotion, and its accomplishment devotion's reward. The narrative voice is dispersed among bones scattered in the desert. Though God asks "shall these bones / live?" the bones remain apart—although, in honor of the Lady who honors the Virgin, they "shine with brightness." (They too participate in the Light, but it is difficult to say whether they are wrapped in it or radiating it.) But if, as Heidegger says in a passage marked with many folds, "memory is the gathering of recollection ... thinking back. It safely keeps and keeps concealed within it that to which at any given time thought must first be given in everything that essentially unfolds,"[8] then they are permitted to remain in the forgetfulness for which the speaker has prayed, to which the bones are offered: "And I who am here dissembled / proffer my deeds to oblivion, and my love / to the posterity of the desert and the fruit of the gourd." The bones, the deeds, and the love are not re-collected. But this dissembling holds us for a moment— is there something dishonest in this resolute focus, in this utter separation, not only from God, but from self? Or is the speaker, passively, dissembled, at a remove from the truth?

Perhaps—especially if that truth is here, as in the gospel of John, a truth of desire, a truth made flesh and word at once.

Forgetfulness is portrayed in this section as the reward for devotion, forgetfulness that lets go of the past and so unanchors the future, blowing prediction away with retention.

> so I would forget
> Thus devoted, concentrated in purpose. And God said
> Prophesy to the wind, to the wind only for only
> The wind will listen.

This forgetfulness is already beginning to offer us a way out of the trap of time: the past is lost in it. And it is a forgetfulness demanded of flesh as well as word; what "atones to forgetfulness" is not intellectual contemplation nor meditative prayer, but "the whiteness of bones." We must, however, be cautious in what we declare to be the case here; the "chirping," singing bones bring forth to the Lady a song of contradictions:

> Calm and distressed
> Torn and most whole
> Rose of memory
> Rose of forgetfulness
> Exhausted and life-giving
> Worried reposeful

And so we begin to suspect that under this exhausted desert the life-giving water nonetheless lies; that in this forgetfulness inheres a memory too. The bones declare themselves "glad to be scattered," but we are warned that "neither division nor unity matters." Perhaps this is because division and unity alike are illusory: all we have is the fold, an imprecise crease along which bringing-together (crossing the divide without uniting into the same) is made possible.

The turnings re-turn in the third section, where the image of *stairs* echoes that of Deleuze's two-story Leibnizian house in *The Fold*, in which a sort of metaphysical staircase pleats together matter and soul.[9] Though the narrator does not hope to turn, he does turn anyway (a first turn away from hopelessness?)—turning as he proceeds upon the ascendant twists of the stairs.

> At the first turning of the second stair
> I turned and saw below
> The same shape twisted on the banister

A shape, he tells us, struggling with "the devil of the stairs," wearing "the deceitful face of hope and of despair." Here, though the ascent out of hopelessness has begun, we are still within sight of the struggle between despair and hope—both, however, equally deceitful. The way out of resignation is not *hope*, at least not in the usual sense in which hope directs itself to the future and leaves this world unblessed, but *faith*, which twists the profane world together with the sacred.

> At the second turning of the second stair
> I left them twisting, turning below;

Here the imagery goes dark; "there were no more faces."

But it is a very specific darkness, a darkness not at all beyond the evocation of despair, still caught in the relentlessness of time, "like an old man's mouth drivelling, beyond repair, or the toothed gullet of an agèd shark."

> At the first turning of the third stair
> Was a slotted window bellied like the fig's fruit

The figure seen through this window is not yet Mary, but a "broadbacked," peasantlike figure in blue and green. What is seen through the window of the third stair is a promising image of flesh in the world—blossom, tree, pasture, a Maytime enchanted by flute music, lilac, blown brown hair. The scene is a distraction, but an evocation too. The speaker of the poem climbs on, finding "strength beyond hope and despair." Here the overtly linguistic movement also begins, as the speaker asks worthiness or redemption through language: "Lord, I am not worthy ... but speak the word only." These lines adapted from both Matthew (8:8) and Luke (7:6–7) into the liturgy of the Mass ("Lord, I am not worthy to receive you, but only say the word and I shall be healed") evoke the redemptive power of language, the word that gathers the bones, beginning the slow process of re-collection against the forgetfulness that is resignation's ideal.

The Line of Inflection

Do not be ignorant of me.

For I am the first and the last.
I am the honored one and the scorned one.

—"Thunder, Perfect Mind"

The fourth section, invoking folding most strongly, opens with the most overtly Marian image so far:

Who walked between the violet and the violet
Who walked between
The various ranks of varied green
Going in white and blue, in Mary's colour,
Talking of trivial things
In ignorance and in knowledge of eternal dolour
Who moved among the others as they walked
Who then made strong the fountains and made fresh the springs

    Made cool the dry rock and made firm the sand
In blue of larkspur, blue of Mary's colour,
Sovegna vos

    Here are the years that walk between, bearing
Away the fiddles and the flutes, restoring
One who moves in the time between sleep and waking, wearing

    White light folded sheathed about her, folded.

This figure, walking in and evoking images of worldly nature (fountains, springs, rock, sand, larkspur) yet enfolded in a light almost certainly sacred, is an exemplary figure of folding. The fold, says Deleuze, is always between: "It is because the Fold is always between two folds, and because the between-two-folds seems to move about everywhere: Is it between inorganic bodies and organisms, between organisms and animal souls, between animal souls and reasonable souls, between bodies and souls in general?"[10]

The robed woman is a folding figure. Between violet and violet: violet is itself a color-between, the color of the day as it darkens, "the violet light,"[11] when blue turns to black. Blue, the blue of larkspur, the blue of the sky, is Mary's color. Violet is blue on the way to black—the night sky. Mary's colors are blue and white, but she is enfolded in the night as well; in iconic imagery she sometimes stands upon the crescent moon,[12] stars on her sky-blue cloak, folding up night into day.

Between green and green: Green is life and fertility, suitable if scarcely traditional for the mother of divine flesh; but in this stanza it is the green of the yew trees ("The silent sister veiled in white and blue / Between the yews"), standing as a symbol older than Christianity of eternal life or of rebirth from death. These yews hold the Word, shaken loose from their leaves in a whisper—"Till the wind shake a thousand whispers from the yew," a whisper we are now too noisy to hear—"And after this our exile." Here is another prayer incompletely unfolded; the "Hail Holy Queen," which finishes the fifth of each set of Rosarian mysteries, asks, "and after this our exile show unto us the blessed fruit of thy womb, Jesus." Is there hope here, in the words yet to come, or is there a renunciation of that hope in the cutting short of the prayer? Thus the color traditionally associated with the newness and natality of spring is also the shade whispering toward absence, forgetfulness, and loss—after this, we are reminded, our exile.

This figure walks between others walking—between their walking and her own. Finally, simply, "between," bearing away and restoring. Violet folds night into day; green folds life into death. But though violet itself might be a color at a fold, where blue enters into black, what would be between violet and itself, between green and green, however varied its ranks? What comes between a thing and itself? This can only be a fold, a demarcation within, which nonetheless does not change the thing into something else or cut it apart from itself, but only complicates it.

What finally enfolds this figure, however, is white—all colors of the spectrum and the absence of all pigmentation, the whiteness of light. White also enfolds the oblivion we would more commonly label black: "Let the whiteness of the bones atone to forgetfulness." Black may be more commonly interpreted as the shade of absence and dark and evil, but here it folds into the goodness of white, the prayed-for forgetfulness finally granted by God. The movement of the figure in white and blue is between opposition: trivial ignorance and deepest knowledge, strong fresh fountain and spring and dry cool rock and sand; sleep and wakefulness; remembrance and forgetting; bearing away and restoring. She is, we recall from the poem's second section, the rose of multiple coexistent contradictions. What suits her so uniquely well to this bringing-together? Perhaps: the light itself.

The enfolding light, white against the black at the far side of blue, wraps this figure improbably. What could it mean to be, as we are told with the emphasis of repetition, enfolded, ensheathed,[13] in light? We are perhaps more accustomed to thinking of being shrouded in darkness, or shadowed;

this figure is anti-shadowed, her illumination not setting her off *against* her background but somehow seeming to lend her the security of enwrapping. If this light is the Light, there has been in time a reversal of enfolding; if she is the mother of Christ, she has borne the flesh enfolded in her body, wrapped in her own flesh and fed with her blood until birth. Now the flesh made light wraps her and she walks between, gathering up opposition into her impossible moment, the pure point-event of inflection. She folds as well as being enfolded; the poem is inflected along the line of her walking. She is the line of folding and the point of inflection, the very reason for the fold. Inflection is where we begin the fold: "Inflection," says Deleuze, "is the ideal genetic element of the variable curve or fold. Inflection is the authentic atom, the elastic point."[14]

This is unlikely to make immediate sense. We need to think inflection, and for that matter eventfulness, with more care. " 'Predicates or events,' says Leibniz (*Discours de métaphysique*, sec 14). . . . Whence the path . . . from inflection to inclusion. Inflection is the event that happens to the line or point."[15] Inflection, the indentation that begins the fold, happens to the surface at a point, along a line; tracing a path to inclusion: the world folds that it may enwrap. More elaborately, Deleuze writes:

> Bernard Cache defines inflection—or the point of inflection—as an intrinsic singularity. Contrary to "extrema" . . . it does not refer to coordinates: it is neither high nor low, neither right nor left, neither regression nor progression. It corresponds to what Leibniz calls an "ambiguous sign." It is weightless; even the vectors of concavity still have nothing to do with a vector of gravity, since the axes of the curve that they are determining oscillate around it. Thus inflection is the pure Event of the line or of the point, the Virtual, ideality par excellence. It will take place following the axes of the coordinates, but for now it is not yet in the world: it is the World itself, or rather its beginning. . . . An event that would await an event? That is how the inflection already moves through virtual transformations.[16]

If the Marian figure in "Ash Wednesday" is a point of inflection, she is the point between opposites—the point at which they will be folded together. She is the inflection of oppositions; she is the point at which two sides come together. And we who think and speak are ourselves points of inflection, Deleuze suggests: "The subject ... is to be created on each occasion, like a focal point of resistance, on the basis of the folds which subjectivize knowledge and bend each power."[17] A point of inflection may be perceived equally well as active or receptive, as the point that draws the surfaces into folds or the point created by the folding surfaces. This suits well the notion of subjectivity that Deleuze draws out of Foucault: not simply a passive surface, still less a simple absence (despite the commonness of both of these misreadings), but a point at play in a world of complication and motion. The veiled figure is the point at which time participates in eternity—if, at least, we read the eternal redemptively,

> restoring
> With a new verse the ancient rhyme. Redeem
> The time. Redeem
> The unread vision in the higher dream
> While jeweled unicorns draw by the gilded hearse

Time redeemed folds death into youth again, the gilded hearse drawn by creatures mythically linked with images of purity—indeed, of virginity.

The time of the fold is nonlinear, just as was the time of touch. It is the time of eternity and recurrence. The sacred enters the profane. As Mark Taylor remarks in glossing the Nietzschean sense of the eternal: "Never attempting to overcome time by returning the temporal to the eternal, Nietzsche acknowledges the eternity of time by collapsing the eternal in the temporal in such a way that every possibility of recovery vanishes."[18] Like the puzzle of Christ's body, the puzzle of return, of folding back, is one of eternity in temporality. Nietzschean eternity is return, which means not that anything stays but that everything, infinitely many times, passes away. We cannot really get out of time, but we can fold eternity up within it. Time contains eternity imperfectly, as that which exceeds it; that with which it is interleaved but not that which it may contain.

The Marian subject is the beginning of the world, in a strange sense: she is the redeemer of time, if time can be redeemed; she is the bearer of the Word that was before the beginning. If, in keeping with Johannine imagery, the word is also light, then the lady of Eliot's "Ash Wednesday" is wrapped in words or Word as well as luminosity, and though this reading stretches the limits of reasonable interpretation, it does open up—it unfolds—some intriguing possibilities. That flesh once enfolded in her own is in the world as Word. And, folds always within folds, Nancy suggests that the Flesh enfolds words: "Literature, and with it, once again, the relationship between literature and philosophy, is a long sequel to the mystery of the Incarnation, a long explication of it, a long implication within it."[19] To explicate and to implicate: to unfold, and to be folded within.

If the fourth section is infolding and cautiously optimistic, the fifth startles us with its rending apart. Here nothing is right, neither time nor place, silence nor Word. The Word *is*, but it is "unspoken, unheard." And though "the light shone in darkness" and Word centers world, we are told, "*Against the Word the unstilled world still whirled / About the centre of the silent Word*." We are, as I suggested, too noisy: "No time to rejoice for those who walk among noise and deny the voice." No one in the fifth section seems able to hear the Word, either that within the world or that calling from the paternal portion of the trinity.

Word is infolded in world, at the center, but in tension rather than the secure enwrapment of the sheath of white light. And pulling in the other direction, those who appear in this verse are not infolded as inflected points, but "torn on the horn between season and season, time and time, between / Hour and hour, word and word, power and power." The word too is torn away, away from those who might hear it. A line that appears biblically as God's righteous and clearly communicated wrath—"For the Lord has a plea against his people, and he enters into trial with Israel. Oh my people, what have I done to you, or how have I wearied you? Answer me!" (Michah 6:2–3)—is rendered instead, like the "Ave Maria" and the "Hail Holy Queen," ambiguous and despairing:

Will the veiled sister pray
For children at the gate
Who will not go away and cannot pray:
Pray for those who chose and oppose

O my people, what have I done unto thee.

Will the veiled sister between the slender
Yew trees pray for those who offend her

And are terrified and cannot surrender

. . .

O my people.

The veiled sister, who brings together opposites, may or may not suffice to heal this rift in which the people's despair is echoed by their God's. There is no hearing here, and if God has said the healing word, it has gone unheard. Yet the despair is scarcely unambiguous. The people are terrified, but the voice is calling to them regardless. In an intriguing additional fold, the line draws the poem across the mournful interval of Lent. In the Good Friday liturgy we read repeatedly in the responsorial:

> (The Lord says)
> My people, what have I done to you?
> How have I offended you? Answer me!

Thus Ash Wednesday, the first day of Lent, touches Good Friday, which opens its final triad of days.[20] The Word is, after all, in the world; and we may not know whether the veiled sister prays, but she is there, and she just may; and after the long vigil in darkness, Easter may finally dawn. But not just yet.

Spiraling toward Redemption

> But with freedom there also comes the moment when a soul is won over to itself and can whisper with a convalescent's astonishment, "My God, what did I do in all of these years?"
>
> —Gilles Deleuze, *The Fold*

And so the sixth and final section returns, subtly altered, to the opening hopelessness of the first:

> Although I do not hope to turn again
> Although I do not hope
> Although I do not hope to turn

Although, not *because*. And this makes all the difference: the presence of the Word is not hope for some uncome time. The rifts transfigure into intersections: "In this brief transit where the dreams cross / The dreamcrossed twilight between birth and dying"; "The place of solitude where three dreams cross." The brokenly nonfunctional wings of the first verse—"Why should the agèd eagle stretch its wings?" and those wings which were "no longer wings to fly / but merely vans to beat the air" are now transformed: "The white sails still fly seaward, seaward flying / Unbroken wings." Here there are careful stirrings of renewal in the midst of loss.

> And the lost heart stiffens and rejoices
> In the lost lilac and the lost sea voices
> And the weak spirit quickens to rebel
> For the bent golden-rod and the lost sea smell
>
> . . .
>
> and smell renews the salt savour of the sandy earth
>
> This is the time of tension between dying and birth

Not, we note, between birth and dying. This is a re-birth. And a re-jointure:

> Even among these rocks,
> Our peace in His will
> Sister, mother
> And spirit of the river, spirit of the sea,
> Suffer me not to be separated
>
> And let my cry come unto Thee. [21]

The meditative forgetfulness of the bones in the desert gives way to the imagery of water and renewal. The spirit of the sea works even among the rocks.

The poem folds back upon itself, but the first and last verses do not become identical at the points where they touch. The hopelessness of the first stanza is accompanied by what seems a grim, weary determination—"because I do not hope"—while that of the sixth allows the slightest possibility of amelioration—"although I do not hope." It is Ash Wednesday still, with Lent ahead, but there is the slightest evocation of the renewal of spring here, the Easter at the end of it.

Note that we do not get an answer, do not *know* for certain whether the veiled sister has interceded, do not know whether the cry is answered—or even heard, if it comes to divine attention at all. The transition is not to factual knowledge but to the knowing that is faith, to sustained desire in the infolding of sacred and profane. The infolding figure of Mary, divine intercessor par excellence, intricately layers the senses of the poem. And she does so in body, Word-bearing flesh with special access to the ear of the Father. In reading the Johannine stories of resurrection, we saw a touch of the sacred in the profane, a world blessed not by fulfillment of every desire (nor even every good desire, however defined) but by the figure of desire perfectly sustained. In "Ash Wednesday," too, we find the divine in this world. Here sacrality is figured not as touch but as something infolded, mutually enwrapped and interleaved. This is not a pantheistic infusion by which everything is God. "Ash Wednesday" is full of dark places and fears. An interleaved sacred may be found throughout the world, but nowhere are sacred and profane identical. But as the narrator steadily, though never straightforwardly, ascends—as he, constantly twisting, turning back upon himself, forgetting, dissembling, perversely praying not to hope, ascends toward language and reaches for the word—as he ascends, the light-enfolded figure of the Marian woman walks across.

She never does speak so that we hear her, but the Light that wraps around her must also be Word. We never hear her words, only those of the narrator, and the bones, and the saddened distant God addressing a stubbornly inattentive people. It is a question left open whether she between the living yew trees will pray for all those caught up in the desperate twists of their own logics, those who "are terrified and cannot surrender," because here too is no *fulfillment* of hope.

Faith, if we are to continue with our Kierkegaardian reading, is not hope. Hope is at best the optimistic far side of resignation, directing itself toward some future where the joy that one lacks in the present may be restored. But faith as present joy delights in the moment; it has, as Kierkegaard famously proposes, just what it also gives up.[22] It is not to be confused with gratification; it is much more nearly a sacred, delighted desire.

Ascent and transversal are each redemptive modes. Both in fact are necessary, the speaker's movement toward the word and the precise inflection of the quietly pacing body. In fact, the fold will bring the two together. To fold across is also to fold up or down. Try it on a written text yourself—or with, for that matter, any foldable object.

The ascent rises through resignation to, in fact, assent, longing for forgetfulness, determined despite its lack of hope, upward on the spiral (always folding, twisting through the horizontal plane), until the final section's revelation. The speaker has already, like Kierkegaard's knight of faith, all that hope could have given him. The hope, after all, is for re-turn: *Because I do not hope to turn again.* Curiously self-defiant, always turning, he moves toward the word he desires.

While the veiled sister, her veils less a denial of the flesh than a doubling of the fold, is rose of memory and forgetfulness—she inflects the flesh, she redeems the time. She forgets the offense of "those who offend her"; she remembers the prayer. We do not hear her intercessory words, but we see her form folding up the world, enfolded in the divine, and we know.

Here those alert to nuances of gender may feel a prickling of caution. After all, are these not dangerously traditional, perhaps reactionary, associations: the man with language and the intelligent, intelligible communication it offers; the silent woman with flesh—man with transcendence and ascent; woman with immanence?

There is no question they could be, and my own love for Eliot's way with language does not lead me to clear him of all possible political taint. But the poem and its images, whatever the author's intent, suggest something more, indeed other, than this potentially risky and at best oversimplified division. They suggest, not the annihilation of gender, but its multiplicities and ambiguities (as did Christ's penetrable body in John,[23] and as the story for the final section of the present work, that of the sacred and immaculate hearts, will do still more strongly)—even a doubling and temporal reversal of birth.

The ascending figure moves in a clearly teleological fashion, through resignation toward faith, evoking Word. Are we to see that the progress is all and only his? In a sense, yes—but with the caution that this sense is deeply strange.

Faith is not ascendant (nor progressive) but present; not teleological but sustained. The silently moving sister has no need for ascent; she already knows all there is to know of the sacred in the world. She is the fold between the lines of life in the living yews, of profane nature and divine grace. We do not hear her speak, yet all that is efficacious in the poem is hers—even the beauty of the bones, which shine in her honor. She bears the divine within and is enwrapped by the Light from without. She remembers those in need of her intercession; she remembers to forget. She is inconceivably sinless; sin sustains damnation. Sin, says E. M. Cioran, is the impossibility of forgetfulness.[24]

No ascent without inflection; no inflection without ascent. This is not something so simple as mutual usefulness or need; this is mutual implication. There is no simple gender order here. The poem's deep longing is eroticized, but not along recognizable gender lines of either sameness or difference. Rather, it keeps folding and twisting: interior and exterior, word and flesh, sacred and profane. Word still longs for flesh, and flesh for language. There is always more; always longing for more without any insufficiency in what is already granted.

I am not going to argue anything so absurd (or contentious) as that "Ash Wednesday" is, simply, a poem about folding. But it does evoke the themes of the enfolding of words and flesh that will be important in the next chapter: inflection and articulation, repetition and memory (in an odd relation to desire), and in the final line reaching across and bringing to: "Suffer me not to be separated / And let my cry come unto Thee." Here the Old Testament Psalms ("let my cry come unto thee") meet the late middle ages (at least) of the "Anima Christi" ("O good Jesus, hear me. / Within Thy wounds hide me. / Suffer me not to be separated from Thee").[25]

The body in the poem is never revealed, always enfolded, sheathed, veiled. Yet we do not doubt its presence beneath the veiling, its power to fold together sacred and profane; its power to pray, to make language with this world-crossing power. In the fashion of all labyrinthine folding, it is a bringing together and branching off; winding within yet never wholly sealing off, never radically disjoining inside and out. It hints at recurrence and at memory, correspondingly, at temporal redemption. It is at once, to give Deleuze his due, baroque and rhizomatic.

It is time to turn from the stories to the fold itself.

Fold

What is there to see on the surface of the image? "No longer what there is to see behind it, but whether I can bring myself to look at what I can't help seeing—which unfolds on a single plane."

—Gilles Deleuze, "Letter to Serge Daney"

As words touch the skin, so too do bodies enfold language, and vice versa; as tactility may be found in both word and flesh, so too may the figure of the fold. Several writers have hinted at the continuity of thought between touch and fold. Irigaray writes, "Touching must remain sensuous, join the near, without dissolving it in the surroundings. Touching must reach it and, as a result, close it again, withdrawn. Enfolded in a proper, which does not make it imperceptible to the other but reveals it to the other, while preparing a proximity between us."[1] For her the fold is a figure of desire, too: "Approaching involves an irreducible distancing. This distancing lies, insurmountable, in the drawing near to one another, like an elusive mystery that we transgress ceaselessly in an anticipation of desire, but of which the preservation is necessary in order that desire unfold toward a blossoming which does not happen without withdrawal."[2]

I have said that touch is always double, always on the edge of confusing the active and the passive, action and passion. It excites and disturbs surfaces, but always finally leaves them to themselves, leaves its subjects ungrasped. The fold would seem to be more nearly prehensile: the move from touch to fold also suggests that from the caress to the embrace, from the brush of words at the tips of fingers to the enwrapping within arms and descriptions, from the touch at the boundary of the sacred to the in-corporation that wraps divinity into every thing without identifying sacred and profane. But to fold, even to enfold, is still never quite to grasp securely, never to dig our minds or fingers in; to wrap around still somehow (however reluctantly) respects those edges, those surface limits (otherwise, we are in the realm of horror films). Language, we are accustomed to think, is inscribed upon bodies. What if it is also folded around bodies, and folded up in them?

My intention here is to show that language and flesh are mutually implicated, folded up together as well, and that both may be theorized in the figure of the fold. In looking at body and language in terms of the fold, four attributes emerge as being of particular importance. The first is exploration—the branching and unfolding of the path before us, in a rather clear connection to the exploratory traits of touch. The second is articulation, both the fineness of folding up and the fluidity of unfolding—the creasing and complication that permit unfolding and enfolding. Though bodily and linguistic articulation can in some ways be understood together, we must also note the tendency of corporeal experience to render us inarticulate. The third is enwrapping, what we might in this context call (if the pun may be forgiven) wrapture, as the movement of enveloping or folding in, folding around, enfolding. Enwrapping involves not only this sense of both sheath and embrace, but also the verbal workings of memory, and links us back both to the attempt to touch upon idea and experience and to the effort to grasp. It turns out, at least in temporal terms, to be far closer to the former. The fourth is once more repetition, the movement of folding back upon. Touch implies repetition, but folding demands it—not only in its function as memory, but as a necessary moving back. The implication of mobility in each of these modes or attributes is no doubt apparent already, and I shall make more of it in exploring each in its turn.

Complex Explorations

I know something about labyrinths. Not for nothing am I the greatgrandson of Ts'ui Pen. He was Governor of Yunnan and gave up temporal power to write a novel with more characters than there are in the *Hung Lou Meng*, and to create a maze in which all men would lose themselves. He spent thirteen years on these oddly assorted tasks before he was assassinated by a stranger. His novel had no sense to it and nobody ever found his labyrinth.

—Jorge Luis Borges, "The Garden of Forking Paths"

Tactility touches upon the surface; the fold complicates it. Touch tends to repetitious patterning; folds tend to multiplicity and complication. Folding draws surfaces and portions of surface together without their ever quite fusing, though they may be brought into contact, brought to the point of touching. Like the infinitely renewable preoccupations of touch, the fold's wrinkled complications of the surface are no less absorbing than the profundities of depth. Moving from touch to fold we move from brushing across the surface to wrapping around it, from touching upon the possibility of meaning to folding around the space where meaning would be.

Any surface folded is more complex than a smooth surface can be. Folded back upon itself, human meaning in word and flesh alike becomes labyrinthine. As Bataille writes:

> With respect to men, their existence is linked to language. Each person … knows of his existence with the help of words.… Being is mediated in him through words, which can only arbitrarily give themselves "autonomous being" and only profoundly as "being in relation to." It suffices for a short time to follow the trace, the repeated course of words, in order to perceive, in a sort of vision, the labyrinthine constitution of beings.[3]

The labyrinthine structure makes a certain conversational sense of words. In conversation, we seldom if ever have the paths and twists of the interchange thought out (and when we do, we frequently find that our conversational partners refuse to follow the directions we had in mind for them). Instead, we wander down those that open to us, opening further conversation by query, sometimes returning to a main track or subject. Literature gives us labyrinths of words as well. The works of such wonderfully word-smitten word-smiths as Borges and Eco offer labyrinthine libraries in which one can get lost in one's reading rather more literally than is customary. Both, interestingly, make their labyrinths exceptionally vast libraries, containing rare treasures in words. It is as if the libraries of Babel and of Eco's Benedictine abbey are the houses of language itself, manifesting in their spaces the impossibly complex possibilities of words.

Writing, perhaps more than reading and at least as much as conversation, proceeds in a decidedly labyrinthine fashion. When I begin to write, often I have in mind a not unclear (if seldom perfectly lucid) sense of where it is that I want my words to go; what topics I aim to address, and how I shall proceed in addressing them. But in a surprisingly large percentage of my efforts, as I write toward my goal and set down my claims, an unexpected path opens to the side, and I find (sometimes with delight and other times with dismay) that I must explore it as well. This exploration is not simply a sidetracking or derailing; it is a complication, because I retain my goal in writing—that is, I must now fold this side-path back into the story. This does not mean refusing to follow it, but figuring out both how to follow it *and* how to return from it, to a line of thought that is no longer straight at all, but complicated and indefinitely (if not in fact infinitely) complicatible. And, just as in a labyrinth more commonly conceived, some of these pursuits will be dead ends, whereas others may lead to places in thought far more intriguing than those toward which I had originally directed my words. Nor does this seem to be an idiosyncratic experience. Asked why he had abandoned his elegantly planned series on the history of sexuality after announcing it in *The Archaeology of Knowledge* and turned his work on the subject in a new direction entirely, Foucault replied, in essence, that it is terribly boring to write if you already know what you're going to say.[4]

Human being—we must perceive the existential as an active verb—is bodily and linguistic. It is visible and articulable, though we must not make the mistake of lining up the former only with body and the latter likewise with language. The two are folded up together and across one another. But if Bataille is at all right about our labyrinthine constitution, then we encounter here one of the puzzles and frustrations of folding: How do we articulate the labyrinthine? Articulation, after all, is not simply a matter of folding up and complicating, of division and recursion. We think of the effort to articulate as working in the service of clarity, but the labyrinth is also an unfolding.

The philosopher who has been most explicitly attentive to the fold is of course Deleuze, who finds folds everywhere. In his work the question of the fold is closely allied with the fundamental philosophical inquiry *Which one?* Studying the fold in all its baroque complexity, Deleuze writes of the Leibnizian preoccupation with perspective and its implications for "truth"—surely one of the few things Leibniz shares with Nietzsche:

> Leibniz's idea about point of view as the secret of things, as focus, cryptography, or even as the determination of the indeterminate by means of ambiguous signs: *what* I am telling you, *what* you are thinking about, do you agree to tell *him* about it, provided that we know what to expect of *it*, about *her*, and that we also agree about who *he* is and who *she* is? As in a Baroque anamorphosis, only point of view provides us with answers and cases.[5]

The point of view is the point at which the fabric is folded; it is the *Which one?* of Leibnizian, but still more of Deleuzean, philosophy. Nor, as I have suggested, is Leibniz the only source of Deleuze's thoughts on folding:

> It's in Foucault himself that surfaces become essentially surfaces on which things are inscribed: this is what utterances being "neither visible nor hidden" is all about. Archaeology amounts to constituting a surface on which things are inscribed. . . . Surface isn't opposed to depth (from which one resurfaces) but to interpretations. Foucault's method was always opposed to any interpretative method. Never interpret; experience, experiment. . . . The theme of folds and enfolding, so important in Foucault, takes us back to the skin.[6]

Foucault is not, Deleuze argues, a philosopher of the depths beneath surfaces, but of the complexities of the histories traced upon them, where surfaces and depths are not opposed. As I've noted, Foucault's method is in the Nietzschean sense genealogical, a tracing of lines in their complicated branching. A study of folds, then, like a study of touch, must trace across surfaces—the inscription and the crease are not to be identified, but they are less clearly distinguished than we might have supposed.

For Leibniz, Deleuze says, matter is "spirited,"[7] alive inseparably from itself, in motion—the motions of rippling, wrapping, folding. Word and flesh are not artificially brought together but always, as animate, mutually implicated.

Articulation

Oh no, I've said too much. . . . I haven't said enough.

—REM, "Losing My Religion"

Articulation suggests both a folding up and an unfolding, and in each a certain accuracy or precision; it suggests language and body, and in each a certain realized capability. I shall take up in turn each of these points of inflection in this particular fourfold.

As we have seen, Deleuze addresses articulation not only in his work on Leibniz but also in his discussion of Foucault, for whom discourse is as vital a theme as power, for whom only the articulable is properly known.[8] Intriguingly, Deleuze plays the articulable off the visible—more precisely, he argues that in Foucault's work articulation encounters the light:

> Therefore there is a "there is" of light, a being of light or a light-being, just as there is a language-being. . . . The one makes visibilities visible or perceptible, just as the other made statements articulable, sayable or readable. . . . Just as the visible cannot be reduced to a perceptible thing or quality, so the light-being cannot be reduced to a physical environment: Foucault is closer to Goethe than to Newton. The light-being is a strictly indivisible condition, an *a priori* that is uniquely able to lay visibility open to sight, and by the same stroke to the other senses . . . for example, the tangible is a way in which the visible hides another visible.[9]

Here we recognize something of the Johannine light: not the visible thing, but that by virtue of which visibility may be. By virtue of what, correspondingly, might articulation be? Perhaps language, which in its mutual enfolding with the body makes flesh. But it is not the case that language acts upon body as upon passive matter. Deleuze is careful not to set agent against object as if we returned to the subject-object poles of a simplified phenomenology.

> The spontaneity of language and the receptivity of light. . . . It was not enough to equate receptive with passive and spontaneous with light. Receptive does not mean passive, since there is as much action as pas-

sion in whatever light reveals. Spontaneous does not mean active, but rather the activity of an "Other" which acts upon the receptive form.[10]

Language and light, then, are analytically distinct, but found folded up together, always entangled. If in John's gospel the Word makes Flesh of body, we find in Deleuze's reading of Foucault a concern with the doubleness of flesh—that is, with the articulate and articulated body, a body without an interior (rather like the famous Deleuzean body without organs) but not thereby simply set forth on a single plane. To open out and to wrap in belong alike to folding.

In a rather different context, Denis Hollier remarks upon this when he distinguishes the Bataillean and Foucaultian depictions of prisons:

> Bataille's prison derives from an ostentatious, spectacular architecture, an architecture to be seen; whereas Foucault's prison is the embodiment of an architecture that sees. . . . Bataille's architecture—convex, frontal, extrovert—an architecture that is externally imposing, shares practically no element with that of Foucault, with its insinuating concavity that surrounds, frames, contains, and confines for therapeutic or disciplinary ends. . . . One represses (imposes silence); the other expresses (makes one talk).[11]

Articulation in this sense belongs as much to silence as to speech, folding language within rather than simply unfolding it into the world. Nor, as this connection reminds us, is the articulated always rational.

We find silence associating itself with madness as voice does with reason, but a certain somatic articulateness nonetheless "speaks" this madness:

> That the essence of madness can be ultimately defined in the simple structure of a discourse does not reduce it to a purely psychological nature, but gives it a hold over the totality of soul and body; such discourse is both the silent language by which the mind speaks to itself in the truth proper to it, and the visible articulation in the movement of the body.[12]

We can only *know* the articulable, the spontaneity corresponding to the receptivity of the visible—and, indeed, the body here renders articulation visible. But since knowledge need not be a reasonable thing, the body offers its own powerful knowledge whether it speaks or is silent. What is visible to us, visible and tangible, draws our speaking, asks to be articulated; what we say articulates the visible, and so we may know what we see. When we articulate what we know, we fold our words around the known, as much as unfolding our knowledge in words.

Of course knowledge is never fixed, and we must always be unfolding and rearticulating our words. Articulation belongs not only to knowledge in the sense in which we might, as if visually, fix it. It belongs also to *power*, and to power's infinite motility. Power is always *between*, always inflected. "Power," says Deleuze of Foucault, "is diagrammatic: it mobilizes non-stratified matter and functions, and unfolds with a very flexible segmentarity. In fact, it passes not so much through forms as through particular *points* which on each occasion mark the application of a force, the action or reaction of a force in relation to others."[13] Power, for Foucault, is never a *thing* but always and purely relational. The forces constituting the subject are those folded up within, those exerted upon the surface of the body, but also those of the body in response to that exertion—its points of inflection.

We may find a thing or at least the trace of a thing that is the fold, the point of inflection and the line of distribution; we may find it illuminated and articulable. But we are always working genealogically, tracing not an object but a movement. Inflection, we recall, is not only point but event.

We must hold on to our awareness of this eventfulness, of the fold as an act, "to fold" as a verb. Foucault writes, in *The Order of Things*, "All nominal propositions conceal the invisible presence of a verb."[14] The fold, even nominally, implies an action. It is a double action of folding and unfolding— both enfolding and, endeavoring to articulate, unfolding the surface to follow the traces of the folded.

Articulation is, in this sense, always in act. Its action, however, is (not unexpectedly) strange. The term has two seemingly opposed meanings, which, upon reflection, turn out rather to reflect differing levels of intelligibility. The first is a matter of precision in divisibility; the second is a matter of fluidity, even of expertise.

To the first: in language, articulation often suggests enunciation. Here it is the precise relation of proximate syllables that presents itself. Each phoneme and each syllable is, in the articulated ideal, clear in itself—crisp and precise. Just as important, each is in proper relation to the others: at once distinct from them and fluidly linked to them. That is, a speaker whose words or syllables are slurred one into the other is said not to be articulating well or properly. But neither would a speaker whose pauses or stops between syllables, words, or sentences are exaggerated or excessively long be articulating well. Indeed, the long pause reflects the second sense of being inarticulate, as I shall explore below: the sense of being unable to unfold, blocked in the unrolling of verbal segments. Articulation in speaking is a matter neither of the straight line nor of the cut but of the fold, of precision in inflection, marking a difference without entirely cutting asunder. Following the line of thought that links knowledge to both speech and silence, we might say that a proper relation between silence and sound is implicit in the articulation.

Corporeal articulation is less often spoken of, except by biologists and dancers. The "flexible segmentarity" that Deleuze attributes to power is characteristic too of articulate bodies. The articulation of bones is inextricable from their motility—it is the way they move against one another at the joints, set into motion. Dancers speak of articulation of backs or feet. Implicit is not only the segmentarity of the spine or the extraordinary multiplicity of the foot bones (Martha Graham used to claim that dancers have more bones than other people), but also the boneless-seeming fluidity of the balletic body. There, too, articulation implies two traits at once. The first is not only being-in-segments but something of an isolability of those segments. Articulation of the feet demands not only the ability to point them strongly but also to flex strongly and precisely at the ball of the foot alone, at the ankle alone, or both—the breaks and angles as clearly defined as the curve and arch of the full extension. The articulation of the back allows the arch of the backbend, the lift of the leg *en arabesque,* and the curl of the Graham contraction; it is the suppleness and precision of the movement of the spine, which is fundamental to the possibility of movement. (All movement, classically trained dancers will tell you, comes from the base of the spine.)

Likewise, when we say of someone that she is articulate, with the more common verbal implication, it may not be enunciation that we intend—at least not enunciation alone. We are more likely to imply a facility or ease with language. Someone is articulate if words at least *seem* to come easily to her, if she is not at a loss for them, does not find herself somehow stranded without them or at a loss between them. This smoothness of language is curiously dependent upon its precise divisibility—sufficiently fine divisions are required if the whole is to unroll smoothly.

Articulation, then, implies this dual quality of folding: that division and smoothness are mutually implicated. This play of division and connection is apparent between bodies and words as well.

Nancy suggests that at the extremes bodies divide discourses: "But 'God is dead' means: 'God no longer has a body.' But there remain the bodies themselves, and a discourse divided by them. One should not stop speaking about what cannot be said."[15] At times it seems, even, that we *cannot* stop speaking, and yet that however we twist and fold our words we have not quite gotten it right. We babble, we stumble over the broken bits of our thoughts, we say too much and end up having said nothing that we intended. Or else we astonish ourselves by our flights of eloquence or, more likely, are astonished by those of others, listen as the words unfold—and still find that we have not quite grasped it. Articulation folds and unfolds, but it does not serve to take hold or consume.

Bodies are perhaps divided by discourses as much as vice versa, but words can also draw us together, fold up the space between us. Such is a possible description of conversation, which never quite brings us together, but draws us close and may unfold for us some mutually new perception. We draw together our initially distant perceptions to move toward some understanding (which will never, of course, reach the limit of mutual comprehension). But it is the delight of conversation that we never fully grasp an other, never know what she will say nor even how we shall respond. And the unanticipatable response opens a new possibility, reveals, unfolds, articulates, and renders suddenly articulable. Just as all that is touched touches back, so too there, where we articulate with an other, responsivity is vitally important. As a friend of mine puts it, "sometimes . . . I'm overwhelmed by how everything means something different to those who hear it than it does to me. I feel folded in upon myself."[16] The effort to articulate, to unfold along a line of thought, more happily encounters not breaks but wrinkles, lines that unfold in directions unexpected and unexpectable, but perhaps, and at their best, welcome. The line of unfolding, which may be blocked by our neuroses, frustration, or incapacity, may be blocked from the outside, as well. We find it hard to continue to speak when we sense that we cannot get through (these blocks), cannot get across (our meaning).

Articulation has always to do with expression, yet not necessarily with an expressive subject. (Here too we should avoid giving in to the "illusion of expressivity.") For Leibniz, Deleuze argues, the body is "a clear zone of expression." This idea already acknowledges the interactivity of self with world. Beyond the baroque, however, where the windowless interior of the monad is broken open, "kept half open as if by a pair of pliers,"[17] subject and world cannot be so neatly separated in our very acknowledgment of their interaction. Self-expression changes the world; the world draws out that expression. Christ changes the world when he invites Thomas's hands, but it is Thomas's need that draws that invitation from him. Response, even potential response (that of a reader, for example), invites one; responding to that invitation, one just may become articulate. Much depends on the mutual possibilities of response.

In this, verbal and somatic articulation share a great deal. Dancers and athletes, gymnasts and martial artists can attest to sessions and performances of perfect flow and of impossible blockage, a sense often significantly intensified by the presence of a partner or corps. Even if one is moving well, the awkwardness of another can impose itself. The lack of another's focus forces my concentration out of the flow of movement and causes me to reflect, to step back and think about, in a manner inimical to either smoothness or precision; to think at a distance from my body.

On the other hand, articulate movement seems utterly to overcome this Cartesian mind-body divisiveness. One of the dance teachers of my childhood, for example, told us continually that good dancing requires getting the mind out of the way of the movement. A yoga teacher's utterly non–New Age advice was to put your consciousness in your toes, or your elbows, or wherever you needed to attend—not to pay attention *to*, but *with*, the body. When mind lacks focus and precision, movement lacks accuracy and crispness. And just as speaking or writing on an unaccustomed subject or in a novel style can lead us to stumble, so too can dancing, sparring, or moving in an unaccustomed space or with an unaccustomed partner force clumsiness upon the body.

At best, unblocked, we experience articulateness as freedom. A free act, in the Leibnizian sense, is one that clearly expresses the subject in the world, properly inhabits that "clear zone of expression." Articulation is one such sense of freedom, a sense also close to that of Nietzsche: freedom not as deliberation or even volition, but as force and action, unfolding and contin-uing without being stopped, balked, blocked.[18] Freedom and unfreedom alike belong to process.

Speaking is an *event*, in the sense that Deleuze has both Whitehead and Leibniz give to the term: "That is clearly the first component or condition of both Whitehead and Leibniz's definition of the event: extension. Extension exists when one element is stretched over the following ones, such that it is a whole and the following elements are its parts."[19] An articulate speech has the seamlessness of the unfolding, extended event, but it is artic-ulated by the precise distinction of its parts.

Deleuze, as I have noted, emphasizes this *eventful* nature of the fold. Thinking along these lines, we may trace out the thought that articulation is peculiarly *processual;* it is an event and not a thing, or perhaps more prop-erly it is adjectival, a quality of events. Speaking, I may be, or may feel, articulate or inarticulate. My speech may be smooth or stumbling, coher-ent or fragmentary, precise or rambling, as it unfolds or stops abruptly short. But afterward, become a part of the past, it is no longer articulate nor inarticulate. If I say of it—or of myself—that I *was* inarticulate, what I recall is precisely the experience, the process. I recall the search for words that eluded me, the making of choices that turned out to have been stun-ningly inept; I recall running into barriers or breaks, concrete walls and uncrossable voids. I recall shame and frustration as the qualities of this experience of failure. But the inarticulation is not a *thing accomplished* or even a failure of accomplishment, any more than the rare and pleasurable sur-prise of finding myself articulate is a goal achieved. Articulateness stretches over the unfolding of my speech, or snaps and breaks and fails, but it is not an object.

This eventfulness may be even more obvious in writing. In process, I encounter the same experiences of articulate outbursts and inarticulate pauses, ramblings, hopelessness. Afterward, my writing may read as some-thing coherent or incoherent, but it is not articulate or inarticulate. That happens *as* I work, not in the work insofar as it, or any work, is ever accom-plished. To articulate is to experience the eventfulness of the flow of lan-guage. Again, I may be inarticulate as I write or as I try to speak, but having written I do not feel the force of the need for words, the frustration of their breakage, or the sheer force of their flow.

If writing seems less an event of articulation than speaking does, this is perhaps because we have the opportunity, with writing, to return and alter the outcome of the process, and only then to present its consequences to others. But this in no way renders it less processual.

Even with language, this experience remains peculiarly corporeal. I may feel inarticulate in my writing, certainly, but it is not clear that this is not an extension—or, more properly, a variant—of the somatic verbal experience. What is clear is that articulateness or the lack thereof is a state felt in motion and in the body.

We feel the impossibility of speaking in our very flesh—a failure in the throat and at the lips. We may also gesture angrily, hopefully, or hopelessly, reaching out as if to grasp the elusive word or chopping angrily at the air as if to cut off the world into which we cannot speak. Even writing, again, we feel in the muscles and the sense of blood flowing, the pleasure of words as language articulates itself, unfolds so effortlessly that it scarcely seems to be our own doing—or we feel the stiff blockage of inarticulate frustration. If I have been writing badly, I do not stand to pace with any kind of smooth grace. I shove my chair back impatiently or rise awkwardly from the floor, where I often sit or lie to write, in abrupt, disgusted movements. My pen stops, my fingers halt over the keyboard—and this, too, is writer's block. Writing is never solely an intellectual enterprise. When words come I am excited, aroused; I pace, I jump, I perform inelegant but exuberant small dances near my desk. And as an unfolded surface still bears the traces of the folds it bore before, so too the written text bears the traces of my articulation, of language never wholly divorced from the flesh.

Besides this, often we experience—at any rate, I experience—somatic inarticulateness in its own right. The unwillingness of the body is a constant frustration, its clumsy refusal to grasp the simplest series of movements a trial. Inflexibility and weakness in the flesh mirror the limitations of syntax and vocabulary, but it is in the absence of smooth coordination that I feel most profoundly inarticulate. Touching we may find ourselves clumsy, unable to trace along and around the skin of the other an exchange of comfort, or healing, or desire—to express along the skin of the body. In articulation, touch is likewise enfolded. So too we stumble to express such things in words, to articulate them in a way that will touch the one who hears.

This phenomenon of inarticulation is by now familiar, the double effect of intensity. Need or desire, mine or that of another (recognizing by now that both the possessive and the distinction are problematic), may draw me smoothly, as the sadness of someone who matters seems so inevitably to call forth my touch, or as lust draws my hands with an inevitability of purpose I find lacking when I try to feign desire rather than to express it. But even the most solitary gesture may find itself inarticulate. What does one do with intensity—affective, corporeal, intellectual—so great that one cannot articulate it with or as the body any more than with words? The strongest corporeal experiences may be those of profound folding up, the fetal position protecting my flesh from the world, and an equally pronounced unfolding, an exuberant opening out, arms wide and head back. But these are limit expressions. I reach through space, toward, across; I draw it around me, I unfold into it. I articulate in space or in words—or I fail.

"That which I express clearly," Deleuze writes, "the moment having come, will *concern* my body, and will act most directly on my body, surroundings, circumstances, and environment."[20] Meaning is not disembodied; it is made both by and on the speaking and listening subjects around whom power and knowledge fold. And because power and knowledge always concern the body, so too do we most clearly express, we could argue, where our bodies are most involved.

Except that we know we do not. We are already familiar with such classical problems as the articulate expression of sensations such as pain. (Wittgenstein writes, "A cry is not a description. But there are transitions. And the words 'I am afraid' may approximate more, or less, to being a cry. They may come quite close to this and also be *far* removed from it."[21]) But apart from these we face the fact that where our embodied, fully incarnate selves are most involved, we so often feel most strongly that we have run up against the limits of our language and its ability to express at all: "I feel stunned into silence by the other person's beauty. Beauty does have that effect on me. It takes away all the words and all the thought in words."[22] Deleuze, in writing of a "free zone of expression," does not refer strictly, not even primarily, to expression in language, but what are we to make of the questions that this raises—those of language at the limit of the flesh?

The intensities of language of which I spoke in discussing touch might well be—and not infrequently are—those which render us inarticulate. The fragmentation of ordinary speaking, when we stumble upon or over our words or find them missing altogether, might be regarded not unreasonably as poetry's inarticulate cousin, language cracked by stumbling frustration rather than smoothly unfolded in confident precision or opened in generous evocation. The Leibnizian fold, says Deleuze, implies a plenum, a fullness of space rather than places with emptiness between. Inarticulateness reveals an emptiness to us, verbal space not folded but broken.

We may well be rendered inarticulate, broken by the inadequacy of our words in the face of what must surely exceed their—and our—grasp. But sometimes we do seem to express the intense with startling clarity; sometimes passion may inspire unexpectedly articulate outbursts. We may be surprised, afterward, by what it is we have managed to say. Sometimes, where we love or loathe or desire most, we find our words drawn irresistibly forth; just as often, we find them shattered and forestalled by the spaces they cannot fill.

Where language borders on body, as it so often does at its most intense, we may find ourselves inarticulate. When we try to speak our own somatic experience, words tend to fall as short as do gestures substituted for language. Writing of her own experiences with bodybuilding, Kathy Acker notes just how elusive that writing has been. "I shall begin describing, writing about bodybuilding in the only way that I can: I shall begin by analyzing this rejection of ordinary or verbal language. What is the picture of the antagonism between bodybuilding and verbal language?"[23] Acker notes that the gym is not a haven of verbal language, remarking upon the stereotypically inarticulate athlete. (We might conversely remark, of course, upon the stereotypically unathletic intellectual or writer.) Bodybuilders perform a simple "language" game of names and numbers, sets and repetitions. This is a meditative, breath-based language. Bodybuilding, Acker writes, is the coming face-to-face of control with chaos, the unknowability, the edge of failure of the body.[24] And here where body courts muscle failure, language fails too.

Interactively, where corporeal articulation is most nearly shared and subjectivity problematized by it (by the sense that it isn't quite clear that a given movement has an agent or a possessor), we find it difficult either to speak or even to know who is speaking, any more than to pinpoint a singular agent to whom the movement belongs.[25] The sacred, joy, pain, and corporeal process frustrate and elude language, yet they may stimulate it as well; as I have already noted, we want so much to speak at the edge of the impossible—to say the body, to say God. If the desire proper to the fold is, as Deleuze claims, the desire to go on unfolding, small wonder the desire to articulate should be so intense at the edge of silence, where utter frustration is at the same time an infinite space of possibility. Because every once in a while the words and the movements happen: at last, I think (though it never does last), I have wrapped my inadequate words around a thought.

Wrapture

> Thus it is a very simple intuition: Why would something be folded, if it were not to be enveloped, wrapped, or put into something else?
>
> —Gilles Deleuze, *The Fold*

It never does last. The fold, like touch, is a figure of non-Hegelian desire. Touch, I suggested, both gratifies and creates, both soothes and sustains, our communicative desire. Touch eludes grasp. The movement that leads to touching is itself an enfolding—more precisely, the reaching toward which the desire for touch initiates may be seen as a kind of folding. To reach toward is to bring into proximity, to pull two surfaces together, to fold the space between them in two (if not always precisely in half).

Deleuze points out that for Leibniz folding is a process of infinitely increasable proximity in which the distance never quite becomes zero:

> Between the two points A and B—no matter in what proximity they may be—there always remains the possibility for carrying out the right isosceles triangle, whose hypotenuse goes from A to B, and whose summit, C, determines a circle that crosses the straight line between A and B. The arc of the circle resembles a branch of inflection, an element of the labyrinth, that from an irrational number, at the meeting of the curved and straight lines, produces a point-fold. . . . The fold is Power, as we see in the irrational number that appears by way of an extraction from a root. . . . Force itself is an act, an act of the fold.[26]

Here we are told that any two points, however proximate, may still be folded more nearly together or unfolded to greater distance. Deleuze reminds us of the *act* (and, as we have noted, the event) of the fold; this point is not a thing but the active (and therefore interactive) force of power. That is, for Leibniz (as for Zeno), distance is never quite closed. It might seem at first that touch contradicts folding in this sense. Surely, we think, *contact* of skin or of sense, membrane or mind, implies an absence of distance. But desire tells us otherwise. The distance between is not annihilated; it will unfold again. Perhaps this knowledge is implicit in the very possibility of desire, and even in contact some trace of it remains. Folding implies envelopment within, but not interiority. Desire does not annihilate; it wraps within without thereby sealing off. This peculiar, never quite interior sense of *within* bears some discussion.

On at least some readings, the purpose of exploring the labyrinth is to find not the exit but the center. Such is often the religious sense of the labyrinth. "Centered" does not necessarily suggest self-contained. There is always a tension between self-sufficiency and openness to the outside, but there is as well a necessary, difficult-to-articulate relationship between them. The religious sense of centeredness seems to have something to do with precision of focus (not altogether unlike that of articulate bodies), but also with a sense beyond isolation, whether of "oneness" with or simply relatedness to something beyond the singular self. Acker gives us a bluntly biological version of this need in "The City": "There's a definite difference in my physical being or body between when I'm being fucked and I'm not being fucked. How can I say anything when I'm totally uncentralized or not being fucked?"[27] That is, it is only by an experience sometimes conceived as invasive, more positively conceived as an experience of enfolding (with) another, that the somatic self becomes centralized. To get to the center of the self is necessarily to open the self to the outside.[28]

It is in this sense that Derrida can write of Bataille's "inner" experience: "This experience above all is not interior: and if it seems to be such because it is related to nothing else, to no exterior (except in the modes of nonrelation, secrecy, and rupture), it is also completely *exposed*—to torture—naked, open to the exterior, with no interior reserve or feelings, profoundly superficial."[29]

As the image of the labyrinth might already suggest, ours is not a properly Leibnizian or baroque fold, in which exterior remains always outside and interior properly inside. ("Such is the Baroque trait: an exterior remains always on the outside, an interior always on the inside.")[30] We have no more interiors that we might sharply demarcate from the outside. We only fold up, enwrap without ever quite interiorizing, fold layer upon layer, without assimilating or annihilating.

Philosophically, we might say that we do not probe depths, staying in the same place, but nomadically trace the intricacies of surfaces. This, of course, is a transition that may be met with hostility, implying, as it may well, the lack of a fixed, deep truth. But it may be a source of pleasure too. Or both at once, as in this example:

> The notion of an ideal feminine appearance which was in some way an outward expression of an inner identity has been partly displaced by a self-conscious manipulation of possibilities in which excess, stylization and irony are brought to the fore. The ways in which this game is played both by producers and by consumers of media images mean that it is difficult to make any straightforward assumptions about the influence of the body imagery in circulation on women's conceptions of self.[31]

To claim that we have no proper interior or exterior, though, is not to claim that we do not wrap within. It is rather to discover "new ways of enfolding" that change the meanings of withinness. To be inside the labyrinth is quite distinct from being outside of it, yet the labyrinth is always open to the outside. (Hence the way out of it, if one lacks Ariadne's thread, is, as its creator Daedalus knew, to fly.) In a discussion of the fold in its relevance to twentieth-century arts, Deleuze writes:

> The question always entails living in the world, but Stockhausen's musical habitat or Dubuffet's plastic habitat do not allow the differences of inside and outside, of public and private, to survive. They identify variation and trajectory, and overtake monadology with a "nomadology." ... We are all still Leibnizian, although accords no longer convey our world or our text. We are discovering new ways of folding, akin to new envelopments, but we all remain Leibnizian because what always matters is folding, unfolding, refolding.[32]

This does not mean that there is no outside at all, only that it remains relative, and that the tidiness of our distinctions will never hold for very long.

Deleuze remarks upon the puzzle of exteriority as a point of continuity between Foucault and Blanchot:

> Foucault always acknowledged a debt to Blanchot. This, perhaps, in three respects. First of all, "talking isn't seeing . . . ," a difference that means that by saying what one can't see, one's taking language to its ultimate limit, raising it to the power of the unspeakable. Then there's the primacy of the third person, the "he" or neuter, the impersonal "one," relative to the first two persons—there's the refusal of any linguistic personology. Lastly, there's the theme of the Outside: the relation, and indeed "nonrelation," to an Outside that's further from us than any external world, and thereby closer than any inner world.[33]

What these newer, nomadic versions of folding suggest is that enwrapping is never a simple matter of interiorizing, as desire is never a simple matter of consumption. Rather, in a constant and sometimes contradictory mobility, the enfolding is also an unfolding, and inside and outside approach infinitely in their proximity. This odd doubleness is characteristic of language and body alike. Both are in some sense *me*—my material self, my descriptions, my voice—and yet both are precisely what link me—more, what make me a conduit—to the outside. That is, it is by being a body that I am active within and acted upon by the world; it is by speaking and hearing and reading and writing that word and idea are transferred to and from and through me. That which is *me* is the very condition of openness to not-me—and vice versa.

I have already indicated that the sense of that which is impossibly far and yet utterly immanent, intimate even, is linked to the sense of desire. My desire is only in a very limited sense really mine; the desired is always in some sense exterior to me, yet there is little that seems to get so precisely to the heart of that same self. Bynum points out that desire may itself be conceived as enwrapped; even, as for Bonaventure, "at the heart of the person."[34] Indeed, desire seems to be wrapped in both body and soul: "A complete substance composed of its own form and matter, soul nonetheless needs body for completion; longing for body . . . is thus lodged in its very being. . . . Bonaventure seems sometimes to assert and sometimes to deny that matter yearns also."[35] Aristophanes rightly points to the lovers' impossible quest for fusion, a quest we may feel in word as in flesh: hear this *just* as I mean it, hear all that I mean by this, let my meanings become for a moment your own. But you cannot, of course. My fingertips on your skin unsettle the boundaries between us, and there is no question that your skin surface touches back—but it is my skin on yours and vice versa, and we no more dissolve epidermally into one another than do our minds meld, though myths of physical or mental fusion will always attract us. At most, you will wrap some part of my meaning into yourself.

We cannot merge in flesh or in spirit, but we can enwrap, and in wrapture enfold our desire. Here too we can recognize language at its limits. Eros may be definitionally a desire for union, but just as it is experientially a desire for touch, so too it may be experienced as the desire of the fold. I seek to wrap around what and whom I love, but not to fix or imprison (though we are all familiar with the risk that intense affect runs of becoming an imprisonment or entrapment), nor to incorporate or ingest that which I desire. Rather, we seek a contact so extensive, omitting so little, that interior and exterior are problematized, entwined, entangled, and enfolded. Eros at its most intense *pulls* the touch into the fold, points of contact transmuted to points of inflection. To touch is not enough; we want to bring the inside out, to touch what is hidden (to be wrapped within the body and, as I shall later argue, the language of those we love) and to be wrapped around (to embrace, to swaddle, to hold safe against pain and loss).

Nancy writes of this unfolding of touch: "Being exposed, exposing: it is the skin, all the various types of skin, here and there open and turned into membranes mucous, poured out inside of itself, or rather without either an inside or an outside. . . . But the skin is always exhibition, exposition, and the minutest look is a touching that brushes against it, and exposes it once more."[36]

Skin, but not only skin. It is not only as if I have fingers at the tips of my words, but as if my sentences were enwrapping arms. Speaking lovingly to a child, I may be reassuring, providing with my words comfort against a cold world, as if I were to wrap the child in a soft blanket; or I may attempt to provide a safe space, a strengthening framework, or any other structure for the child's well-being. Speaking in love entangled with desire, I endeavor with my words to wrap around and reassure, but also to enter in, to be understood but as well to interleave my desire with that of the other, to call forth her desire with my own, to tangle us one in the other like vines.

Bodies can be enfolded by words in less overtly desirous senses as well. That bodies are inscribed by language is, as I have said, something of a commonplace by now. The notion of bodies wrapped in language is somewhat different, and potentially (if scarcely necessarily) more comforting. It implies a greater fluidity in that relation—it is easier to open a fold than to erase an inscription. Writing of body image among women—an area of discussion famous for its pronounced negativity—Michelle Henning asks:

> Must it inevitably be a negative message that I am offered? Could the internalized other of ... gendered subjectivity perhaps be instead the introjected loving parent, adoring boyfriend, benevolent woman friend or friendly mirror telling me I look great, and hence offering a considerable degree of narcissistic pleasure? This may be worth speculation on, though the tone of moral disapproval ... may incite even more women to deny their own possible pleasure in themselves.[37]

Narcissism here suggests less a tendency to review with pleasure one's own reflection than an enwrapping with the benevolent words of others. We cocoon ourselves in loving words just as we wrap ourselves in comforting clothing (fuzzy sweatshirts, gentle compliments, oversized robes, admiring asides); we wrap others in words just as we wrap our arms around those in need of comfort. And to some extent too we become the words that describe us. Tamsin Wilton writes, "'Biological' sex and 'cultural' gender are all too often mistakenly seen as natural fact and cultural artifact. . . . A focus on the erotic enables us to recognize that they are, rather, co-dependent and mutually reinforcing."[38] The sex and gender debate is perhaps the paradigmatic debate over biology and culture, and as Wilton rightly notes there is gross oversimplification in the division. Language is not precisely culture, but I think we would be hard put to disconnect them; bodies and words make one another.

Description challenges our self-sufficiency. Bataille writes, "The sufficiency of each being is challenged unceasingly by those who surround him. Even a look expressing admiration is attached to me like a doubt."[39] What holds for looks holds even more for the more directly connective senses and for the words used to us and about us. Self-sufficiency implies self-containment, a wholly interiorized ego. But we are never, being human, wholly alone. We may be wholly lonely, reading and writing, but others are implicated in the making of our very selves.

Cutting words—we even use the phrase in everyday language—may incise us, but may also cut us apart. We feel wounded by them, broken or torn, disrupted. Incising language scars us. Enwrapping language may well stifle and inhibit us, but it can give us a sense of safety and pleasure as well. Such words may hold us together, however broken we remain inside them; perhaps they even offer us the reinforcing strength that we need in order to heal. Nor do we desire only to be enwrapt. The other's words are as much an object of my desire as the other's body, drawing my words and my flesh alike. I want to wrap my language around the other. Seduction, at least verbal seduction, is precisely this: to unfold a space of possibility, to fold the space of separation slowly smaller, to enwrap the other in words.

I have just suggested that we may wrap words around us. But so too may we wrap ourselves around words. Memory too is an instance of wrapture. When I remember, I fold up the remembered but do not wholly interiorize or incorporate it. If I did, if I could, there would be no forgetting. To forget is one kind of unfolding, a loss of the wrapping power of language; to bring forth from memory to presence is another, an unwrapping as of a treasured possession.

Repetition

You know where I am bringing you? You remember?

—James Joyce, *Finnegans Wake*

A final sense of the fold remains, evoked by memory, echoing one of the conspicuous traits of touch. The echo is appropriate, as the trait is that of repetition.

The desire proper to touch, I suggested, is a desire that repeats and a desire to repeat: the desire to touch, the desire sustained by touching, repeats indefinitely as the desire to recur to the surface. The desire proper to the fold too, says Deleuze, is to sustain, to repeat—to continue, to go on folding or unfolding. The fold, like the touch, is at once an expression and a source of desire. There is always more to the surface, complicated by the infinite possibilities of folding: "A fold is always folded within a fold, like a cavern in a cavern. The unit of matter, the smallest element of the labyrinth, is the fold, not the point, which is never a point, but a simple extremity of the line."[40]

This always-more has the particular and peculiar form of the always-again. This same-again (never quite the same, if only because qualified with the "again") appears for Deleuze's Leibniz in the relation of matter to spirit: "Pleats of matter, and the folds in the soul" echo one another.[41] Likewise soul and world: "The soul is the expression of the world (actuality) but because the world is what the soul expresses (virtuality). Thus God creates expressive souls only because he creates the world that they express by including it: from inflection to inclusion."[42] Inflection is the bending and drawing point of the world. By inflection, crucial to articulation (the word properly inflected), we draw toward and draw around, from inflection to envelopment. Inflecting we include within.

To say much more of repetition would be itself repetitive. The repetition of the fold occurs in matters already touched upon. To fold brings back across the point of inflection. To unfold opens up the path that we trace. Like touch, folding offers us a mobile figure of body and language, a figure, as are both of these, of both the singular yet shifting locality of the subject and the excesses of desire. Body and mind echo one another, repeat without sameness one another's articulation.

The temporal complexities of memory's embrace have a great deal to do with repetition. We know, of course, that to remember is never to repeat exactly; events once past are famously elusive, and recollection famously creative. When we fold up and unwrap words, events, images we deepen the creases, change the picture, never refold quite the same. The fabric of our selves is different at each moment; memories may be those treasured enwrapments, but they are the foldlines too, the traces of event-lines along which refolding is just a little more likely.

The time of memory is repetition. It is not past—it is *here* that I remember. But neither is it present—it is *then* which I now recall. This pleat in time is the mnemonic fold, such that moments are themselves inflected, in sensory and verbal recollection both. The figure of the fold, then, works in many ways like that of touch. It indicates movements by which the labyrinthine complexities of body and language are each expressed and explored: articulation, a process delightful in its success and frustrated in its blocking; enwrapment, which may as easily be care and security or claustrophobic threat; and repetition, the folding back and folding up of words and bodily memory. It suggests, too, not merely these similarities but the sharedness of mutual implication: bodies are folded in words and words articulated by bodies, each repeating the other, always altering in repetition, each unfolding slightly new.

A final shared figure of speech is more blatantly excessive and more generally disturbing. It is to the cut that we turn now.

Sacred Hearts

The avoidance of anachronism is not, perhaps, my strong suit as an exegete.

—Stephen Moore, *God's Gym*

As both touch and fold evoke particular stories and images, so too does the linguistic figure of the cut. When I tried to think of stories that made sense of the cut between and across language and body, the first vague thought to come to mind was that the story for this figure should have something to do with tattooing. This literal form of writing on the skin is an inscription created by a series of minute incisions, using an electrical stylus (or, in the most traditional forms, a small hammer and a pointed stick) to slice and stab ink into the dermal layer. In keeping with the imagery of the wounded and risen body in the gospel of John and the light-enfolded Marian figure in "Ash Wednesday," the tattoo design that came to mind, one which is currently quite popular, was also canonically Christian—the sacred heart of Jesus, with the variant forms of the sorrowful and immaculate hearts of Mary. To give some sense of how deeply this idea has come to be associated in popular culture with tattooing: a jewelry company that sells sacred heart designs categorizes them, not with other religious symbols such as crosses, but under "totally tattoo," alongside dice, horseshoes, tribal designs, and tiny tattoo machines;[1] shirts with flaming heart designs bear the tag "tattoo shirt" at any number of East Village shops, and one of my correspondents remarks of her fondness for sacred heart iconography, "As you know, it's rampant in the 'new-school' style tattooing."[2]

To figure out what this flaming heart, and its closely related and surprisingly numerous variant forms, are doing on so many skins, we need first to figure out what they were about before making their way into the subcultures of the epidermally enhanced. Accordingly, I'll begin here by exploring the history and early visions of the sacred heart (of Jesus) and the closely parallel immaculate heart (of Mary), with notes on the less well known Marian heart of sorrows as well, and by noting common themes among them: intense passion, often symbolized by fire, incorporation by ingestion, and entry into the wounds themselves, suggesting a fluidity of inside and out, and exchange of body parts between visionaries and envisioned. These visions feature both literal writing and figurative inscription. They also, as I'll go on to note, show interesting parallels with contemporary tattooing, where these heart images are particularly appropriate to such artwork because of a shared flamboyance, an urge to bring inside and out together, a confusion of some traditional ideas about gender (as both touch and fold have also shown us), and a play between corporeality and inscription.

A Brief History

> The heart is never far away.... absolute intimacy of the limitless secret, no eternal border, absolute secret, secret for oneself of an untouchable self-interiority, secret of that which symbolizes the origin of life, within the body, by its displacement of it (metabole of the blood).
>
> —Jacques Derrida, "To Touch"

There are three distinct heart iconographies in Christianity: one of Christ (the Sacred Heart) and two of Mary (the Immaculate Heart and the Heart of Sorrows). The devotions to the images of the sacred, immaculate, and sorrowful hearts emerge entangled with one another, and their images are wildly intermingled—even in traditionally religious devotions, if not quite so spectacularly as they will be in tattoo work. In their most common forms, the Sacred Heart is shown either visible through Christ's chest[3] or held in his hand, on fire, bleeding, wrapped in a crown of thorns; the Immaculate Heart is shown against Mary's chest or in her hand, afire or radiant, wrapped in roses; and the Heart of Sorrows is shown likewise in or on the chest but not, so far as I know, in the hand, pierced by seven swords, and bleeding. Though my focus here is on the Sacred Heart, I hope that the juxtaposition with the hearts of Mary will prove revealing.

Prior to any of these is the devotion to the wounds of Christ, which appears alongside meditations on the Passion as early as the fourth century. This early devotion is focused, however, not on the externalized heart (still less on the smilingly benign images of Christ and Mary gesturing toward their exposed hearts for our viewing pleasure that will become popular many centuries later), but specifically on the bleeding injuries of the crucified god. Such devotions and meditations are initially caught up in the imagery of blood and water flowing from those wounds. Inside and out cut across and flow into one another, as not only is the body opened to the outside but, in the thinking of some of the Church Fathers, water becomes symbolic of baptism and blood of the Eucharist, the one flowing over or around and the other being taken within.[4]

The wound in the side, especially, as the opening both onto and even *into* the heart, rapidly becomes an object of considerable interest and even obsession. (Not only is the wounded side an opening onto the heart, but the heart itself is viewed as wounded and thus opened, the spear having apparently been quite deeply thrust.) The extraordinary vulnerability of this damaged divine body becomes a source of both strength and comfort to its worshippers, just as the woundedness of Christ's resurrected body grants to the least believing of his disciples the strength of faith. In the eleventh century, the devotion to the fluid-issuing wounds narrows onto the wounded heart, taken (as hearts often are) as symbolic of love, but love in what is to contemporary sensibilities quite a disturbing form, as we shall see.

The image of the immaculate heart of Mary is caught up from the beginning in its relation to that of the sacred heart, and, despite distinct offices of observation, it is often conflated with the heart of sorrows. Like the devotion to the Sacred Heart, this one presents delicate doctrinal issues of the nature of the body and the possibility of idolatry:

In order that, properly speaking, there may be devotion to the Heart of Mary, the attention and the homage of the faithful must be directed to the physical heart itself. However, this in itself is not sufficient; the faithful must read therein all that the human heart of Mary suggests, all of which it is the expressive symbol and the living reminder: Mary's interior life, her joys and sorrows, her virtues and hidden perfections, and, above all, her virginal love for her God, her maternal love for her Divine Son, and her motherly and compassionate love for her sinful and miserable children here below. The consideration of Mary's interior life and the beauties of her soul, without any thought of her physical heart, does not constitute our devotion; still less does it consist in the consideration of the Heart of Mary merely as a part of her virginal body. The two elements are essential to the devotion, just as soul and body are necessary to the constitution of man.[5]

The *Catholic Encyclopedia*, source of this cautiously phrased exegesis, suggests that devotion to the Immaculate Heart is intended less to focus on Mary's love than to bring the devotee, by imitation of Mary, to love of Christ.[6] However, what we find in these images and devotions is less imitation in love than love of imitation—not only in the devotees' *imitatio Christi*, but a love as well of the modes in which the bodies of Christ and his mother are rendered curiously interchangeable, if never quite indistinguishable.

As meditation on the wounds is justified by reference to the gospels' Passion stories, so too is devotion to the Heart of Mary begun in meditation upon the crucifixion. "It was, so to speak, at the foot of the Cross that the Christian heart first made the acquaintance of the Heart of Mary. Simeon's prophecy [of Mary's sorrows] paved the way and furnished the devotion with one of its favourite formulae and most popular representations: the heart pierced with a sword."[7] Here is a clear instance of the conflation of immaculate and sorrowful hearts, but also a sense of the confluence of Marian and Christic hearts: the devotion to each begins in the focus on this particular moment of most intense, incomprehensible pain. Somewhat startlingly, Mary in her capacity as suffering mother is sometimes named "co-redemptrix," even by so orthodox an authority as St. Augustine, who declares that "she cooperated through charity in the work of our redemption."[8]

This cooperation extends to parallelism. Simeon's prophecy, as given in the gospel of Luke, intriguingly parallels the prophecies of Isaiah and Zechariah, which Christ is supposed to have fulfilled. These Old Testament prophecies read, "But he was pierced for our offenses, crushed for our sins; Upon him was the chastisement that makes us whole, by his stripes we were healed" (Isaiah 53:5) and "they shall look on him whom they have thrust through, and they shall mourn for him as one mourns for an only son" (Zechariah 12:10). The fulfillment of these is declared in the gospel of John, "They will look upon him whom they have pierced" (19:37). Simeon, speaking to Mary, says, "And you yourself a sword will pierce so that the thoughts of many hearts may be revealed" (Luke 2:35). The translations of this passage vary, not all of them making mention of hearts. Sometimes spirits or simply thoughts are revealed, but in every case some mode of interior revealing is included. It is clear that the cut of the sword *opens.* This wound too is a revelation.

As the sword piercing Mary's side reveals the thoughts of many hearts, so too later versions of the devotion to the Heart of Sorrows multiply this heart-piercing sword into seven, each representing a particular moment of sorrow in the Virgin's life. The celebration of the corresponding feast, expanded from its initial devotion only to Mary's sorrow at the crucifixion, "was enacted by a provincial synod of Cologne (1413) to expiate the crimes of the iconoclast Hussites,"[9] whose gratitude or lack thereof has not been recorded. In the late fifteenth century, the scope of the devotion gradually expanded to encompass the seven now standard sorrows.[10] An official and specific devotion to the Heart of Sorrows had to wait until 1668, when the right of observation was granted to the Servite order (which had promoted the observation of the seven sorrows since 1239, though it had first emerged as early as the eleventh century in a sermon by St. Bernard).[11] The devotion to the seven sorrows developed by the Servite order echoes the Good Friday Stations of the Cross rite, and indeed we find in devotion to the hearts and wounds of mother and son any number of curious echoes and cross-cuttings. (Intriguingly, we also find the best-known devotees of the Sacred Heart of Jesus to be female, and those of the Immaculate and Sorrowful Hearts of Mary frequently to be male.) Thus this devotion to the maternal heart cuts back across the devotion to the Passion from which the Sacred Heart devotions arose.

The *Stabat Mater*, the hymn to the sorrows of Mary, has become famous in innumerable versions and was around at least early enough to be banned by the Council of Trent in the mid-sixteenth century (though probably on grounds of distracting musical complexity rather than any more explicitly doctrinal suspicion).[12] The earliest hymn to the Sacred Heart appears in the thirteenth century, as visionary devotion to the image intensifies. This time of intensifying devotion to the heart icons—the eleventh to fourteenth centuries, roughly—is also one of increasing focus, especially among women, on the intensely corporeal aspects of Christianity.[13] Explicit devotion to the Immaculate Heart also begins in the late eleventh or twelfth century, first becoming public and widely propagated in the seventeenth century. Around the sixteenth century, the highly adaptable sacred heart image makes the move from mysticism, as an object of vision, to asceticism, as an object the pain of which is desirably imitable; at the same time, as befits the relatively defined rigors of asceticism as opposed to the unpredictability of the mystical, "it was constituted an objective devotion with prayers already formulated and special exercises of which the value was extolled and the practice commended."[14]

The first feast of the Immaculate Heart is celebrated in 1648, by St. Jean Eudes, a fanatical devotee of the Heart of Mary. It seems, especially at first, not to have been wholly distinguished from the devotion to the Sorrowful Heart.[15] Eventually, in 1855, "the Congregation of Rites finally approved the Office and Mass of the Most Pure Heart of Mary without, however, imposing them upon the Universal Church."[16] Its iconographic popularity is enormous. My own, highly informal, experience has been that it is far easier to acquire images of the immaculate heart, ringed in roses, than of the sword-pierced sorrowful heart—quite possibly because the implicit violence of the swords is too discomfiting to contemporary Christian sensibilities. (Late images of the sacred heart are also less likely to show the heart as bleeding or otherwise visibly wounded.)

In 1670 the first feast of the Sacred Heart is celebrated, at Rennes, due in some measure to the visions—and the sheer stubborn persistence—of St. Margaret Mary Alacoque. Interestingly, it seems at first to have been piggy-backed upon the devotion to the Immaculate Heart of Mary,[17] though the latter would ultimately be the less officially successful devotion. Despite the cautious hesitation of Church authorities, who feared that such devotion to an image verged uncomfortably upon idolatry, the feast of the Sacred Heart was finally made official in 1875.[18] There is certainly a chronological element at work here as well; visions of Mary become popular very late. Our Lady of Guadalupe is said to have appeared in 1531, but many apparitions of the Virgin seem to occur in the nineteenth century or later.

In contrast to the often-envisioned heart of Christ, the hearts of Mary are objects of devotion but less often of vision. Mary speaks *of* her heart in the visions at Fatima, and the children who experience these visions see a blood-dripping Host above a chalice, but they do not see Mary's heart, or even her blood.[19] And in the famous appearance to Catherine Labouré, in which the vision of the miraculous medal was granted, Mary *describes* but does not *show* her sword-pierced heart.[20] Perhaps because Mary's humanity is not conspicuously miraculous (though exceptionally spotless), it is not flesh but word that is remarked in her manifestations; or perhaps because entry into the female body is not considered exceptional, hers is flesh most remarkable for its closure. Perhaps in this Mary shares with the miraculous quality of certain saints' bodies, bodies that exuded fragrant oils or odors but were most remarkable because they "were also wonderfully closed; they did not eat or waste away, excrete or menstruate, sicken or stink when death arrived."[21]

There is more to this inwardness. Luke also tells us twice "that Mary kept all the sayings and doings of Jesus in her heart, that there she might ponder over them and live by them."[22] If Christ is Word made Flesh, Mary is correspondingly Flesh holding word, inscribed and revealed as Flesh itself. As the Light enfolding the veiled figure of "Ash Wednesday" suggests a reversibility of folding, the mother wrapped in the son she once carried within, so too the Word born of human flesh reinscribes itself in that very flesh, so that despite exteriorizing the body of Christ Mary retains interiorly the Word, retained within her heart even when it is pierced. If we did not in reading folds already suspect the flexibility and even reversibility of inside and out, we would surely be forced to do so in reading the cut.

Visions

According to thy word.
They shall praise Thee and suffer in every generation

With glory and derision,
Light upon light, mounting the saints' stair.
Not for me the martyrdom, the ecstasy of thought and prayer,
Not for me the ultimate vision.
Grant me thy peace.
(And a sword shall pierce thy heart,
Thine also.)

—T. S. Eliot, "A Song for Simeon"

In exploring this mutual implication and reversibility, it is worth attending to the early visions of the Sacred Heart. Among the less disturbing is that of St. Gertrude: "Allowed to rest her head near the wound in the Saviour's side she heard the beating of the Divine Heart and asked John [who was also present in her vision, which famously occurred on his feast day] if on the night of the Last Supper, he too had felt these delightful pulsations, why he had never spoken of the fact. John replied that his revelation had been reserved for subsequent ages when the world, having grown cold, would have need of it to rekindle its love."[23] Already we see the importance of the later imagery of the heart in flames: this sacred heat is invoked against the chill of an unloving world. We have grown cold, and these flames express a dual passion of insatiable love and the rage of frustration. We risk increasingly growing disincarnate, as I have elsewhere argued. Here is a first link to the images' contemporary popularity: ink in flesh forcibly reinscribes our corporeality, inscribing in the image of fire the passion of the Incarnation.

The notion of a god frustrated by love unrequited persists in later visions of both heart and wounds. In a vision of uncertain authorship from the fourteenth century, Christ details the wounds he has suffered and adds, "I opened my Heart to thee, and gave thee the rosy blood of My Heart to drink. What more askest thou of me? Tell me, I pray thee, how I may soften and turn and draw thee to My love, and of a truth I will do it unto thee."[24] In his discussion of the visionary St. Lutgarde, Thomas Merton writes, "The true sorrow, which gave the saints a taste of Christ's bitter chalice in Gethsemane, is a participation in the anguish of infinite love, seeking to give souls joy and peace and everlasting life, and yet rejected by them."[25] The *Catholic Encyclopedia* declares, "Devotion to the Heart of Jesus is especially directed to the Divine Heart as overflowing with love for men, and it presents this love to us as despised and outraged."[26]

These envisioned hearts are those of bodies beyond the norms of human bodies, passionate (in many senses of the Passion) beyond the norms of human passion. Outraged, suffering, unrequited, and yet, astonishingly, insufficient. As the wounds remain unhealed even when the body miraculously rises,[27] so too the demands of divine desire push beyond the options of satiation, that "closure" supposedly sought by all emotion-stricken human beings. This intensity is made explicit in much of the commentary on the visions. Christ tells St. Catherine of Siena that the principal cause of his wounds is this: "My desires regarding the human race were infinite and the actual time of suffering and torture was at an end. Since my love is infinite, I could not therefore by this suffering manifest to you how much I loved you. That is why I will to reveal to you the secret of my Heart by letting you see It open."[28] To St. Margaret Mary he declares that "My Divine Heart ... is so inflamed with love for men, and for you in particular that, being unable any longer to contain within Itself the flames of its burning Charity, It must spread them abroad by thy means and manifest Itself to them in order to enrich them."[29] This inexhaustible self-consumption of the heart, so far in excess of the conspicuously finite possibilities of human love, suffices to burst the boundaries of the body yet retains the nature of the inarguably corporeal. Indeed, merely metaphorical devotion to the hearts is often considered insufficient,[30] even though literal devotion must run the risk of idolatry—again, this risk for some time kept the devotion to the Sacred Heart under official Church censure. (Late medieval Christianity had far more room than later versions for intensely somatic forms of piety, but such corporeality was never universally comfortable, and the officially established has always recognized with apprehension the unsettling possibilities in the ecstatic.) As we noted in the exploration of touch, excess—here in the sense of the uncontainable—may imply fragmentation, as the boundaries of that which would contain, whether body or word, are burst. The heart comes to us as a part that is at once insufficient—only a part—and yet excessive.

The idea that *we* are responsible for these bleeding wounds, though most often a source of blame for us, can also take on a positive spin. Gilbert of Hoyland writes in the twelfth century, "The Lord Himself bears the wound of violent love.... Do not cease, O spouse, to seek out thy Beloved with such darts. The glances of love are like so many arrows to both.... Be not content to wound thy Beloved once, but give wound after wound ... How much more is it when His Heart is not only lightly touched, but is wounded."[31] Cupid's arrow becomes a sword, and this duality of devotion and outrage plays into an *intensity* that is likewise in the image. Both blood and fire express this intensification fueled by impossibility.

After the flaming intensity of frustrated passion, a second common element in the visions is that of incorporation by ingestion, specifically the consumption by drinking of Christ's blood. St. Lutgarde writes: "At the door of the church Christ appeared to her, nailed to the cross and bleeding. And lowering one arm he caught her as she went by, and drew her mouth to the wound in his right side. And there she drank such sweetness that ever after she was stronger and readier in the service of God."[32] In the thirteenth century Angele of Foligno "speaks similarly of Christ placing her mouth on his wounded breast and feeding her in that way; and after"—the first element we've noted appears again—"she is granted an apprehension of 'the acute pain which was in Christ's soul' because of 'his immense love of humanity.'"[33] Catherine of Siena famously envisioned drinking the blood from Christ's side, following her "real world" drinking of pus from a leprous or cancerous human sore.

This exchange complicates, rather obviously, the notion of selfhood for the visionaries, who might echo Nancy's consideration of his heart transplant: "Strangeness did not have to come from the outside; it first appeared from the inside."[34] Suddenly one must look at oneself as not only oneself. Nancy's account is again evocative: "A gentle slipping separated me from myself. I was there, it was the summer, I had to wait, something detached itself from me, or this thing appeared in me where nothing had been before: nothing but the 'proper' immersion in me of a 'myself' which was never identified as this body, much less this heart, and which suddenly looked at itself."[35]

There are intriguing Marian or at least maternal elements in some of the visions of the Sacred Heart, and, as I've suggested, in the contemplation of sacred hearts gender becomes very complex, fluid, and downright weird. Mechtild of Magdeburg, in a somewhat similar, though more strange and elaborate, vision, makes evident the gender blurring of such experiences: "They were both opened, his wounds and [Mary's] breasts. The wounds poured out and the breasts flowed, so that the soul quickened and was even cured. As he poured the bright red wine into her red mouth, she was born out of the open wounds and was quickened."[36] Birthing participates here in both temporal and gender reversibility, as the son gives birth to his mother. But even Mechtild has nothing on Julian of Norwich, who declares:

> The Mother may lay the child tenderly to her breast, but our tender Mother, Jesus, He may homely lead us into His blessed breast, by His sweet open side, and shew therein part of the Godhead and the joys of Heaven, with spiritual sureness of endless bliss. And that shewed He in the Tenth [Shewing], giving the same understanding in this sweet word where He saith: Lo! how I loved thee; looking unto [the Wound in] His side, rejoicing.
>
> This fair lovely word Mother, it is so sweet and so close in Nature of itself that it may not verily be said of none but of Him; and to her that is very Mother of Him and of all.[37]

Bynum points out in *Fragmentation and Redemption* that "miniatures and panel paintings [of the thirteenth and fourteenth centuries] showed Christ exuding wine or blood into chalices or even into hungry mouths and drew visual parallels between his wound and Mary's breast offered to sinners."[38] Incorporation and ingestion reverse into a most peculiar process of birthing and lactation.

Hadewijch, in her poem celebrating blood drinking and flesh eating, also points to a third common element in these visions: the exchange or transfer of hearts.

> So that each knows the other through and through
> In the anguish or the repose or the madness of Love,
> And eats his flesh and drinks his blood;
> The heart of each devours the other's heart. [39]

St. Lutgarde likewise "concluded her mystical espousals with the Incarnate Word by an exchange of hearts with Him."[40] In other visions, Christ pierces the heart of the visionary; St. Gertrude the Great prays, "Through Thy Wounded heart, dearest Lord, pierce my heart so deeply with the dart of Thy love that it may no longer be able to contain earthly things."[41] In a rare male version, Henry Suso envisions an angel giving his (that is, Suso's) heart over to Jesus.[42] Margaret Mary Alacoque, like Lutgarde, envisions Christ *asking for* the exchange: "After this He asked me for my heart, which I begged Him to take. He did so and placed it in His own adorable heart where he showed it to me as a little atom which was being consumed in this great furnace and withdrawing it from His Heart it was like a burning flame in the form of a heart. He restored it to the place where He had taken it."[43] As a reminder of this exchange Margaret Mary had a pain in her side for the rest of her life, heartburn at its most literal. It is not merely in terms of gender that bodies are startlingly plastic; even vital organs, wholly or in bits, may be exchanged, on a temporary or lasting basis.

Finally, the open wound, in the side and/or in the heart, reveals a space which the visionary is often encouraged to enter, an invitation suggesting that in these visions eros runs along lines about as straight as those of gender. St. Bernardine of Siena makes a metaphorical shift from the heart to love, remarking, "The deepest mysteries of the Divine Heart have been revealed to us, sparing nothing; the cruel lance has gone within . . . [ellipsis in original] The open side reveals the Heart, the heart that loved unto death. We are called to enter into this ineffable love which made Him come down to us."[44] But Angele declares more literally that her soul "enters within that wound in the side of Christ and walks there with delight."[45] Lutgarde felt that she "rested in the wounded side of Jesus like a baby in her cradle."[46] Catherine of Siena exhorts Raymond of Capua: "Rest in the cross—with Christ crucified. Delight—in Christ crucified; delight in suffering. Be a glutton for abuse—for Christ crucified. Let your heart and soul be grafted into the tree of the most holy cross—with Christ crucified. Make his wounds your home."[47]

That this resting place might not be altogether comfortable is evident in the words of Ludolph of Saxony, a fourteenth-century Carthusian monk who declares that Christ was wounded "that . . . we might enter through that open wound into His heart and there live inflamed with His love, just as iron cast into the fire becomes incandescent."[48] Glorious, even ecstatic, but scarcely restful.

Inside Outness

When surface consumes depth, everything is turned inside out.

——Mark C. Taylor, *Hiding*

Each of these modes has in common a strange fluidity between interior and exterior, an excessiveness that pushes to the destruction of boundaries. As we've seen, some considerable measure of this fluidity is expressed in gender terms. It is as if Christ and Mary must each be allowed what the other has as well as what we might more commonly attribute to them somatically. If Christ has a visible heart, so shall Mary, even without a wound. If Mary nurtures through fluid from the side of her torso, so too shall Christ, even without milk ducts. Christ's divinely androgynous body invites entry; Mary's immaculately sinless body exteriorizes—gives birth—without being entered (in fact, when the midwife of the *Protevangelium* attempts to enter Mary's body in examination, her hand bursts into flame). Thus the Word is, as Nancy might have it, exscribed into the world, as flesh: everyone's flesh, with word within.

As Bynum has pointed out, late medieval medicine—that is, the science of the body—has a highly labile concept of physiological sex. No one seems to have seen it as bizarre that so many women were identifying with Christ's male body.[49] Essentially, persons of any gender are leaky bodies, male and female differing in being one another turned inside out. And to leak, to bleed most particularly (as Christ so conspicuously does), is already inside out, a bringing to the surface of the body and the presence of the outside world a most essential inwardness.

Nancy writes in "Corpus" of the dangers of modernizing and tidying the messiness of the Incarnation:

> Discharges of writing, rather than surfaces to be covered by writings. Discharges, abandonments, retreats. No "written bodies," no writing on the body, nor any of this graphosomatology into which the mystery of the Incarnation and of the body as pure sign of itself is sometimes converted, "modern style." For indeed, the body is not a locus of writing. No doubt one writes, but it is absolutely not where one writes, nor is it what one writes—it is always what writing exscribes.[50]

The body eludes writing; it may be written out and written on, but it is always beyond what is written. What the visions of the passionate wounds suggest is a less simplistic affiliation. The discharge itself is body: blood, water, milk. And the inscription of the body later transforms it into flesh. This turned-inside-outness is perhaps the most fascinating element of the heart icons. Of course, neither the binary views of sex in late medieval medicine nor the exteriority of the sacred hearts is properly or fully inside out; if they were, then either women or men would wear the linings of their organs outside their skins, ultimately surrounded, I suppose, by bone marrow; while the heart would turn itself inside out and surround the body. But the fluidity of the externalization and internalization nonetheless implied appeals to a third-millennial sense of excess and transgression, of writing on the body that always remains, nonetheless, that which eludes writing. All the visionary modes linked to the Sacred Heart—the entry into the wounded body, the exchange of hearts, the drinking of the flowing blood, the thrusting of the spear—offer images of an intense participatory physicality, and a profoundly somatic understanding of Word.

Excess

Such a mode of speaking, that is, excessively, properly belongs to the divine scriptures. Everything divine, as such, is immense and not subject to measure. . . . The excellence of divine things does not allow them to be offered to us uncovered, but they are hidden beneath sensible figures.

—Meister Eckhart, Latin Commentary on John

As Stephen Webb points out in *Blessed Excess*, there is something inherently excessive about religious expression, which shares with erotic language a necessary hyperbolic character—a "saying too much in order to say just enough when everything else is insufficient"[51] that is practically unacceptable in language elsewhere. "Hyperbole," Webb writes, "does not emphasize and magnify; it conjures and reveals."[52] Revelation and conjuration, of course, are in a certain tension with one another, and Webb notes that religious discourse makes it especially difficult to distinguish what language creates from what it explains or shows.[53] The passion of the heart invites the opening spear. This creation defines boundaries precisely by cutting across them. Hyperbole, in the need to say what it cannot, rips across meaning itself. However joyous, it is shredded language, the language of ecstatic woundedness. Ascetic devotion wounds the flesh literally, while the visions of the mystics do so imagistically. In such flesh the Word is made hyperbolic, excessive, sacred.

But it isn't (just) wounds that we read, as I shall suggest in the next chapter; it's scars—the lasting traces of woundedness. As I suggested in the reading of John's gospel, it is precisely in being scarred, carrying forth into eternal life the story told by his wounds, that Christ's body reveals its miraculous vulnerability. Mary's body is gifted with scars not received in the flesh: her heart too a sword will pierce, but not necessarily from without.

Thus the incarnate Word is literally transgressive. Transgression has to do with boundaries, and specifically with the act of crossing them. The word originates from the Latin, via Old French, "to step across,"[54] ultimately traceable, for those who might care, to the Sanskrit *ghredh-*, "to walk, or go"—a curious return to touch. We have the urge to cross boundaries because this crossing is both the expression and the act (both the revelation and the conjuration) of being most fully alive. As we noted in reading the gospel of John, the notion of eternal life "stresses quality of life rather than duration"[55]—*intensity* of life, as I have argued, rather than extension.

At the scene of wounding, Christ's words emphasize his vulnerability; he speaks (at least in the first two gospels) as one abandoned: *My God, why have you forsaken me?* Nancy's discussion brings the abandoned together with the abundant, and so perhaps abandonment at its utmost—God's own loss of God—is also a barrier-bursting abundance: "this speaking in multiple ways is abandoned, is in abandonment, and it is abandon (which is also to say *openness*). It so happens that 'abandon' can evoke 'abundance.' There is always a *pollakos*, an abundance, in abandon: it opens on a profusion of possibilities, just as one abandons oneself in excess, for there is no other modality of abandon." [56]

Abandoned—cut away—and cut open, the wounded figure of the corporeal God opens onto infinite possibilities of life. Flesh and Word burst into fragments as meaning breaks its limits. Bringing the sacred into the profane world is inherently transgressive; so too is tearing the heart from its place beneath the skin. To exceed oneself, however secularly expressed, is a profoundly religious impulse, whether its mode of expression is serious or in every sense comic. Nancy associates self-exceeding with joy:

The empty identity of an "I" can no longer be based on simple adequation (on its "I = I") as it expresses itself: "I suffer" implies two "I"'s, the one a stranger to the other (even though they touch). The same goes for "I enjoy" (it could be shown how that is indicated in the expressed pragmatics of the one and the other). But in "I suffer," one I rejects the other, while in "I enjoy," one I exceeds the other. They are as alike as two drops of water: no more and no less.[57]

The sacred heart is an image of corporeal self-exceeding.

This remains uncomfortable language, and much of the kitsch factor of this imagery in its later instantiations comes of the attempt to make such an image, from intolerably somatic medieval piety, into one tolerable to the clean-scrubbed sensibilities of much later centuries. As Bynum points out, there is an inherently comic element in the worship of body bits, though "The comic is not necessarily the pleasant.... Its goal is the pluralistic, not the total. It embraces the partial as partial."[58] Images and texts devoted to fragments, she writes, "are surely comic in the common sense meaning of the word as well as in the more literary meaning.... They evidence what Henri Bergson sees as crucial to the comic: a moral response to the 'recalcitrance of matter.'"[59] The sacred heart is seldom regarded as a comic image, yet when its fragmentation, its excision from the body, is focused upon, it does become comic in both senses.

Wearing the Heart on the Skin

The skin-mind relation is far from unidirectional. As mind is inscribed on skin, so skin influences mind.

—Mark C. Taylor, *Hiding*

These attributes revealed in the sacred hearts—those of a corporeality that is passionate, excessive, fragmented, fluid, and full of words—make the hearts appropriate third-millennial religious images, and may well account for their popularity in secular circles as well—particularly, as I have suggested, their association with tattooing.

For some contemporary tattoo devotees, precisely the excessiveness of the image appeals. Excess can mean passion or kitsch with equal ease. One fan writes, "It's more the kitsch factor than anything. It really does seem absurd to associate something so tacky ... with something supposedly so almighty."[60] But another declares, of a sacred heart tattoo he co-created for himself, "The heart itself is love. I know it sounds simple and even cheesy, but my wife introduced me to love. It's an emotion that I now retain. . . . Without her I probably never would have experienced this, at times intoxicating, emotion. The fact that this tat resembles the sacred heart . . . is to represent that faith, I feel, that has brought us together as well as tied us together for life. . . . The flames burning hot represent a real intensity, passion, . . . the flames are also a physical, earthly tangible ring of protection."[61] Tattooing, grounded in a strong sense of the malleability of flesh, makes a singularly fitting art for the image of so many kinds of somatic inversions. The image of the sacred heart has been popular in Western tattooing for decades, but it may be more so now than ever; perhaps the image and the medium are unusually mutually appropriate.

Interestingly, religious symbols were also the first choice for earlier tattooed skins—those of the eleventh- and twelfth-century crusaders, who wore these symbols home on their skins as a sign of their having reached the Holy Land. This marked the return of tattooing to the Christian West after it had been banned for centuries, since the Emperor Constantine's order against it in 325—not on Old Testament grounds (see Leviticus 19:28), but because the practice was seen as disfiguring bodies made in God's image.[62] This return happens about the same time, we notice, as the heart-shaped devotions really catch on. The late medieval era is a time of intense, and to our sensibility often quite disturbing, physicality in Christian practice and observation. With the attention to the body of Christ comes an attention to the bodies of Christian worshippers, including the possibility of wearing Christian symbols not only on but in the flesh.

I should be clear about the nature of this "symbolism" in contemporary imagery. Though there are signs of affiliation in gang, prison, and biker tattooing, very often contemporary Western tattoo imagery is not directly symbolic. Where it is, that symbolism is often highly individual, and this very fact is important within at least some segments of the tattooed community. Thus, for example, this advice from the very popular *BME* (*Body Modification Ezine*) Web site, in response to an inquirer seeking "some classic designs that represent mourning for a loved one after their death":

> I think that you should speak to an artist and have a design that means
> something to YOU. Getting a design just for the supposed "meaning"

is not going to help you cope or represent the loved one that you are mourning. Personally, when my mother passed, I had my artist design a sacred heart using the colors and motifs that were her favourite. Every time I look at this piece I am always reminded of her and it makes me smile. So think of the things that your loved one represented to you and have a beautiful piece created. Believe me, it will be better and bring you more closure.[63]

That is, there is no neat system of correspondence by which to declare the significance of particular images, and I certainly would not wish to claim that the sacred heart "means" in the sense that a simple cross might have indicated a visit to the Holy Land. Rather, as an image and in its history, it signifies and suggests many things, any or none of which may be the source of its appeal for a given individual, the combination of which is behind its present remarkable popularity.

As overdetermined as most cultural phenomena, the sacred heart seems to have entered tattooing from a number of different angles. The image appears in very early tattoo flash (that is, images of already-designed tattoos displayed on the walls of studios—flash designs are generally distinguished from unique custom work); for instance, a George Bigmore version from the 1920s appears in Lyle Tuttle's collection at the Tattoo Museum in San Francisco, and Coney Island flash sheets from the 1940s offer numerous variations. Pierced hearts, more often run through by Cupid's arrow than by swords or thorns, appear in the flash sheets of tattooists like Brooklyn Blacky, Bill Jones, and "Cap" Coleman, who worked on sailors, Bowery bums, and other stereotypical early tattooed white guys.[64] But the specifically Christian versions seem more likely to have entered tattooing through another of its primary sources, Latino tattooing. (I must note that this is speculation on my part, based on my best observation of the available historical material.) As Margo DeMello notes, in the fine line work of "classic Chicano tattooing," images of Christ, the Virgin of Guadalupe, and other religious symbols "tend to represent loyalty to community, family, women, and God—very similar in theme to the nationalist designs seen among sailors, but stylistically, a world apart."[65] Christian imagery was so closely associated with Latino communities that Sailor Jerry Collins, one of the most famous American tattooists, remarked rather disturbingly in a letter (June 18, 1971):

I don't have any religious stuff at all. Stayed away from it, except for a full back Christ Head, as I didn't want the pachuco and wet-back trade and out here the Puerto Ricans. Don Nolan does them, and when Christ looks like a hippie, the guys want to tear his ass up. Not worth it—I'll stick to Egyptian & Indian hieroglyphics & the Taoism and Buddhism but no Christianity for me—those greasers are too emotional about their fucking saints, etc., and I don't want no part of it.[66]

In a rather more positive mode, the Dutch tattooist Henk Schiffermacher also notes the Latino influence behind Christian tattoo imagery and suggests that people choose religiously iconographic tattoos "to honor the lord. Or maybe as a passport into heaven."[67] The New York tattooist Matty Jankowski points out that such an image can express both faith and penance, both celebration and guilt.[68] With all of these possibilities so plausibly read into the image, one can see some of the ground for its widespread popularity—the sheer diversity of its appeal.

Today the image is most closely associated with what's called "new school" tattooing, a style noted for the use of bright colors and thick black outlines.[69] "New school" tattoos are less different from "old school" (traditional designs such as those associated with American sailors or military personnel) than from tribal, Celtic, or other more overtly "artistic" styles. They tend to pay homage to those traditional, old-school, often American designs, but with a more personal or even ironic spin. Certainly one ground of this image's popularity is its enormous adaptability to personal quirks of style. Roses, thorns, flames, and swords are freely up for combination and exchange. In the space of perhaps twenty minutes' search through two contemporary tattooing magazines, I found hearts pierced with swords, flaming hearts pierced with crosses, thorn-wrapped hearts topped by winged crowns instead of flames, flaming sacred hearts topped by crosses, roses and thorns intermixed encircling flaming hearts, many versions of the sacred and immaculate hearts with wings, several variations on the thorns, especially barbed wire; and one heart encircled by roses and thorns, topped by a cross, and pierced by a sword, though without flames.[70] A contemporary flash sheet multiplies the meanings of the flames in an image that has "heaven" scripted above the heart and "hell" below. Another replaces the customary radiant light with a halo of nails or spikes, neatly referring us back to the originary devotion to the wounds.[71] Sometimes hearts are literally screwed, rather than sword-pierced;[72] in some, the heart is rendered in a more anatomically correct fashion, while others include an eye in the heart or the flame. Inscriptions such as "mom" or "mother," or "faith," "passion," "love," and "hate," may be added in old-style banners. The image is an unusually strong one in simply visual terms as well as associatively; it can take a great deal of creative modification without losing its impact. The multiplicity and fluidity marking the original images continues full force.

Tattooing, like hyperbole, "conjures and reveals." Though it is an aspect often downplayed, tattooing wounds the body, thereby re-creating it, revealing it to be more than mechanical matter. Revelation is implicit in the cutting open of the body, whether to the depths or only into the dermal layer, as in the fiery illumination of the heart. Conjuration too is present in a great deal of tattooing, the creation of a new skin, the transfiguration of the flesh into art—and, in a term not infrequently evoked by tattooists and devotees alike, the sacred.

Here as in the ancient visions, the passion that wounds is also the love that protects. The sacred heart is polysemic, with equal ease profoundly devout and outrageously camp. Wearing the image may express devotion or profanation. Consider it: a heart not only torn from the body, but cut through and bleeding; not only bleeding but set on fire. An image of love beyond bearing, of a god who so loved the world that he sacrificed to it his person in the flesh—or an image of the utterly ridiculous, as if one were to think that the only proper expression of one's devotion to the King would be to paint his image not in muted colors on rough canvas but luminously against the luxuriance of velvet.

Tattooing is transgressive not in the rebellious sense—though that differs according to social context—but in some of the same senses in which the sacred hearts are transgressive. It is gratuitous, excessive. It messes with our senses of inside and out by making the skin surface an expressive site, its inscriptions imposed from without but chosen from within. Originally very masculine in its associations, Western tattooing has come to be worn, and increasingly performed, by all genders. One of the tattooists with whom I have worked suggested in conversation that many men bring to tattooing a fantasy of surrender and vulnerability, traditionally the least macho of attributes, yet precisely those which combine with passion to confuse the bodies of visionary and Christ—vulnerability and wounded-ness forming for each an expression of that passion and a surprising source of strength.

Though "transgression" has come to take sin as one of its meanings, we may well see grace as likewise transgressive; the sacred can cross into the pro-fane as well as vice versa. To put the heart on the skin is to transgress the boundaries of the body, bringing the inside out; to transform some portion of the skin into a religious symbol is to give to oneself a postmodern vari-ant on the stigmata, a sign of identification with love and suffering, with religious excess, in an era when, as Webb notes, "Under the pressures of civility and moderation, Christianity has prepared the conditions that disal-low its own most distinctive contributions. Agape becomes trust and respect, the demands of Christlike love are generalized as expressions of sociability and mutuality."[73] As I've noted, to exceed oneself, however secu-larly expressed, is a profoundly religious impulse, whether its mode of expression is serious or wholly comic.

The heterodox use of sacred heart imagery suggests in excess and trans-gression secular versions of the religious craving for something exceeding the limits of the self. The religious imagery of the sacred and sorrowful hearts is that of bursting the flesh, and it is an image of eros as well as agape—an image suggesting, especially when we take the visionary details into account, that these two are not neatly distinct. Again, if Webb is right, religious language shares with erotic language this *need* to push words beyond their meanings in order to make them mean what they must; that is, this is a language of necessary hyperbole, precisely visualized in the ridiculous excesses of great hearts afire. And yet all writing must be in some measure hyperbolic, must both reveal meaning and conjure speech.

"Religion," writes Webb, "is nothing less than that which is excessive, that which is, by definition, more than what can be known or felt, described or contained. And yet, perhaps this excess itself fulfills a need, satisfies a defi-ciency—stakes a claim to truth. Of course, we know that we do not need religion anymore. Nevertheless, we cannot settle for anything less."[74] The sacred hearts are precise indications of what exceeds measure, hyperbolic images designed for that excess which is the least for which we can settle. We do not *need* religion any more; we can never be said to need the excessive—it is precisely what must necessarily be gratuitous, an act of grace.

Contemporary secular manifestations of divine hearts, cross-cut with multicultural, trans-stylistic, high and low cultural, utterly pomo referentiality, are in their way as excessive as their ecstatically originary forms, forms off limits to the queasily polite sensibilities of third-millennial Christianity. These hearts burst out of the body and take their place on and in the skin, defiantly glorious, inside out, genderbent, fucked up, queerly passionate and flamboyantly inexhaustible. They write of scars that neither heal nor close; they write of rupture that cuts open but not apart: "The divine is always the dissonance of unity and of separation," Nancy declares; "The divine *is* thus the dissonance of the divine and the human."[75] Mark Taylor writes:

> Tattooing inevitably slips between polarities customarily used to organize experience and structure knowledge: nature/culture, savage/civilized, regulation/transgression, simulation/dissimulation, socialization/marginalization, interiority/exteriority, veiling/unveiling, materialization/dematerialization, differentiation/unification, and so forth. By repeatedly alternating between unreconcilable opposites, tattooing marks and remarks a boundary that cannot be fixed. Forever superficial, even when its wounds are deep, the tattooed body is the incarnation of a seam that never mends.[76]

Bodies thus inscribed leave our coolly rational comprehension in fragments, the unmended seam marking a dissonance beyond fusion. The divine body rendered synecdochally in the image of the sacred heart is likewise dissonant, an image of male and female (at least); body and word; fulfillment and frustration; agony and joy. In both its classic instantiations and its contemporary variations, this image cuts through boundaries of inner and outer, flesh and word; and in its flamboyant excess remains profoundly religious.

Cut

we too
kept on drinking, soul-crossed, two swords,
stitched to heavenstones, born of wordblood,
in the nightbed.

     Paul Celan, "In Prague"

The final figure of speech to be explored here feels at first somewhat out of place. To begin with, the connotations of the cut, in word and flesh alike, are largely negative. Touch can make us flinch, enfolding can suffocate, but most of us have a sense too of the touch of word or flesh that pleases, arouses, or reassures; of the pleasures of a minute's skillful articulation or (even if we must go back to childhood for the memories) the securities of wrapture. It is far easier, more nearly automatic, to see either in a positive light than it is to place a positive value on cutting. The modes of the cut presented here—disruption (and the absence linked to it), wounding (and the scarring that comes from it), and even inscription bear or have come to bear unpleasant implications. The pleasures of incision come always with an admixture of pain. This, of course, plays no small part in contemporary (as opposed to early) uneasiness regarding the imagery of the sacred and sorrowful hearts. The problem now is not the risk of idolatry, but the viscerality of the opened body, the untidiness inherent in blood.

What's more, while both touch and fold complicate a surface, cutting appears to destroy it, at least along the length of the cut itself, to open it onto the depth that we commonly believe superficiality opposes. We may question whether it makes sense to speak of a ruptured surface. But if we answer in the affirmative, we are turned not to the contrast of depth but to the language of fragmentation and disruption. What we find in the cut is not depth so much as complication; not a singular revealed interior but a multiplicity of fragments. Taylor quotes Yukio Mishima thus: "If the law of thought is that it should search out profundity, whether it extends upwards or downwards, then it seemed excessively illogical to me that men should not discover depths of a kind in 'surface'. . . . Why should they not be attracted to the profundity of the surface itself?"[1]

The first element of the cut explored here is that of disruption or fragmentation, the sense of being cut up or cut apart. The second element is that of inscription. As we shall see, inscription need not imply either the negativity (power is bad) nor the passivity (bodies are helpless) often attributed to it. I shall note as well the palimpsestic quality of inscription (a pretentious way of saying that no surface, whether page or body, is really blank). Finally, I shall take up the image of the wound and scar, tracing its narrative and identity-constitutive (naming) functions—its ability to write and to tell a story on the flesh.

Despite—or, in some cases, because of—the disruptive quality that makes cutting always a bit out of place, some thinkers have seen the cut as perhaps the most fundamental in our triad of figures. The cut at the heart of language is remarked most often where words are written. Blanchot writes in *The Infinite Conversation:*

> —To write is not to give speech to be seen. The game of common etymology makes of writing a cutting movement, a tear, a crisis.
> —This is simply a reminder that the proper tool for writing was also proper for incising: the stylet.
> —Yes, but this incisive reminder still evokes a cutting operation, if not a butchery: a kind of violence—the word flesh is found in the family, just as graphy is a scratch.[2]

Writing here evokes not only cutting but flesh, violence on or against the flesh, a dermal scratch or slice sharp enough to break the surface of the skin.[3] For a moment the sheer physicality of this description is surprising in Blanchot, an author much more often given to spacing and evocation—until we realize that the space can itself be a cut across. Violence is likewise surprising in one who writes, "I will say rather: nothing extreme except through gentleness."[4] And since we are inclined to identify body with person, we may also be surprised by such physicality (still more, such violent physicality) in the work of one who so insists on the absence of his own identity. But then, why should the body be more personal than words? Both create the self at the interface with the world; both, despite a widely held conviction that bodily dishonesty is impossible, can, being creative, also lie. As Taylor vividly points out, it is not even the living corporeal self that generally meets the world: "Death, like life, is not a momentary event but is an ongoing process whose traces line the body. At the point where I make contact with the world, I am always already dead."[5] Only almost always, I would say instead: I am alive at the point of the cut, where I bleed, where interior life pours out into a world unprepared for it. (Small wonder Lutgarde feels forever invigorated by her draught of Christ's blood, or that such myths emerged inverted as tales of blood-drinking demons irksomely absent ordinary mortality, continually fed on life itself.)

What Blanchot says here of writing, Anne Tomiche will say of reading as well, bringing into her discussion (primarily of Nancy) other famous names: "That writing (and reading) depends on a process of *cutting* rather than on a more conventionally conceived process of healing has been stressed by Derrida, who, in his discussion of Philippe Sollers, writes: 'the operation of reading/writing goes by way of the blade of a red knife.' Reading and writing are operations structured by mutilation, a 'cut,' in which the 'presence' of the text paradoxically establishes itself."[6]

And what is said here of writing and of reading is true, though not identically so, of speaking, where language seems to be closer to the body. In fact, Gary Shapiro notes: "These are voices in which interruption and the bodily base of the voice have become operative principles."[7] Body and language, mutual limits, are also, as we have already begun to see in the discussion of articulation, mutually disruptive. They are not fixed limits, natural boundaries, but limits nonetheless for all their shifting. Bataille, though not writing of speaking directly, places the cut at the heart of all communication: "Through what could be called incompleteness or animal nakedness or the wound, the different separate beings *communicate*,"[8] and again, "For those who understand communication as laceration, communication is sin, or evil. It's a breaking of the established order."[9]

I do not intend here to be disingenuous about Bataillean "communication," which we know well is not the transmission of information, by words or other means, as we ordinarily think it. But Bataille must transform our understanding of language if he is to have any sense at all.[10] And it is with and as words and bodies that we communicate—that is, cross for an instant the distance marking the distinction of self from other. Communication occurs in bodies and in words too, in speaking and in the contact that requires an impossible intersection of impenetrable surfaces—that requires that we be cut open. The wound, laceration, breaking—all are forms of the cut.

The rhetoric of cutting, then, startling as it is, is at the same time nearly commonplace, at least within certain kinds of poststructural theory. But as Shapiro's wording rightly suggests, this near-everydayness does not quite render the figure conventional. It is hard to conventionalize what is always, definitionally, displacing and fragmenting, from which some measure of violence seems inextricable. Nancy, whose philosophy, like that of Blanchot, is more commonly notable for its gentleness, points this out. But he pushes the violence to the level of *thought* itself, thought which, as he remarks, "cannot give up signifying the body, assigning signs to it—except by allowing itself to be brought back to its own thinking matter." And thus, returned to the matter of the body, thought acquires *weight*:

> A gram of thought: trace of this pebble, of this calculus, engraving, tiny incision, notch, cut hard point of a tip, engraver's stylus, body of the first cut, breached body, body separated by *being this body* that it is and by existing it. . . . Of course, there is violence and pain in this thought. It never stops banging into itself, hard, resistant, impenetrable, being destined to think its hardness by means of that hardness itself, impenetrable by dint of essence and method.[11]

Thought of the body, at least where we assign words to it, speaks in seeming contradictions: impenetrable and notched, hard and incised, separate and breached. Thought of the body can be brought only to an unsettled and unsettling speech.

Disruption: Fragmentation

To write the sign of oneself that does not offer a sign, that is not a sign. This is: writing, finally to stop discoursing. To cut into discourse.

—Jean-Luc Nancy, "Corpus"

In keeping with this opening emphasis on unsettledness, I shall turn first to the cut as disruption. As Blanchot's contrast of writing with speaking suggests, language may cut language. Writing, by inscribing on the page the evanescently corporeal ebb and flow of the breath, cuts into speaking. But this cut is at the same time—not only, but also—a bringing forth. To write cuts into language, cuts words into a page, but it brings forth language too. One of the important realizations when we think the cut between flesh and word is that the spaces opened by slicing may be creative, their emptiness the fullness of possibility. Of course, where writing cuts across writing, or speaking across speaking, disruption can become interruption, and then it most often becomes something hostile. If I cut you off when you are speaking, I assert my disinterest in what you have to say, or the relatively greater importance to me of my own words. Such interruption cuts *off* or cuts *into*. But disruptive rather than coercive interruption as the opening of spaces between words opens up the possibility of interaction.

Again, we may turn to Blanchot to find a particularly precise description. Writing of Edmond Jabès in an essay titled "Interruptions," Blanchot declares, "The power to speak is interrupted, and interruption plays a seemingly subordinate role. . . . A role, however, so mysterious that it can be interpreted as carrying the mystery of language itself: pause between phrases, pause from one speaker to the other, and pause of attention, of understanding, which doubles the power of expression."[12] Blanchot's own writing, too, is characterized by disruption, by an emphasis in both style and substance upon fragmentation. Such unclosed thought slyly invites the reader into an uncomfortable level of participation. Like a speaker's silence, the gap in writing invites our own language (as the wounded body both enters its insides into the world and invites the entry of another). Fragmented writing poses questions and endlessly reopens what might have been answers; it grants answers so elusive as to draw perpetually further questions.

Here we find the cut as, to mix metaphors atrociously, the flip side of the fold. That is, as articulation links together, acknowledging a distance but never quite cutting apart, disruption breaks apart the articulate unfurling. It cuts in. Yet in this breakage and disruption we find certain positive possibilities of language, of conversation rather than monologue. Where one self breaks off its flow of words, there is room for another, who in some sense may well be the source of those words' very possibility, the reason for our speaking and writing. Surely we have all faced the phenomenon of an articulation so perfect and so self-contained as to leave no space for the conversational. The fissure is vital to communication in the mundane as much as in the more dramatic Bataillean sense.

I have suggested above that one reading of disruption is fragmentation. We have seen already the fragmentation of both body and text in the visions and descriptions of the sacred and immaculate hearts, a fragmentation that leaves language and body open along the lines of rupture. (As I shall later suggest, even in apparently unfragmented or mended bodies and texts, we may read the remnants of fragmentation in scars.)

Fragmentation is often linked with evil. Bynum cites James of Voragine: "James thus asserts that—whatever the historical events—the good are intact when divided, while the evil fragment or decay even without violence."[13] Christ is represented as a force of good capable of rendering evil into the fragments proper to it: "The divinity which lay hidden in Jesus' flesh shattered the molars in death's mouth, when it rashly bit at the flesh of the Word. Even if it bites us like a snake or a horned serpent, if we have the horns of the cross in our hands … then all that horrible armor described in Job will be destroyed."[14] To part beyond mending, fragment beyond redemption, seems to be the mark of evil, the impossibility of restoration—the wound that goes beyond opening to tear apart. But the mend, the scar, is a sign of virtue, and the scar requires the wound. Good and evil are not so far apart.

As I have argued in more detail elsewhere,[15] these disruptive instants, these silences, are as much vital to language as destructive of it (and we must hold on to the realization that they are both). Several thinkers have linked the cut to silence. Derrida, for example, writes of Bataille, "From one to the other, totally other, a certain text, which in silence traces the structure of the eye, sketches the opening, ventures to contrive 'absolute reading,' absolutely rends its own tissue once more become 'solid' and servile in having been read."[16]

Here we are drawn back to those places, those spaces and borders alike, where language falls most often, and most conspicuously, silent. Body and language call to one another, but only in silence can the call be heard. The word cannot resound where there is not enough silence. Nancy, as we earlier noted, remarks upon the ungraspability of the body by the word. Taylor remarks upon the mysterious quality of this elusiveness, the seductive disappearance of the flesh just where we would speak (of) it:

> Language, it seems, is the appearance of the disappearance of the body. If the word is the death of the thing, the mystery of language *always* involves a missing body. The search for the body (and the effort to establish its identity) is the search for a signified—transcendental or otherwise—that lends signifiers their thickness, weight, depth and substance. If the body cannot be found, the mystery cannot be solved.[17]

Little, of course, calls us quite so strongly as a mystery. We have seen already that Acker takes on the same questions from the bodily perspective when she meditates on the experience of bodybuilding, with its forgetting of verbalization.[18]

Between them, the citations from Taylor and Acker suggest at first that body and language are mutually *impossible.* And in some sense they are— they can never coincide—but they are just as much mutually necessary. Each emerges as the disappearance of the other, but neither exists simply in the other's absence; they are called *by* the pause, by the moment of disappearance. Where it (nearly) reaches the body, language falls silent; where it (nearly) comes to speaking, body stops short, becoming more than only flesh.

Silence breaks, but it too can be broken, and not only by words properly speaking. Here again we encounter amorous intensity, as Roland Barthes writes: "so that a long series of verbal contentions (my 'politenesses') may suddenly explode into some generalized revulsion: a crying jag (for instance), before the other's flabbergasted eyes, will suddenly wipe out all the efforts (and the effects) of a carefully controlled language. I break apart."[19]

I break apart. Breaks are not always violent outbursts. Stillness too is a disruption of speaking, moving, writing that, in the breaking of the active self, invites an other—another body, another text, or body to text, text to flesh.

The disruption of bodies is less evident. Bodies are "disrupted" most literally by the entry of matter—from a spear thrust into the side to a stone scraped over a shinbone in an inadvertent stumble. They are inscribed by language, too, made in some measure by their descriptions, made interpreted flesh. They disrupt speaking as well, not only in halting the flow of words but in being beyond description. Bodies and language intrude upon one another, as Nancy says of the heart that remains an intruder while becoming his own: "Everything in this will come to me from elsewhere and from outside—just as my heart, my body came to me from elsewhere, and are an elsewhere 'in' me."[20] This heart remains for him "something troubling in the midst of intimacy"[21]—something preventing intimacy from becoming a smooth wholeness. The scar and the internalized elsewhere are literal for Nancy, at least in these passages, but what he literalizes is true for any-body, every scar and marking, every inscription.

Where language reaches its descriptive limits, one may resort to the imagery of the cut and the life that flows from it. Artaud writes:

> When the soul lacks a language or language a mind, and the rupture ploughs a vast furrow of despair and blood in the sensory field, this is the greatest pain: for it subverts not merely the bark or the skeleton, but the very STUFF of the body. . . . this uselessness is like the moral tone of this abyss and of its intense stupefaction, and the physical color of it is the taste of blood spurting in cascades from the orifices of the skull.[22]

Returning to such vividly violent imagery, Artaud urges as well the return of cruelty to poetry, to language, which ought to be at the extreme but has been purged by the false gentleness (really the mediocrity) of modernity. "First let's make a poem, with blood,"[23] he urges. And writing is compared directly to the cut of the flesh: "The air is full of pencil strokes like razor strokes or the etching of a magic fingernail."[24] The pencil writes, the razor cuts, the nail—skin at its hardest—scratches open meaningful flesh. Derrida interprets Artaud as a thinker of scarring: "Artaud initially dreamed of a graphism which would not begin as deviation, of a nonseparated inscription: an incarnation of the letter and a bloody tattoo."[25]

But the impossibility of this dream soon becomes apparent; every cut cuts apart: "The traces inscribed on the body will no longer be graphic incision but wounds received in the destruction of the West, its metaphysics and its theater, the stigmata of this pitiless war. For the theater of cruelty is not a new theater destined to escort some new novel that would modify from within an unshaken tradition. . . . The stigmata and not the tattoo."[26] The stigmata, however, is not wholly novel but is the reassertion of something ancient, less the destructive overthrow of the West than a reminder of an uncloseable space within it, the bleeding of the god who is so commonly supposed to totalize all meaning.

Artaud is not alone, of course, in bringing word and blood together at the limit of meaning. Paul Celan, not infrequently accused of impenetrable linguistic abstraction, makes a poem in blood, or leads the "shadows" of words to the body's bleeding:

All those sleep shapes, crystalline,

that you assumed
in the language-shadow,

to those
I lead my blood,

those image lines, them
I'm to harbour
in the slit-arteries of my cognition—
my grief, I can see
is deserting to you.[27]

Here language meets its limit where the life of the body, and the tolerance for that life, meets its limit, where speaking and bleeding alike encounter the other (where language and body enter into the world) and then, finally silent, finally stopped, leave behind their absence. In one more point of paradox, disruption meets stillness. Torn apart, the body is finally led to the shape of sleep. But here where grief has led it the body no longer speaks, and the *you* to whom the poem is addressed, perhaps the "approachable you" of a more optimistic moment, is left deserted as the word falls silent.

Here the cut of word and flesh appears in its multiplicity. There is a fissure between self and other, an image-line to be harbored in the artery.

"Making me a stranger to myself," Nancy writes, "does not bring me closer to the intruder. It would seem, rather, that a general law of intrusion is revealed; there is no single [law] and as soon as there is one, it multiplies, it identifies itself in its renewed internal differences."[28] Cutting open the neat boundaries of self, one makes space for the other; again, we have all known those without openness, hermetically sealed against human connection. But extremes meet; cut too far and one is again cut off, the possible connection fragmented when there is no longer a self who might connect (even if it is to be undone in that connection: we begin this recurrent process *as* us, as selves). Edmond Jabès writes of this paradox as it appears in his own poetic language: "The whole work, in effect, takes place in this 'one' and is finally canceled out to become this 'nothing.' This reveals the essence of the fragmentation."[29] In the same passage, Jabès writes of language in terms remarkably evocative of desire—desire in language for language itself: "This work of cutting is at the very heart of the writing, at the very heart of writing itself. Why? Because in words there are things that attract and repel each other. . . . Tensions and relationships arise from the fact that they have the same letters, or because there is some kind of sonority or assonance."[30]

Body and language disrupt themselves and they disrupt one another. Language calls to language, body to body, and word and flesh to one another. But there must be space for the call to reverberate—this space-making too is a function of the cut, which never cuts *only* apart. There is both gentleness and violence, both pain and joy in this thought. The thought of incision disrupts every understanding we have of surfaces.

Inscription

Of course it can't be any simple script; you see, it's not supposed to kill straight away, but only after a period of twelve hours on average; the turning-point is calculated to come at the sixth hour.

So the actual lettering has to be surrounded with many, many decorations; the text itself forms only a narrow band running round the body; the rest of the body is set aside for the embellishments.

—Franz Kafka, "In the Penal Colony"

From a conservative perspective, disruption must be negatively valued: fragmentation must always be evil, in a way that never implies redemption. It unsettles, or it makes unsettling possible. It opposes the neat stability of a coherent and lasting order. To many of us, of course, this unsettling and opposition sound like very good things, or at a minimum like potentially good things. Yet the cut in another of its modes, that of inscription, tends to be taken negatively precisely from the radical and, to a lesser extent, liberal perspectives that more positively value disruption.

For the widespread acceptance of "inscription" as the manifestation of social forces on the body, and for the nearly automatic politicization of the reading of such inscription, we can undoubtedly thank (or blame) Foucault. It is not at all my intention to argue against him in this, but rather to caution against certain limitations in the uses to which his theory has been put, the ways in which it has been developed. Foucault steadfastly refuses to see power as negative, resistance itself being just as much a form of power as hegemony. But this nuance seems easy to forget. Bodies are inscribed by power, necessarily—there is no space outside power—but this necessity is *not* necessarily negative. That something is unavoidable does not make it undesirable, however strongly this sentiment runs up against our individualistic senses of freedom.

Still, negativity is most remarked here (though it is by no means the case that all readings of inscription are negative). Ruth Salvaggio writes, in "Skin Deep: Lesbian Interventions in Language," of inscription even within language as negatively affecting discourse along with bodies: "What's worse is that these [reductive] categories continually inscribe themselves in discourses, so that the very language of a particular discourse reflects the unquestioned assumption 'that what founds society, any society, is heterosexuality.'"[31] Salvaggio gestures beyond these unquestioned assumptions, though; hers is work on the very possibility of cutting into this discourse with a new inscription. (The palimpsestic possibility of inscriptions complicated by overlay is one I shall take up below.) Consideration of corporeal inscription has been particularly developed in feminist theory, though here, again, the negative effects are the most examined. In "The Body and the Reproduction of Femininity: A Feminist Appropriation of Foucault," Susan Bordo makes extensive use of the idea of inscription, writing in a section titled "The Body as a Text of Femininity":

The symptomatology of these disorders [hysteria, agoraphobia, anorexia] reveals itself as textuality. . . . Working within this framework, we see that whether we look at hysteria, agoraphobia, or anorexia, we find the body of the sufferer deeply inscribed with an ideological construction of femininity emblematic of the periods in question. That construction, of course, is always homogenizing and normalizing, erasing racial, class and other differences and insisting that all women aspire to a coercive, standardized ideal. . . . The bodies of disordered women in this way offer themselves as an aggressively graphic text for the interpreter—a text that insists, actually demands, it be read as a cultural statement, a statement about gender.[32]

I do not mean to argue that such a reading of inscription is mistaken—indeed, I think such readings are both important and valuable. I wish only to emphasize other, coexistent possibilities. These too have their place in feminist and gender theory, though they may be approached there with some wariness. Jean Arthurs and Jane Grimshaw write with a certain ambivalence of a "new androgyny," which assumes that "The body can be 'written on' in any way that one chooses. The denial in much academic writing of the 'naturalness' of the body and the stress on its discursive construction is played out in some of the more transgressive forms of sexual politics, notably in 'queer' theory and activism, which have aimed to deconstruct gender binarism and subvert gendered norms of dress and bodily presentation or representation."[33]

Such wariness is not unfounded. It is much more appealing, both aesthetically and politically, to look at transgression than at the forces favoring conformity, but the play between central text and marginal annotation is always important. In an essay in the same volume, Tamsin Wilton notes that margin and center alike can be read inscriptively:

Thus the current social crisis in gender is marked by a veritable epidemic of body-transformative actions intended to assert control of the gender-speaking of the bodied self. Bodies are exercised, starved, depilated, shaved, pierced, tattooed, cut, stapled and stitched. Skin is bleached with chemicals or darkened with radiation, fat is vacuumed out of breasts, thighs, stomachs and buttocks, bones are cracked, hair is shaved or removed, breasts are stuffed with gobs of plastic. Despite the degree of attention paid to subcultural practices such as scarification, piercing and tattooing, body transformation is overwhelmingly a set of practices undertaken in utter docility to heteropolar scripts of gender. Much is also carried out in the interests of conforming to white racist notions of acceptability, notions which are themselves gendered. For every goth or queer dyke whose shaved labia are (transgressively) bedecked with multiple piercings there are innumerable women whose desperate obedience to the doctrine of femininity is signaled by the scars of plastic surgery.[34]

Bodies have and are their own power; they too enter into the relations that are all there is of power (at least according to both Nietzsche and Foucault)—indeed, it is paradigmatically bodies that are thus related. Bodies do not exist uninscribed, but they give to inscription not only its surfaces but its possibilities. And at the same time, they resist, eluding disciplines and words alike, always exceeding.

Inscription need not be static as opposed to processual. Inscription carries forward signs of process, but the body is less typeset page than complex palimpsest, written and overwritten. Wilton writes, "The attempt to erase one set of embodied speech acts—those that speak 'man' for example—and to replace them with another set—those that speak 'woman'—is not and cannot be successful."[35] Without addressing the significant and clearly central issue of whether this denies the possibility of successful gender transition or reassignment, I would voice instead my suspicion that *no* "set of embodied speech acts" is ever simply and wholly erased or replaced. Arthurs and Grimshaw suggest as much in their introduction to the anthology: "Rather the body is itself the subject of constant social inscription; it is discursively constructed and 'written' on by innumerable forms of social discipline: there is no possibility of a sharp distinction between 'nature' and 'culture.'"[36] The page invites the print and sets its possibilities. Writing on the body is further from the typesetter's labor and closer to the tattooist's art, including the cover work designed to conceal an undesired but permanent image in the skin by creating another on, around, or over it. The body is no more singularly inscribed than read only once.

But words too are rewritten in the moving eyes and hands of their readers. Body like text is constantly re-cut, torn open again, opened to communication with the outside even when the skin remains intact. The text giving itself to be read must, in a sense, be reinscribed: reading is constitutive of inscription just as writing is, if not just as much. And this giving, this inscribing, is also a rending, each rendition a violent tear in the stability, the solid fixed stolidity of language.

Little would seem so permanent as inscription. But as Derrida also writes, "The page is white but it has been written on from time immemorial; it is white through forgetfulness of what has been written, through erasure of the text on which everything that is written is written. And yet nothing is truly written, all this can change at every moment, and it is still and determinably the first time (one ought to write, 'the first time')."[37] That is: every inscription starts anew but not afresh (*you did not write it first and neither did I*); we never write on a virginal surface but neither can we ever trust our words to stay written, nor our inscriptions, however carefully disciplined, to remain in place unaltered.

In this, as the reader will have gathered by now, I have been more literal than Foucault, seeking those places in which bodies are inscribed, incised, marked by that which does not merely touch the skin surface but intersects it, cuts across it, opens spaces in it. Inscription is often understood as if it cut off possibilities, as if by writing on a blank surface we cut off our freedom to interpret that surface, or the surface's own freedom to express. But of course a truly blank surface neither expresses nor invites; it remains in the most uninteresting way unreadable. For body and language alike, that inviting, subtly seductive surface is vital. We are always overwriting an at most incomplete erasure.

To write, as Blanchot has suggested, "is not to give speech to be seen." But it is to give language to be read, to make of words an inscription upon a surface—"the proper tool for writing [is] also proper for incising." In some sense we speak *as* the body, we write *on* the body, we as inhabitants of language *are* not only body but flesh. Where speech comes to be inscribed on the body, it makes the move from speaking to writing as surely as it does on the page. Your spoken words may inscribe themselves on, eventually as, my flesh—I may come, self-fulfillingly, to fit the descriptions I am given—and from that flesh I speak my own words, to be reinscribed in the flesh of the world.

Not to give speech to be seen, but to create an incision into its flow and movement. Writing changes the time of speaking, making it both more and less lasting: more, because the word on the page can be recurred to in a way in which the passing voice cannot; less, because the word on the page can be erased or blacked out as the spoken word cannot. Writing sets down, it cuts in. The beginning and end of any act of inscription are in some sense arbitrary: "So make some incision, some violent arbitrary cut ... the scission, far from being an inaugural act, is dictated by the absence—unless there exists some illusion to discount—of any de-cisive beginning."[38] Even speaking, though, cuts into the fabric of language. This is less evidently so than for writing: Speaking too begins and it ends, picks up and leaves off, with any given speech act begun in a broken silence and cut off before it must be. Speaking and writing, though, share a participation in what Blanchot calls the "infinite conversation." Writing's conversation can go on longer—I can, if I have the intellectual skill, put my words into conversation with Plato's. Speaking's conversation can be richer in corporeal textures, from tonality to touch. Like writing, speaking, when it is conversational, seeks openings. As Edmond Jabès notes, when we part from conversation for a time, it is with questions that we return.[39]

If we permit ourselves a bit of Heideggerian illegitimate etymology, to write the body is not merely to incise but, with the stylet, to give style. Bodily meaning is complex in its semiotics, not merely referential or symbolic.

To give style to the body—and to give flesh to the text. There is something irresistibly somatic in textual style, in the recognizable (even when depersonalized) voice. Style is in no small measure the rhythm and cut, the breath and pause of the text. Does it teach us, as Eliot prayed, to sit still, absorbed, attentive—and if so, are we alert, alive in every nerve, or numbed to our own flesh? Do we feel it as rising, pacing, dancing; does it run or crawl, does it persuade us to join in? Writing we inscribe words, but more: we reinscribe speaking, we inspire what will respire, the voice and breath of the reader. However profoundly abstracted, no text is wholly discorporeal.

Inscription reminds us of the cutting quality of language and of the lasting quality of the cut. The body inscribed is stylized. Thus it is altered, but only from another inscription. There are no bodies "natural," uncultured, unread. The text inscribed is no less bodily than the spoken word; it gives the style of speaking to the voice of the reader. Body and text alike are palimpsestic; nobody is natural, no one writes the first word.

Though I have been, as I've said, more literal than he, there remains considerable common ground with Foucault: this incisive disruption of the culturally constituted body is not limited to the merely somatic, as if we could somehow disconnect the body from the world. We do not slice into our skins without making trouble in our worlds. We do not rend language without troubling our flesh, however thoroughly we try to ignore the ability of words to arrest and disrupt us. A palimpsest is written over, but not in the manner of a computer screen in which text can be so obliterated as to leave no trace on the screen.[40] Even erased lines, even healed cuts, leave marks—usually too obscure to be read, no doubt, but capable in turn of rendering subsequent as well as precedent text more obscure.

To think the cut as inscription tells us two contrary-seeming things. First: that we need not think of depth to see the surfaces of flesh and word as layered in their complexity. Every body and every sentence comes to us as a palimpsest, overwritten in shadowy layers of a history we cannot quite read or say, but which alters no less the presentation before us, as the once-present always does. Second: that every inscription is an incision, slicing open language, body, any surface at all. This slicing is a revelation, not of depth but of space, of the open, the between, which is needed if we are to read or write or say at all; if we are to interpret or express. The opening is violence but it is also possibility. It may cut us off from one another, but it may open us to one another instead, or too. The closed is silent, invulnerable and unavailable. "The grace of a body offering itself is always possible,"[41] Nancy declares, but we *can* close ourselves to this possibility. If we are truly to explore the lasting cut, then we have to return to the wound. More exactly—more lastingly, more tellingly, to the mark of the open, however written-over—to the scar.

The Wound, the Scar

> She would have destroyed herself many a time at their stirrings and have been damned with them in Hell, and in witness thereof, she bit her own hand so violently, that the mark was seen all her life after.
>
> —*The Book of Margery Kempe*

In literature, in inherited writing and written speech, we find some remarkable stories of scars. Early and exemplary among them is the scar left by the wild boar on the thigh of Odysseus. As Dennis Patrick Slattery points out in *The Wounded Body*, this scar serves multiple narrative functions: it is initiatory, destiny revealing, and identifying. The initiatory aspect of the scar brings body explicitly into conjunction with language: Odysseus is scarred in the same episode in which he is named.

The name and the scar form parts of the pattern of his destiny, the thread of his life. Rightly noting the importance of the thread—spun, woven, and cut—not only in the hands of the fates but in the intersections of Odysseus's tale with Penelope's, Slattery metaphorizes the scar as its own thread, "a threading marker."[42] Tracing this line of thought etymologically, we may follow this thread, *suture*, to the path followed (the Hindi *sutra*, path or way, is itself a thread). The scar is tied to the story, and the flesh to the words that tell it. The story line is drawn—"The boar scar that initiates the young Odysseus through his fresh wound is about Odysseus the wanderer trying to return home decades later."[43]

The sight and, significantly, the touch of that flesh will reveal the identity of Odysseus, will let him be called by name, when after so many years of wandering he returns to his home. The servant woman Eurycleia, washing him, touches the scar and knows the man—"When she traces her fingers over the scar she immediately retraces, or retrieves the life of the man she is cleansing."[44] "The scar tissue reveals ... who he is,"[45] Slattery says, and Eurycleia's touch calls him by name.

Later tales give to scars still stranger functions, marking the bearer's body not only by cross-cutting through the time of the world but by carrying the mark into eternity. Paraphrasing Ephraim, Bynum writes, "Body expresses what is important about the self. . . . risen flesh reflects who we are and what we deserve. The martyrs will rise with gifts in their hands and the marks of tortures still on their bodies."[46] Gregory of Nyssa tells of the miraculous cure of his sister Macrina, suffering from breast cancer: "both she and her mother prayed, and she made an ointment of mud and her own tears, and the tumor disappeared, leaving only a tiny scar. . . . the scar remained, in death as it had been in life, 'a memorial of the divine intervention.'"[47] Macrina's scar functions, as Burrus notes, as "a metonym both for Macrina's body ... and for the text itself."[48] The disruption becomes the sign of the "whole" that it disrupts. Suffering as well as healing is marked: "But we also rise as Jonah did from the whale, without a single hair or eyelash lost ... and the flesh that rises bears the specific marks of our suffering as Christ's bore his wounds."[49]

Augustine argued that saints who suffered physical damage and dismemberment in this life would rise restored, but marked by seams; whole, but still more glorified by the narratives of suffering inscribed on their skin.[50] Here Augustine seems to echo the sentiment quoted earlier from James, for whom "the good are intact when divided, while the evil fragment or decay even without violence."[51] The very ability to scar tells the necessary story, establishes the virtue of one's identity. Indeed, for those who mightn't be marked by worldly forces, God "puts 'the mark of glory most of all on those members by which it is earned.'"[52]

What is so special about scars? Are they simply to be classed with other "distinguishing features," or "identifying marks," whether or not these carry over into carnal resurrection? They *are* distinguishing marks, of course, readable distinctions too, as we might argue (correctly if facilely) that the marks on a page set it apart from other pages, so that we know, returning to a book, if we have already read the page to which we open (at least we do if we were paying attention the first time through). But there is more to scars than distinction, something making these marks other in kind from such descriptive attributes as height or hair color or the patterns memorialized in dental records. Scars are bearers of memory, memories carried forward in the skin even when we forget or repress their stories. Like words, they do more than specify; they mean in ways that cannot be reduced to designation.

Unlike other identifying features, scars are also unlike stamps or signs that might be placed on products to tell us what they are. They identify not simply by being unique to our bodies, but by constructing our identities themselves, telling the stories of how we became what we are. At the origin of each scar, as I shall note again below, is a wound. Note the peculiarity of these statements in conjunction: it is wounds that make us who we are. This is not, or at any rate not merely, to argue for the long-asserted, character-giving value of suffering. Rather: this mark that both says and makes who I am—this mark by which the *I* is written—is a mark made by a brief and partial absence of the very body that I am, that becomes me. For a moment—for a time that may range from minutes to months—there was an opening in the surface, in my corporeal self-containment. For that moment, the skin was cut apart, peeled off, burned, abraded, damaged, and my flesh left open to the world. I become *I* (again) as I heal, but only as my healing is imperfect, only as I carry the marks of my own rupture. We are who we are by virtue of these places in us that have been not-us, those marks that remind us that we can be broken, and that the *I* who is healed is not who I was. Nancy writes after his heart transplant: "The strangeness of my own identity, which was always very much alive [to me], never touched me so poignantly. 'I' has clearly become the formal index of an unverifiable and impalpable chain [*enchainement*]."[53] By such marking we need not mark sadness or harm, though we cannot rule out the constitutive power of such things either. Rather, we are disrupted and reclosed, as much by intensities of joy as by sorrows, if much less often.

It is likewise an absence that carries writing forward. Stories like scars proceed in nonlinear time. Slattery makes this point clearly: "The wound and its memory, the scar can, like words, conjure something that has been absent into the present. Here is what words and wounds share—their relation to the past and to the memory of the past being brought forward into the present. . . . Words, like the scar, can conjure absence into presence."[54] This is the operation of writing, as well; as Blanchot puts it, writing is always "in obscure combat" with presence.[55] Writing is an effort to make a memory into a future, losing the very present it would seem to mark. Like the scar, it tells of a space of loss, but makes of that loss a mark that draws us irresistibly. Hyperbolically, the scar both conjures and reveals.

The unease we feel before the scar is itself an evocation of memory whether or not we know what the scar remembers, even if the scar is on another body—because that which the scar traces is of course the wound,[56] and wounds are nearly definitional of our unease.

As I have already indicated, Bataille famously links the wound—especially the cut, often using the term *laceration*—to communication. Communication remains impossible so long as two beings are closed to one another. But openness is an impossible risk, "acquiring life by losing it in *communication* with the other."[57] We are who we are by virtue of our boundaries, our skin boundaries not least importantly. To open ourselves is to lose ourselves; to be cut open is to chance scarring, the memory of communication. Because memory is all that the subject can have, certainly all she can retain, of communication, the scar is all we *know* of the wound, the mark in the flesh, the trace of the thought.

Bataillean communication is not, of course, an innocent or affectless informational exchange. He almost always has in mind experiences of limit-intensity. But something of this risk and damage is found in less extraordinary forms as well. Roland Barthes writes of love: "Meaning (destiny) electrifies my hand; I am about to tear open the other's opaque body, oblige the other (whether there is a response, a withdrawal, or mere acceptance) to enter into the interplay of meaning: I am about *to make the other speak*. In the lover's realm, there is no *acting out*: no propulsion, perhaps even no pleasure— nothing but signs, a frenzied activity of language: to institute, on each furtive occasion, the system (the paradigm) of demand and response."[58] Here one wounds, tears open, to invoke or provoke speech (a more aggressive form of the welcoming disruption); speaking in turn may wound, and indeed it may be by speaking that we first evoke that response.

As I've suggested, when we think of the cut, we might more commonly think of being cut apart, rather than being cut open. But, as the images of the sacred heart have already suggested to us, the wound may be an opening onto the world, a willingness to make possible the loss of oneself. Slattery, like Bataille, connects this to intensity: "If only pain has to be confronted, then separation between self and body and even self and world can be maintained. But if the pain moves to wound us deeply such that our own existence is suddenly called into question, then the separation collapses."[59] At this depth the scission no longer separates; the opening makes togetherness possible, but the limit of togetherness is self-loss.

If communication is the risk (delightedly embraced or rejected as unwelcome) of scarring, then too we must realize that scars can both facilitate and block communication. The touch of skin on scars communicates; we can guide memory as we do hands to the places that are marked. Not every scar tells of lasting damage; injury can be willfully received or proudly healed. But some do so tell. Scar tissue is tough. Barthes urges the loved one to speak: "What matters is the physical, bodily, labial proffering of the word: open your lips and let it out (be obscene)." [60] But we may refuse to reopen scars; or they may refuse to bleed even if we do, acknowledging no fissure, giving nothing. Mistrustful, we withhold words, refuse to give of ourselves in speaking any more than in flesh.

Where we are wounded, we are also vulnerable (susceptible to further wounding), subject to infection. Nancy provocatively links infection to intrusion, to strange otherness: "The other stranger can very quickly manifest itself: not the woman or the black or the young man or the Basque, but the other immune system."[61] A perfect, closed identity (an impossible identity, we might say, a self without openness, without longing) is wholly immune; "in any case, what it all comes to is this: identity counts as immunity, the one identifies itself with the other."[62] Immunity is life-protecting, and yet, as Nancy rightly notes, it can be life-threatening, too, as when the body rejects a transplant or, as we may further add, when one attempts to foreclose all intrusion, to make the cut-off self invulnerable, not recognizing that we are already, fundamentally, disunified.

Scars can make us protective, but they protect us, too. The narrator of Acker's "The City" uses the wounded body as a break in language, a disruption that provides time to escape the deeper scarring of words: "When Eddie was kicking me out of his house, I put a razor blade into my right wrist in order to stop Eddie from saying 'You don't know how to love. No man will ever love you.' The people who saved me from death're my friends."[63] The cut speaks as clearly as a word, but perhaps more strongly still, silencing the words that would speak against it—silencing the cutting words that would destroy the possibility of love. The friends who save the narrator from death save her as much by defying those words, by showing the possibilities of friendship (a life-saving care, surely a match if not a replacement for the love Eddie has declared impossible), as by listening to her wounds.

The scar, then, in flesh or as word, identifies—it is the word that *names*. The name is not merely a marker but a thread that traces a strangely nonlinear path, the time of writing, of memory. As Burrus writes, "The scar bears witness, in vain defiance of flesh's corruptibility, focusing the gaze on what is already disappearing, what can only be fixed—what is also always shifting—in the performative act of remembrance."[64] The memory is that of communication—which is to say not only exchange but breakage. To speak and to write, as much as to offer the skin, are to render oneself vulnerable. But by now we should be alert to the strengths of vulnerability. Slattery writes, "Our wounds are connected, therefore, to time, to memory, and to the divinity within the soul; vulnerability and divinity exist close to the affliction, marking us as both."[65] The cut is neither good nor evil, neither sanctifying nor sinful—or, more exactly, it is either, or even both. That is: it signifies an extreme, a vivid mark of sin or sanctity too strong to be denied. Disruption writes on the flesh, keeps it honest. Writing on the body appears mythically as the perfect conjunction of body and writing, a dual revelation that *must* be true, or a revelation of a truth so hyperbolic that it must be said too much, must carve itself into the very flesh.

In *Dissemination*, Derrida reminds us of the vulnerable materiality—indeed, not just existence as matter but power as flesh—of texts, as well. The opening epigraph of the section entitled "The Scission," taken from Philippe Sollers's *The Numbers*, reads as violently as any vision of the bleeding God:

> The virginal folding-back of the book, again, willing/lends for a sacrifice from which the red edges of the books of old once bled; the introduction of a weapon, or letter-opener, to mark the taking of possession. . . . The folds will perpetuate a mark. . . .
> There is a knife that I do not forget.[66]

The knife scars into memory. Derrida here links the scission to time, to the making and marking of beginnings and endings, those violent, arbitrary cuts. Every beginning-to-write is a scission; we begin only when we have read and thought, when we are full of words. We cut into them to start *here*, and we cut them off to end.

When we write, our inscriptions placing words that they might enter the eyes and exit the throats of others, we also trace in hopeful anticipation the line from raised print to cut page. Echoing Blanchot's observation about writing's "obscure combat with presence," Derrida writes, "The pure present would be the untouched fullness, the virgin continuity of the nonscission, the volume that, not having exposed the roll of its writing to the reader's letter-opener, would therefore not yet be written on the eve of the start of the game. But the pen, when you have followed it to the end, will have turned into a knife."[67] Knives make not presences but absences, openings, which later form the seams and scars along which we trace our knowing. We as writers are constantly editing, cutting, inserting; we as readers are constantly re-entering: "Textuality . . . is an undecidable process of opening/closing that re-forms itself without letup."[68] Stephen Moore writes of the arrival of the age of textual (he writes specifically of biblical) criticism, when "the pen took its place beside the scalpel."[69] Incision and suture, slice and scar write and read us into our texts.

Here too we find ourselves in these texts, as Webb suggests when he notes of Bataille that his eroticism is one expression of "a desire for intimacy that necessarily takes the shape of aggression, because the displacement of the self is always experienced as the opening of a wound."[70] Recalling the paradoxes of identity and dispossession, we note that we are made as cutting, too, "like all those whose vital substance is cut from the same fabric as writing."[71]

Cut open or cut from, we bleed into. As I noted in the exploration of the sacred heart, Nancy writes of the "discharges of writing," which only "exscribe," of the body which cannot be the locus of writing: "No 'written bodies,' no writing on the body, nor any of this graphosomatology into which the mystery of the Incarnation and of the body as pure sign of itself is sometimes converted, 'modern style.'"[72] But the discharges of the Word incarnate are bodily: blood and water, the nourishing milk with which they are both conflated. Without being the locus of writing, remaining perpetually elusive as the limit case must, the body is nonetheless the place of the displacement that is intimacy, sharing, communication. The "mystery of the Incarnation," which Nancy warns us against converting to a simplistic graphosomatology, is the mystery of all incarnation.

Thus the extraordinary power of the Christian Incarnation myth and those bodily God-states associated with it. When the flesh of God the son is opened, it bleeds. But, as a biologist of my acquaintance is fond of saying, all bleeding stops eventually. What the brilliance of the idea of Word made Flesh suggests is an open wound that may bleed forth millions of words, not just exegesis as language attempts to enwrap this impossibility, but the longing expressed by mystics and even in more "ordinary" prayer. If love, as Nancy argues, constitutes the very subject wounded by it, then we are returned by these thoughts of ruptured limits to our limit cases of language—to love letters and prayers, and to the permeable, indeterminate boundary between them.

Between body and language the cut serves the function of disruption—in the artifice of beginnings and endings as well as in fragmentation and partiality. It serves as inscription, body or page bearing the mark of its relation to the outside. And in the extreme of inscription, the cut forms the scar, identifying its bearer by serving as a reminder of absence.

The stories that express this inexhaustible longing, this unquenchable bleeding, have little place in a properly contemporary and clean-scrubbed

Christianity, but they remain among the best and most religious elements that tradition has ever had to offer.

The exploration of touch, and of the Johannine stories in relation to it, suggested to us that we do not grasp the sacred so much as brush across it in an encounter with the perpetually elusive and infinitely desirable. The figure of the fold articulates for us a series of twists and entanglements in which we find the profane already layered through with the sacred, as much wrapped around as wrapped up, but always, too, somehow just beyond the next turning. The cut is equally defiant of the possibility of grasping; the sacred may be seen in the openings of possibility,[73] moments of pain and of grace that cut into our world and our words. But it may be also, as the visionaries of the Sacred Heart suggest, our own cutting in return, into the body and word as the revelation of their already-imminent sanctity.

Conclusion: Figures of Desire

> Desiring-machines work only when they break down, and by continually breaking down.
>
> —Gilles Deleuze and Felix Guattari, *Anti-Oedipus*

I have attempted in this series of reflections a pair of movements, two kinds of choreography set in a juxtaposition that is not, I hope, an opposition (though certainly the two are in tension). First is the movement of the corps or chorus, a corporeality of bodies or voices *en masse*. That is: I have tried to trace in word and flesh what is in some manner the *same* movement, in a series of parallel structures. Here the relation is one of amplification by synchronous repetition, as of voices lifted in tones sustained, or of movement when it is performed by groups of bodies. (Imagine the reduction in effect if the chorus line were a single dancer, however spectacularly high her kicks.) I hope to have suggested curious commonalities across these two modes of what, or how, we are. I've tried to show ways in which body and word could be said to follow the same lines.

But a second movement, subtler and more difficult, has sustained itself alongside this choral harmony. However passionately interleaved and entangled, cross-cut and in contact, body and language present limit cases for one another. Each is at the boundary of the other, with the peculiar and frustrating quality of borders: they can scarcely be said to be wholly foreign to one another, any more than countries are properly foreign exactly along the lines that share their division. After all, there they *are*, along the boundary, at the same place, sharing, surely, that suturing (touching, creased, inscribed) line. Perhaps they even trace this very line, in terms of the first kind of movement, in common. Yet the existence of a boundary already tells of separation: over here is (sometimes it is useful to state the obvious) *not* over there. The difference gives meaning to each territory. This idea is old enough to have the flavor of the obvious too: cat is cat because it is not mat or rat or bat or fishing line, said Saussure in his lectures, as early as 1907 perhaps, or, in translation, something at any rate very much like that.[1] But philosophers from Zeno to Levinas and Derrida have hinted to us that difference is infinite, after all, and (perhaps thus) it retains its fascination still. In this second kind of movement, body and language reach toward, touch, enfold, and intercut one another. In this final chapter, we can revisit the opening chapter's connection of desire to limit to suggest that perhaps this makes some sense of the call between body and language, noting how each both makes and unmakes the subjects who tend to think of themselves (ourselves) as in charge of each.

As limit to and for one another, body and language, mutually implicated in their need, also each mark for the other the limit of the possible. Nancy writes in "Corpus":

> *Body* is the total signifier, for everything has a body, or everything is a body ... and *body* is the last signifier, the limit of the signifier, if what it says or would like to say—what it would have liked to have said— is nothing other than the interlacing, the mixing of bodies with bodies, mixing everywhere, and everywhere manifesting this other absence of name, named "God," everywhere producing and reproducing and everywhere absorbing the sense of sense and of all the senses, infinitely mixing the impenetrable with the impenetrable.[2]

Nor is Nancy alone in this startling pairing, limiting language at the surface of the body and at the name of God. Hélène Cixous writes:

> And in telling you this I am trembling in pain and in joy and I am crying in terror, as if I had dared to want to tell god his real name, which

is not simply god: for "god" is the word that enables us to avoid speaking to god directly. For ever since the beginning we have guessed that if we ever managed to pronounce just once the true name of God, all the truth dispersed in all languages and all the truth of lives that is concentrated in the body and reserved for love, would shatter in a single breath, just as if god, who ever since the beginning has not spoken to anyone had always made our name resound in his language, and once the true name rang out, all words in all languages would become unusable, so weak, false, bare, impotent, unforgettably merely words, the straw of thought, that we would no longer wish to speak. Yes, I have also guessed that, I myself, and you too, you remember no doubt, but I have never stopped ignoring it. And when I recall having thought it, it is by flash-memories that are so dazzling that I close my eyes and I forget.[3]

Here "God" as an infinite admixture of opposites names both indistinction and infinite difference, tracing the same lines of movement, as fingertips on flesh, vibratory tone on receptive tympanum, words in the throat. To use such a name reminds us of the sacred character of desire. And, the sacred being always very near the taboo, the use of such a name has itself not infrequently been forbidden.

Small wonder that throughout the history of philosophy desire is conceived, as we saw in the introduction, as both lack (or absence) and overfullness, excess. Desire has everything to do with otherness—which is both what the self is not (hence lacks) and what is beyond the self (as the self reaches over its boundaries into the outside). And yet desire, like the limits with which it is mutually implicated, constitutes self—"The I is the I of desire." Such a self is made by the very limits it must always seek to exceed. More precisely, it is made at once by those limits and by the excesses of desire.

We, we as a shifting set of those I's of desire, are there, not simply bodies nor wholly text, but in their intersection in desire. We constitute ourselves in the inscriptions on and the surfaces of somata, in the touch of words in the throat, in the infinite unfoldings of meaningfulness and sound itself. The question *Which one?*—put into time, *Which one now?*—keeps drawing desire into the world, because it is an open-ended and exploratory question, and the *now* demands our constantly renewed attention. This need and desire for motion—to go forth (*gredh*) and enter into, to take in and be receptive, to have an effect and to be affected—is not a desire of matter in the mechanistic or reductive sense, but of flesh, doubly body and word. My words enter into the conversation that a language is; that conversation cross-cuts and restimulates the flow of my speaking, writing, listening, reading. My body reaches into the world not solely to make happen but to feel, to sense, to receive. Each calls to the world, which calls it in turn; each calls, as well, to the other.

I wrote in the introduction of the tension, within desire, between power and lack. We may perhaps be better positioned now, if not to make sense of this tension, at least to sense it better, to form a better sense of its workings. Desire is first the overfullness reaching toward: the poem, the prayer, indeed, any speaking or writing reaching out to touch someone; as well as the literal movement of touching while being touched back; the articulation of eager words unfolding into the world when we *need* to speak and to write and the rapturous unfolding of joyous flesh when we open ourselves to the possibilities of response, when we incise, inscribe, cut into, leave marks—including those constitutive of ourselves.

But desire is simultaneously lack: the bare or even, in *imitatio Christi*, wounded skin that draws touch, the need of the other to hear the words with which we touch; the inward pull of the inflective point, the pull of those who need to hear, need intercession, need reassembly; the eagerness of the visionary to have her heart entered, and even of the subject to exceed its self-possession.

Desire is the wounding arrow or the deeply striking word, but also the desperate compulsion to be torn open, to communicate. It is the receptivity of the page and skin and the eagerness of the ink. In each case the need that might be characterized as negativity or lack—vulnerability, openness, woundedness, receptivity—is no less desire, no less powerful than those more "actively" characterized as sounding, reaching, scarring, seeking. Lack is power too, and power is as needy as vulnerability. The dichotomy, as the reader will have guessed, is never so strict after all.

Desire does not seek, more precisely, does not ever seek only, satisfaction. What it seeks is instead an impossible pairing, to remain while fulfilled. In terms of the subject, itself both made and unmade by desire, desire seeks to remain self while fulfilled outside self; hence to remain the very self that may be broken or even emptied in that fulfillment. Born of limit, it pushes to break limitation. I have argued elsewhere, and hardly alone, for the importance of what Bataille calls "desire avid not to be satisfied." All desire is impossible: in body, in word, and in the desire that calls the two, one to the other.

It is in desire that body and language call to one another, the desire of self to exceed self. The body, which can never be wholly text, is drawn forth by words; language, which can never quite capture corporeality, tries always to say the flesh. At their most passionate, each encounters its limit in the other. In Winterson's novel *The Powerbook*, a scene unfolds in dual descriptions of hands on skin and voices in conversation. The scene's lover asks the narrator about her current book:

> "What is it about?"
> "Boundaries. Desire."
> "What are your other books about?"
> "Boundaries. Desire."
> "Can't you write about something else?"
> "No."[4]

I must confess to having often felt much the same as the second speaker sounds. Perhaps, writing the body, there is nothing else one could say.

Bodies and words never fuse; they never quite coincide. They go forth, and they touch. They articulate and enfold. They transgress, and they cut. The touch moves on, the fold reforms, the cut scars over. We bear the traces of our own existence as the I's of impossible desire. We work by continually breaking down.

Body and word are in mutual incomprehension, possessed by an inability to grasp. Each reaches endlessly for the other; each marks the limit of the other's significance. Nietzschean *power* is the capacity to give, the inability not to be affected —but that capacity, as we saw in reading the resurrection story from John, is indistinguishable from a perfect receptivity. Desire is utterly generous in its perfect greed, seeking always to touch upon, enfold within, cut open and into and through.

So we return at last to the mutual, impossible craving of body and words. Desire always strives to push past—at its most intense and devastating, to break—limits. But limit, as we have seen, is the very condition, the precise location, of desire. The absence of coincidence between body and language, their mutual exclusion even where they so completely overlay one another, gives breath to the call of each to other. This limit is that *of* both body and language as well as *between* body and language; this is the very limit of communication.

Language, we have seen Nancy claim, reaches its limit at the name of God. But we have seen too that for him, and for others, language reaches its limit at the body. As a communicative medium, language reaches toward and across: across spaces; toward, necessarily toward, its limits. Desire, implicated with limit, is built into communication.

Language is spoken and written outside any of us, yet by bodies, drawing them; it speaks and writes toward the body as the limit that draws it. The body too reaches toward the outside, toward the other to whom it could speak, toward the language that surrounds it and makes it the body of a subject.

Evocation

I am about to make the other speak.

—Roland Barthes, *A Lover's Discourse*

Collectively, religiously, mythically, we fantasize a perfect communication (such may be almost definitional of the "oceanic feeling" to which Freudian psychoanalysis attributes mysticism), but this would annihilate us, body and word alike. To be oneself, as I have said before, is to be only one self. To break our boundaries is self-annihilation. But perhaps this annihilation is central to the fantasy: weary of ourselves, maddened by our own security, we seek what will breach our boundaries for more than a moment. Of course, perverse creatures that we are, we want to be there for our own loss, to be around to enjoy it, to feel what it is to be beyond the limits of our own sensation. Then, of course, we want to tell it, as if our words would not also burst. Or we want to tell—something, it hardly matters what—that *would* already burst language, not only approach but reach that *you*; not only reach you, but enter; not only enter you, but stay to show you this bursting. And yet that impossible, ineluctably singular (unnumbered, innumerable) moment must be enough: an instant's loss from which we return to say *once I lived, like the gods, and no more is needed.*[5]

Perhaps this is something of what we love in words—their very imperfection. They do not communicate perfectly; they seem to struggle against us with all the recalcitrance of matter itself. If we turn optimistically to the flesh (thinking, as I have suggested, that bodies don't lie), we will find the same frustrations: we are limited by our selfhood to imperfect instants; we are clumsy in our motion as in our touch. But those instants may suffice to eternity: your touch may open my sense of self and tear me out of that self not only when it impinges against my consent but far more (and far more gracefully, graciously, evocatively) when it collaborates in drawing in my deep self-weariness, working precisely in accord with it. Flesh and word share this wounding skill. *Let you destroy yourself,*[6] as all writing invites; *lead me to my own destruction,* we ask as we reach out or read. *Take and read,* whispers the voice of Augustine's salvation—but in thus reaching out and taking in, he loses himself in consuming desire, his will torn against itself until he hands it over to the God who sets him on fire with need.[7]

This borderline destructiveness is better expressed not as a Freudian oceanic feeling but as Lacanian bliss, *jouissance* with all its delight in fatality, *ate* as the limit and the space beyond. This term's ambiguity plays out, not as two contradictory meanings we might equally grasp, but as touch and the nothing beyond the touched surface. No matter the direction in which we reach, we can only touch without grasping, without seizing hold.

It is this very play of limit and rupture that gives to the exploration of body and language such a religious resonance. These limit-concerns are, in some wide sense, necessarily religious preoccupations, taken up by that which is always elusive, just beyond our grasp. Just as the oceanic absence of limit marks one understanding of mysticism, so too does that which is at the limit of language, evoking the ineffable, a historically mystical concern with that which draws or calls us without our quite being able to understand it. I do not at all mean to reinscribe this peculiar relation in the context of any particular religious dogma; if I have told Catholic stories, it only reveals the depth at which they have inscribed themselves in (and as) me. Regardless of denomination, religious thought is the place we find such concerns, and so too it seems, for me at least, to be the place where such concerns rather unexpectedly find themselves—it is at the names of God that language finds its limits; it is in calling out those names that we hear the limits of flesh. (And when, after all, are we most inclined to call out the name of God?)

Entry and Invitation

Desire, pure impure desire, is the call to bridge the distance, to die in common through separation.

Maurice Blanchot, *The Writing of the Disaster*

Nor would I posit a metaphysical or topographical distinction between sacred and profane; both are immanent—insofar as the term might, without the opposition of transcendence, still make any sense—in any place, any moment, any body, any text. Yet they are not precisely, not solely, immanent, since immanence does suppose the opposition of transcendence. The possibility of breakage and rupture is integral to the possibility of containment; the impossibility of the perfect communication marks the limit of our ability to destroy limits. But it is all right here, and there is nowhere *else* we might go to get out of ourselves. It is all right here as the very possibility of breaking. We are pulled to the promise of fulfillment in loss: as bodies, to language; as those who come to ourselves in words, to the flesh.

Every invitation, insofar as it invites us out of ourselves, insofar as it draws us beyond the given present—every temptation, every desire—is an invitation to destruction. But destruction can be most inviting when it arises in the ecstasy of desiring delight and not in the loathing of annihilation; when, like sacrifice, it turns upon what it loves, not in hate but in love's own greater intensity. Perhaps this destructive turn is even what makes love possible, in some measure by making possible the loving subject.

We lose ourselves so that we might be. Flesh and word, we seek the very loss by which we say and hear ourselves.

Undoubtedly one of the forces at work in the making of this text was a line I heard Jane Gallop use in a lecture many years ago: "There is a peculiar *calling* relation between body and language," she said, or so, at any rate, I recall it. They call, but this is a call dangerous to answer (dangerous, but in the manner in which promise is dangerous). If in certain modes of poetry we may, as Rilke urges, astonish the angels by telling them of *things*, by giving them *as words* the flesh of our world, then in increasingly dehydrated technical terms and increasingly pointless chatter we wring our language utterly dry of things, and our flesh of the rich resonance of meaning. But something as much in our words as in our flesh—something in their shared desire—resists.[8] Remember Mark Taylor's Hegelian suggestion that language appears as body's disappearance. But body is not just stuff, and there is the heart of the mystery: all that can be found, pinned down and precisely formulated is matter. The flesh of the world is insoluble, impenetrable—and already entered everywhere by words.

This entry is of course multiple and multipliable. Figures of entry-into are everywhere in the mutuality of bodies and words. Speaking in multiple ways, as Nancy says, is *openness*.[9] We recall that for him there is, in self-abandonment, "always a *pollakos*, an abundance ... : it opens onto a profusion of possibilities, just as one abandons oneself in excess, for there is no other modality of abandon."[10]

This excess is curiously indistinguishable, where flesh meets word, from not nearly enough. Nancy's notion of abundance meets the liminal sacrality of Acker's word-excluding gym to suggest to us that the limit is a paradox, where an opening marks the very possibility of closure; where, when "the world and words fuck each other," we must recall our own enfleshing in the world too. Recall, too, the speaker in "The City," who declares, "There's a definite difference in my physical being or body between when I'm being fucked and I'm not being fucked. How can I say anything when I'm totally uncentralized or not being fucked?"[11] Being fucked would scarcely seem to make or leave one "centralized"; indeed, not only does the term imply a boundary-breach that must threaten the security of the center, but fucking, at least if it is any good, tends to have a peculiar effect on our ability to *say anything*—whether we become preverbal altogether or startlingly verbose in terms exceptionally suited to our later detriment or regret. "How can I say anything when I'm ... not being fucked?" asks, I suspect, not about the action or passion of fucking but about the subject's need to be made by those moments that take it out of itself. If we do not forget ourselves sometimes ("what happens during these minutes is that I forget"), we will explode under the pressure of our own containment. If we are not brought to forgetfulness, sometimes, we shall have no words to remember. And this too is characteristic of desire; all love, as Barthes reminds us, is intermittently forgetful. [12]

Particularly fascinating (to me, at least) in this narrator's query is the use of the receptive (I would hesitate to say "passive") voice. "How can I say anything," one might more reasonably ask, "if I'm not fucking, not entering the world, if there's no receptive ear? If I'm totally uncentralized, forced to scatter my energies in the effort to be heard?" By contrast, the formulation of the question by Acker's character reminds us of the mutuality of word/world interleaving, of reach and receptivity. We speak forth into the world only by letting it into us, only by letting its words enter our flesh so that we too can speak, give voice. We can only speak when speaking is double, when we hear as much as we say. This peculiarity, this opening of self to world, this strangeness not of fucking but of being fucked, echoes at once the "inability not to respond" that Nietzsche attributes to Dionysus and the power-giving vulnerability of the incarnate, desiring Christian God, whose wounds beg for entry. We find here again a "lack" that cannot be told apart from power.

Cixous, like Acker, reminds us not to neglect the doubleness, the mutuality, of words and flesh, with themselves and with one another. She writes of the other side, of that in us which reaches out only by virtue of being reached into—"having never been without writing, having writing in my body, at my throat, on my lips ... to me my texts are elements of a whole which interleaves my story."[13] My words enter into the language that forms me; my body into the desirous meanings of flesh: "Skin I am inside that skin, stretched out between its lips and fingers"[14]—among the organs of closest touch, but of speaking and writing too.

Here, once again, we are reminded not only of the ineluctable interleavings of the fold and the rending intimacy of the cut, but of the touch, as well, that does not grasp: "I never dream of mastering or inventing concepts," Cixous writes. "Moreover I am incapable of this. I am overtaken."[15]

Moving after Words

The Languages of the Body.
1. The languages of flux. Of uncertainty in which the "I" (eye) constantly changes. . . .
2. The languages of wonder, not of judgment. . . .

3. Languages which contradict themselves.

4. The languages of this material body: laughter, silence, screaming.

5. Scatology. That is laughter.

6. The languages of play: poetry....

7. Language that announces itself as insufficient.

8. Above all: the languages of intensity....

9. The only religions are scatology and intensity.

10. Language that forgets itself.

—Kathy Acker, "Critical Languages"

Words, overtaking us, set us into motion after them. Cixous links the body in motion to language at its most somatic.

> Mandelstam asks very seriously in his "Conversation about Dante": how many pairs of shoes Dante must have worn out in order to write *The Divine Comedy*, because, he tells us, that could only have been written on foot, walking without stopping, which is also how Mandelstam wrote. Mandelstam's whole body was in action, taking part, searching. Walking, dancing, pleasure: these accompany the poetic act. I wonder what kind of poet doesn't wear out their shoes, writes with their head. The true poet is a traveler. Poetry is about traveling on foot and all its substitutes, all forms of transportation.
>
> Mandelstam wore out hundreds of pairs of shoes. You cannot write such intense, dense poetry without the kind of dance that dances you round the world. Mandelstam himself could not write without walking round and round. When he was prevented from walking he died.[16]

How can I write anything if I'm not out walking? How can I say anything if I'm not being fucked? How can I be read on uncut pages? What is our access to language, if not this motion of flesh in the world, this powerful vulnerable mutuality, this overflowing excess and indrawing space?

It is thus, where matter and word are always reaching for and calling to one another, that the flesh of the world takes on Merleau-Ponty's chiasmatic sense, with its emphasis on the doubleness of touching. The world is spaces for the movement of bodies and words, and they in turn move doubly toward one another. Moore writes in *God's Gym:* "'Read me,' urges the book, 'that you may have life.' 'Eat me,' urges the Word, in the book; 'whoever eats me ... will live because of me.' ... Eat me, drink me ... ingest me, digest me!"[17] What is urged is desire; what is spoken, the desire for desire. *Want me*, words urge, and the hunger they awaken may not be wholly intellectual.

Hyperbolic in the extreme, religious and erotic language point to the unquenchable desire to be the very selves we so urgently desire to exceed. We are words that say too much and yet can never say the body; we are flesh that feels too much and never does more than touch upon the ways to say it. All the possibilities of language are exceeded in our skins; all the strength and grasp of our bodies are eluded by our words. This insufficiency is all we have: and yet (here is the true delight of desire) there is nothing more powerful than this hunger; this not enough is more than sufficient to everything.

Language and body are communicative, outreaching and indrawing. But they are also, importantly, constitutive—constitutive of ourselves. This is perhaps more evident for body, but it is true of language too. Kojève, who calls the human self "the I of Desire," also insists that we become selves by entering into speech: "Man becomes conscious of himself at the moment when—for the 'first' time—he *says* 'I.' To understand man by understanding his 'origin' is, therefore, to understand the origin of the I revealed by speech." [18] When I speak, when I write, I enter into language, but the I who enters does not pre-exist the speaking, and language continues to exceed the self.

Every desire, I earlier remarked, is impossible. What constitutes each of us as a *me* and what takes us out of, away from any possibility of self-containment is in each case the force, the power of desire. We are made selves, we *are*, as the very urgency of exceeding those selves. In our very construction we are open to the outside, not as sturdy Things with holes into our depths but as indefinitely unfolding, profoundly complex surfaces.

Language and body are both constitutive and communicative, yet to communicate is to threaten, at least a little, the very selves who communicate, who were constituted by language and the body as the media of communication. *I am*, a matter of language, but I am only if I have someone to whom I might say so. *Hoc est corpus meum*, declares the Christ of the synoptic gospels, *this is my body*, not long before his death sets so many paradoxes into motion.

Perhaps we can go further: *this body is me*, but unbeheld, unheard, untouched, even the most divine of bodies would be just another object. We enter into language and into corporeality not solely as we enter the visible and audible— though we do that too, we must—but as we doubly touch and are touched, enfold and are implicated, open and scar. We too are word made flesh, and just as much flesh made word; in infinite desire we go on making and unmaking our selves.

Notes

Introduction

1. Jean-Luc Nancy, "Of Divine Places," trans. Michael Holland, in *The Inoperative Community*, ed. Peter Connor (Minneapolis: University of Minnesota Press, 1991), § 32, p. 135.

2. "Speech on the Occasion of Receiving the Literature Prize of the Free Hanseatic City of Bremen," in Paul Celan, *Collected Prose*, trans. Rosmarie Waldrop (Riverdale-on-Hudson, N.Y.: Sheep Meadow Press, 1986), 35.

3. Celan, "The Meridian," in *Collected Prose*, 49.

4. Luce Irigaray, *The Way of Love*, trans. Heidi Bostic and Stephen Pluhácek (New York: Continuum Books, 2002), 2.

5. Gilles Deleuze, *Nietzsche and Philosophy*, trans. Hugh Tomlinson (New York: Columbia University Press, 1983), 75.

6. Plato, "Euthyphro," in *The Collected Dialogues of Plato*, ed. Edith Hamilton and Huntington Cairns (Princeton: Princeton University Press, 1961), 169–85.

7. Plato, "Republic," in *Collected Dialogues*, 575–844.

8. Plato, "Symposium," in *Collected Dialogues*, 526–74.

9. Aristotle, *Metaphysics*, trans. Richard Hope (Ann Arbor: University of Michigan Press, 1952), beta 3 998a20, 999a20, pp. 48, 50.

10. Deleuze, *Nietzsche and Philosophy*, 77.

11. Plotinus, *Enneads*, VI.9. First translation cited is in *Plotinus VII: Ennead VI Books 6–9*, trans. A. H. Armstrong (Cambridge: Harvard University Press, 1989). Second translation cited is in *Enneads*, trans. Stephen MacKenna (New York: Penguin Books, 1991), 535.

12. Bruce Milem, in a personal communication regarding the gospel of John, pointed out to me this duality of *comprehend* as taking in both "understand" and "overcome."

13. Ludwig Wittgenstein, "The Nature of Philosophy," in *The Wittgenstein Reader*, ed. Anthony Kenny (Oxford: Blackwell, 1994), 270.

14. Ibid., 286.

15. Wasily Kandinsky, "The Spiritual in Art," in Robert Herbert, *Modern Artists on Art: Ten Unabridged Essays* (Garden City, N.J.: Prentice-Hall, 1965), 29.

16. Ibid.

17. Roland Barthes, *The Pleasure of the Text*, trans. Richard Miller (New York: Noonday Press, 1980), esp. 9–10, 37, 47–48, 51–52.

18. Maurice Merleau-Ponty, *The Visible and the Invisible*, trans. Alphonso Lingis (Evanston: Northwestern University Press, 1968), 154.

19. Ibid.

20. Wittgenstein, 271.

21. Friedrich Nietzsche, *The Gay Science*, trans. Walter Kaufmann (New York: Vintage Books, 1974), bk. 2, § 84, p. 138; ibid., bk. 5, § 366, p. 322; *Beyond Good and Evil*, trans. Walter Kaufman (New York: Vintage Books, 1989), § 27, p. 39.

22. See especially Michel Foucault, *The Archaeology of Knowledge*, trans. A. M. Sheridan Smith (New York: Pantheon, 1972), and still more Michel Foucault, *The Order of Things*, trans. unnamed (New York: Random House, 1970).

23. Foucault, *The Archaeology of Knowledge*, 200.

24. Foucault, "The Discourse on Language," appendix to *The Archaeology of Knowledge*, 216.

25. Michel Foucault, *Madness and Civilization* (New York: Vintage Books, 1988), 100.

26. Foucault, *The Order of Things*, x.

27. Michel Foucault, *Discipline and Punish*, trans. Alan Sheridan (New York: Vintage Books, 1995), 25.

28. See, e.g., Michel Foucault, "Preface à transgression," *Critique* 195–96 (1963): 751–70; and "Langage à l'infini," *Tel Quel* 15 (1963): 44–53.

29. "We are not to burrow to the hidden core of discourse, to the heart of the thought or meaning manifested in it" (Foucault, "The Discourse on Language," 229).

30. Gilles Deleuze, *The Fold: Leibniz and the Baroque*, trans. Tom Conley (Minneapolis: University of Minnesota Press, 1993), 58.

31. Gilles Deleuze and Felix Guattari, *Anti-Oedipus*, trans. Helen R. Lane and Robert Hurley (Minneapolis: University of Minnesota Press, 1985), 25.

32. Ibid.

33. Ibid., 26.

34. Although the *Symposium* is not the only site of Plato's considerations of desire, it is at least, perhaps alongside the *Phaedrus*, one of the most sustained.

35. Plato, *Symposium*, 189e–193e, in *The Collected Dialogues*, pp. 542–46.

36. Ibid., 200a–b, p. 552.

37. Ibid., 202b, p. 554.

38. Ibid., 203e, p. 556.

39. Ibid., 206b, p. 558.

40. Ibid., 206e, p. 559.

41. Ibid., 211c–e, pp. 562–63.

42. "And remember, she said, that it is only when he discerns beauty itself through what makes it visible that a man will be quickened with the true" (ibid., 212a, p. 563). This suggests, though arguably, that without a sensitivity to worldly beauty we can never hope to ascend to the contemplation of the beautiful itself.

43. G. W. F. Hegel, *Philosophische Propädeutik*, in *Sämtliche Werke*, vol. 3 (Stuttgart: Frommans), § 59, pp. 209–10. Cited in Christopher Gemerchak, *The Sunday of the Negative* (Albany: State University of New York Press, 2003), 253 n. 67.

44. Alexandre Kojève, *Introduction to the Reading of Hegel: Lectures on the Phenomenology of Spirit*, trans. James H. Nichols, Jr. (Ithaca: Cornell University Press, 1980), 3.

45. Irigaray, *The Way of Love*, 11.

46. Kojève, 4.

47. Ibid., 5.

48. As Nancy remarks in "The Intruder": "The stranger has something of the intruder about him; without it, he would lose his strangeness" (trans. Anne O'Byrne, manuscript, 1).

49. Kojève, 76, cited in Gemerchak, 185.

50. Unless, of course, in this absence of desire God ceases to be God at all. Such is at least implied in Meister Eckhart's famous sermon "Blessed are the poor," in which God and self come into existence together in an outflowing of desire from a primal satisfaction. Hegel was apparently much taken with Eckhart. See Meister Eckart, *The Best of Meister Eckhart*, ed. Halcyon Backhouse (New York: Crossroad Publishing, 1995), 74–79.

51. As Freud notes, the ego is in "service to three masters" in its struggle to mesh the demands of id and superego with the reality of the external world. See Sigmund Freud, *The Ego and the Id*, trans. Joan Riviere (New York: W. W. Norton, 1960), 46.

52. This feeling of being one with everything around one, like a drop of water in the ocean, is considered by Freud to be, not the origin of religious feeling, but something that often comes to be associated with religion. He attributes the idea of the oceanic to his friend Romain Rolland. See *Civilization and Its Discontents*, trans. James Strachey (New York: W. W. Norton, 1961), 11–21.

53. Rainer Maria Rilke, *Duino Elegies*, First Elegy, in *The Selected Poetry of Rainer Maria Rilke*, trans. Stephen Mitchell (New York: Vintage Books, 1989), 154–55.

54. Luce Irigaray, "Women-Mothers, the Silent Substratum of the Social Order," in *The Irigaray Reader*, ed. Margaret Whitford (Oxford: Blackwell, 1991), 52.

55. Stephen Moore, *Post Structuralism and the New Testament: Derrida and Foucault at the Foot of the Cross* (Minneapolis: Fortress Press, 1994), 76–77. Quotation from Jacques Lacan, *Écrits: A Selection*, trans. Alan Sheridan (New York: W. W. Norton, 1977), 172.

56. John Leslie, *Fifty Key Contemporary Thinkers* (New York: Routledge, 1994).

57. Gilles Deleuze and Claire Parnet, *Dialogues*, trans. Hugh Tomlinson and Barbara Habberjam (New York: Columbia University Press, 1987), 89–90.

58. Deleuze and Guattari, 26.

59. My thanks to Anne O'Byrne for reminding me of this point.

60. Nietzsche is highly skeptical of the existence of objects as such, rather than of processes, events, and actions. See, e.g., Friedrich Nietzsche, *Will to Power*, trans. Walter Kaufmann and R. J. Hollingdale (New York: Vintage Books, 1968), esp. §§ 484 ff.

61. Friedrich Nietzsche, *Twilight of the Idols*, in *Twilight of the Idols and The Anti-Christ*, trans. R. J. Hollingdale (New York: Penguin Books, 1968), "Expeditions of an Untimely Man," § 10, p. 73.

62. Ibid., § 9, p. 72.

63. Georges Bataille, *On Nietzsche*, trans. Bruce Boone (New York: Paragon House, 1994), xx.

64. Ibid., 22.

65. Though these themes are too frequent in Bataille's work to be cited properly, we might at least note their appearance in the work *On Nietzsche*, e.g., on pp. 22, 54, and 72.

66. Ibid., 22.

67. Ibid., 72.

68. Nancy, "Of Divine Places," in *The Inoperative Community*, ed. Peter Connor (Minneapolis: University of Minnesota Press, 1991), § 22, p. 128.

69. Deleuze, *The Fold*, 22.

70. Ibid., 8. A footnote refers to Leibniz's "letter to Arnauld, April 1687."

71. This notion is at least implicit throughout Baudrillard's *Seduction*, trans. Brian Singer (New York: St. Martin's Press, 1990).

72. Jean-Luc Nancy, "Corpus," trans. Claudette Sartiliot, in *The Birth to Presence* (Stanford: Stanford University Press, 1993), 190–93.

Word Made Flesh

1. *The Catholic Study Bible* (New York: Oxford University Press, 1990), 148, note to John 1:1.

2. See ibid., 159, note to John 6:54–58.

3. On the puzzles of the inaudible Word, see Augustine, *Confessions*, trans. Henry Chadwick (New York: Oxford University Press, 1991), esp. book 11.

4. The distinction between body and soul is not evident in the language of John's gospel.

5. *The Catholic Study Bible*, 159, note to John 6:63.

6. For other portrayals of either vision that compels belief or Christ as luminosity, see also ibid., 149, John 1:18; 150, 1:34; 150, 1:50–51; 152, 2:23; 152, 3:3; 155, 4:48; 156, 5:35; 157, 6:14; 158, 6:30; 159, 6:46; 162, 8:12; 165, 9:37; 167, 11:9–10; 167–68, 11:40; 168, 11:45; 170, 12:40; 170, 12:45–46; 172, 14:9; 173, 14:17.

7. Origen, *First Principles*, trans. G. W. Butterworth (Gloucester, Mass.: Peter Smith, 1973), "Spirit," § 562.

8. See also *The Catholic Study Bible*, 155, John 4:53–54; 159, 6:68.

9. See also ibid., 165, John 10:4.

10. Ibid., 152, note to John 3:15: "Eternal life: used here for the first time in John, this term stresses quality of life rather than duration."

11. See ibid., 150, note to John 1:42.

12. Ibid., 181, note to John 20:17.

13. My thanks to Marcos Bisticas-Cocoves, my source on all things Greek.

14. Carolyn Walker Bynum, *The Resurrection of the Body in Western Christianity, 200–1336* (New York: Columbia University Press, 1995), 27.

15. Christ's "time" is sometimes used in John to refer to the time of death and resurrection—a time that, by restoring eternal life, will break one of the rules of time, that of ending and death. See *The Catholic Study Bible*, 160, note to John 7:6.

16. See ibid., 172, note to John 13:31–38.

17. William of Ockham, *Quodlibita*, III, Qxiii, 4. In *Ockham: Philosophical Writings, a Selection*, ed. and trans. Philotheus Boehner, O.F.M., (New York: Thomas Nelson and Sons, 1957), 144.

18. Let me review a few of the best-known conundrums, because I cannot quite resist—a weakness of my all too human will, perhaps. God's will has always been presumed to be both all-good and all-powerful, thus giving rise to the problem of evil. (That is, does God will that there be evil? How could he? If not, why does evil nonetheless seem to exist?) Then there is the puzzle of human freedom. (How can we be free if God could at any point overrule us?) Or even such logical puzzles as that of the immovable stone. (Can God make a stone so big he can't move it?) Ockham's puzzle (see n. 17, above) provides its own version of this question: "The objection may be made: God can command that He be not loved for a certain time" (ibid.) That is, God can command a necessarily vicious act. Yet this seems utterly incompatible with God's theoretically infinite goodness.

19. This is argued by Pico della Mirandola in his *Oration on the Dignity of Man* (Washington, D.C.: Regnery Gateway, 1956).

20. "Because the will extends further than the intellect, I do not contain the will within the same boundaries; rather, I even extend it to things I do not understand. Because my will is indifferent to these latter things, it can easily turn away from the true and the good; in this way I am deceived and commit sin" (Rene Descartes, *Meditations on First Philosophy*, trans. Donald A. Cress [Indianapolis: Hackett, 1979], 58).

21. Aristotle, *Nicomachean Ethics*, trans. Terence Irwin (Indianapolis: Hackett, 1985), 1094a–1103a, pp. 1–32. That this flourishing will have an impact upon Neoplatonic conceptions of what life ought to be is particularly evident in Plotinus, e.g., *Ennead* I.4.

22. Aristotle, *Nicomachean Ethics*, III.1, 1111a, pp. 58–59; III.3, 1112a31, p. 62.

23. For a concise presentation of the relations of happiness and morality in Kant, see Gilles Deleuze, *Kant's Critical Philosophy*, trans. Hugh Tomlinson and Barbara Habberjam (Minneapolis: University of Minnesota Press, 1993).

24. Immanuel Kant, *Grounding for the Metaphysics of Morals*, trans. James W. Ellington (Indianapolis: Hackett, 1981), Ak11.

25. Ibid., Ak16.

26. Deleuze, *Kant's Critical Philosophy*, 37.

27. Kant, *Grounding for the Metaphysics of Morals*, Ak15.

28. For the suggestion of "sarkic desire," and for scholarly help throughout this chapter, I am much indebted to my colleague Jennifer Glancy.

29. Nietzsche, *Beyond Good and Evil*, §188, p.100: "The curious fact is that all there is or has been on earth of freedom, subtlety, boldness, dance, and masterly

sureness, . . . in the arts just as in ethics, has developed only owing to the 'tyranny of such capricious laws'; and in all seriousness, the probability is by no means small that precisely this is 'nature' and 'natural'—and *not* that *laisser aller*."

30. Aristotle, *Nicomachean Ethics*, III.5, 1113b, p. 66.

31. Ockham, 147.

32. See *The Catholic Study Bible*, 35, note to Matthew 16:18.

33. Nietzsche, *The Anti-Christ*, in *The Twilight of the Idols and The Anti-Christ*, § 33, p. 145, ellipsis in original.

34. Gilles Deleuze and Claire Parnet, "Dead Psychoanalysis: Analyse," in *Dialogues*, 91.

35. See esp. Gregory's commentary on the Song of Songs, which he reads as a parable of endless desire. I am indebted to Bruce Milem for bringing this to my attention, and for his helpful and insightful discussion of divinity and desire more generally. Indeed, much of my discussion here is indebted to him, and any of the ideas that may be any good probably originated in his thought more than my own.

36. Deleuze and Parnet, "Dead Psychoanalysis," in *Dialogues*, 89.

37. Moore, *Post Structuralism and the New Testament*, 44.

38. Gregory of Nyssa, "Commentary on the Song of Songs," 1.4, at http://www.bhsu.edu/dsalomon/nyssa/epekt.html.

39. Bruce Milem, personal communication.

40. Gregory of Nyssa, "Gregory the Wonderworker," at http://www.bhsu.edu/dsalomon/nyssa/epekt.html.

41. See, for a similar perspective, Mark McIntosh, *Mystical Theology* (Oxford: Blackwell, 1998), 56f.

42. Meister Eckhart, Sermon 12, in *Meister Eckhart: Teacher and Preacher*, ed. Bernard McGinn (New York: Paulist Press, 1986), 270.

43. Nancy, "Of Divine Places," in *The Inoperative Community*, § 22, p. 128.

44. Nietzsche, *The Anti-Christ*, § 41, p. 154.

45. Ibid., § 42, p. 155.

46. Ibid., § 43, pp. 155–156.

47. Merleau-Ponty, 133.

48. Ibid., 141.

49. Nancy, "Corpus," in *The Birth to Presence*, 204.

50. See Nietzsche, *The Birth of Tragedy*, in *The Birth of Tragedy and the Genealogy of Morals*, trans. Francis Golffing (New York: Anchor Books, 1956), § 10, pp. 65–69.

51. Deleuze, *Nietzsche and Philosophy*, 62.

52. Friedrich Nietzsche, *Ecce Homo*, trans. R. J. Hollingdale (New York: Penguin Books, 1993), "Why I Am A Destiny," § 9, p. 104.

53. Nietzsche, *The Anti-Christ*, § 39, p. 151: "—The word 'Christianity' is already a misunderstanding—in reality there has been only one Christian, and he died on the Cross."

54. Ibid., § 32, p. 144. I am grateful to James DiGiovanna for directing my attention to this discussion.

55. See ibid., esp. § 34, pp. 146–47.

56. Ibid., § 33, p. 145.

57. Ibid.

58. Ibid., § 35, p. 148, all ellipses in original.

59. Merleau-Ponty, 143.

60. Nancy, "Corpus," in *The Birth to Presence*, 205.

Touch

1. Constance Classen, *Worlds of Sense* (New York: Routlege, 1993), 50.

2. Michelle Lovric, *How to Write Love Letters* (New York: Shooting Star Press, 1995), 16–19.

3. Nancy, "Corpus," in *The Birth to Presence*, 198.

4. Paul Celan, "The Meridian," in *Collected Prose*, 49.

5. Roland Barthes, *A Lover's Discourse: Fragments*, trans. Richard Howard (New York: Hill and Wang, 1978), 77. Barthes does not further specify his source.

6. Kathy Acker, "The Future," in *Bodies of Work* (New York: Serpent's Tail Press, 1997), 173.

7. T. S. Eliot, "East Coker," in *Four Quartets* (New York: Harvest Books, 1974), 28–29.

8. *The Catholic Study Bible*, 148, note to John 1:1–18.

9. In an opposing but structurally parallel orthodoxy, Charles Baudelaire alternates descriptive phrases of kingship with the plea, "Satan, take pity on my misery!" ("Litanies of Satan," in *Flowers of Evil*, ed. James McGowan [New York: Oxford University Press, 1998], 269).

10. Nietzsche, *The Gay Science*, § 84, pp. 138–39.

11. Jeanette Winterson, *Written on the Body* (New York: Vintage Books, 1994), 89.

12. Ibid.

13. "Night" in *Poems of Paul Celan*, trans. Michael Hamburger (New York: Persea Books, 1988), 122–23.

14. Denis Hollier, *Against Architecture* (Boston: MIT Press, 1992), 60.

15. I am alert to the importance of avoiding gender bias, but in my experience this gesture is exclusively male. I remain, however, open to correction upon this point.

16. Celan, "Corona," in *Poems of Paul Celan*, 58–59.

17. Augustine, *Confessions*, 10.27, p. 201.

18. Ibid., 10.6, p. 183.

19. Jean-Luc Nancy, *Being Singular Plural*, trans. Robert D. Richardson and Anne E. O'Byrne (Stanford: Stanford University Press, 2000), 13.

20. Ibid.

21. Marcel Proust, *Remembrance of Things Past*, trans. C. K. Scott Moncrieff and Terence Kilmartin (New York: Vintage Books, 1982), 1:231.

22. Ibid., 227.

23. Ibid.

24. Ibid., 48.

25. Acker, Preface, *Bodies of Work*, ix.

26. Nancy, *Being Singular Plural*, 6.

27. Jacques Derrida, "Le toucher: Touch / To Touch Him," trans. Peggy Kamuf, *Paragraph* 16, no. 2 (July 1993): 143.

28. Barthes, *A Lover's Discourse*, 98.

29. Ibid., 153–54.

30. Nancy, *Being Singular Plural*, 5.

31. Nancy, "The Intruder," 8.

32. See Nancy, *Being Singular Plural*, 12.

33. Nancy, "The Intruder," 14.

34. Classen, 75.

35. Ibid., 54–55.

36. Ibid., 72.

37. Nancy, "Corpus," in *The Birth to Presence*, 192.

38. Jacques Derrida, "Economimesis," *Diacritics* 11 (June 1981): 19; cited in Catherine Vasseleu, *Textures of Light: Vision and Touch in Irigaray, Levinas, and Merleau-Ponty* (New York: Routledge, 1998), 100.

39. *The Catholic Study Bible*, 148. note to John 1:1.

40. Slavoj Žižek, "How to Give Body to a Deadlock?" in *Thinking Bodies*, ed. Juliet Flower MacCannell and Laura Zakarin (Stanford: Stanford University Press, 1994), 64.

41. Winterson, *Written on the Body*, 9.

42. Gabriel Josipovici, *Touch* (New Haven: Yale University Press, 1996), 59.

43. Barthes, *A Lover's Discourse*, 73.

44. Freud, *Civilization and Its Discontents*, 64ff.

45. Barthes, *A Lover's Discourse*, 98.

46. Acker, preface to *Bodies of Work*, viii.

47. See Derrida, "Le toucher," 124.

48. Georges Bataille, *Erotism: Death and Sensuality*, trans. Mary Dalwood (San Francisco: City Lights Books, 1986), 12.

49. Josipovici, 2.

50. Ibid., 129.

51. Classen, 66.

52. Emmanuel Levinas, *Totality and Infinity: An Essay on Exteriority*, trans. Alphonso Lingis (Pittsburgh: Duquesne University Press, 1979), 258; cited thus Vasseleu, 105.

53. Classen, *Worlds of Sense*, 58.

54. Nancy, "Corpus," in *The Birth to Presence*, 203.

55. Bynum, *The Resurrection of the Body*, 329.

56. Derrida, "Le toucher," 127.

57. Barthes, *A Lover's Discourse*, 98.

58. Wittgenstein, "Ethics, Life, and Faith," in *The Wittgenstein Reader*, 296.

59. Bataille, *Erotism*, 12–13.

60. Nancy, "Corpus," in *The Birth to Presence*, 204.

61. Nancy, *Being Singular Plural*, 6.

62. Acker, "A Few Notes on Two of My Books," in *Bodies of Work*, 12.

63. Acker, "On Delaney the Magician," in ibid., 62.

64. Cited in Ruth Salvaggio, "Skin Deep: Lesbian Interventions in Language," in *Cross Purposes: Lesbians, Feminists and the Limits of Alliance*, ed. Dana Heller (Bloomington: Indiana University Press, 1997), 78.

65. Edmond Jabès, "There Is Such a Thing as Jewish Writing," in *The Sin of the Book: Edmond Jabès*, ed. Eric Gould (Lincoln: University of Nebraska Press, 1985), 29.

66. *The Catholic Study Bible*, 162, note to John 8:24.

67. Ibid., 163, note to John 8:58. The verse reads, "Jesus said to them, 'Amen, amen, I say to you, before Abraham came to be, I AM.'" The note in the *The Catholic Study Bible* points out, "the Greek word used for 'came to be' is the one used of all creation in the prologue, while the word used for 'am' is one reserved for the Logos" (163n).

68. Nancy, "Corpus," in *The Birth to Presence*, 189.

69. Irigaray, *The Way of Love*, 150.

70. Nancy, "Corpus," in *The Birth to Presence*, 190.

Unfolding "Ash Wednesday"

1. Deleuze, *The Fold*, 121–22.

2. I am grateful to Marcos Bisticas-Cocoves for pointing this out to me.

3. *Protevangelium of James*, at http://wesley.nnu.edu/noncanon/gospels/gosjames.htm, excerpted from "The Apocryphal New Testament," trans. M. R. James (Oxford: Oxford University Press, 1924), 19:1–2. My thanks to Jennifer Glancy for making me aware of this text.

4. Virginia Burrus, *The Sex Lives of Saints: An Erotics of Ancient Hagiography* (Philadelphia: University of Pennsylvania Press, 2003), 157.

5. Søren Kierkegaard, *Fear and Trembling*, excerpted in *A Kierkegaard Anthology*, ed. Robert Bretall (Princeton: Princeton University Press, 1946), 125.

6. The theological virtues are faith, hope, and love. Often these are attached, respectively, to the members of the Trinity—Father, Son, and Spirit.

7. Deleuze, *The Fold*, 71.

8. Martin Heidegger, "What Calls for Thinking," in *Basic Writings*, ed. David Farrell Krell (New York: Harper and Row, 1977), 352.

9. Deleuze, *The Fold*, 5.

10. Ibid., 13.

11. Cf. T. S. Eliot, *The Wasteland*, "And bats with baby faces in the violet light / whistle, and beat their wings," in *Selected Poems* (New York: Harcourt Brace Jovanovich, 1988), 66.

12. In such imagery she echoes icons of the Egyptian goddess Isis, another figure of memory and recollection.

13. Here we might note with some interest that the word *vagina* means "sheath," and that Mary's is unquestionably a miraculous vagina, capable not only of giving birth to a god but of retaining afterward its virginity. The above-mentioned *Protevangelium* warns us against the literal penetration of this mystery; the midwife who curiously examines Mary to see if her virginity is really intact is punished for her unbelief by having her hand burst into flames. Her immediate repentance earns her leniency: "An angel of the Lord appeared, saying unto her: Salome, Salome, the Lord hath hearkened to thee: bring thine hand near unto the young child and take him up, and there shall be unto thee salvation and joy. And Salome came near and took him up, saying: I will do him worship, for a great king is born unto Israel. And behold immediately Salome was healed: and she went forth of the cave justified" (*Protevangelium of James*, 20:1–4). The ensheathing of the mother in the light emphasizes the double birthing imagery here.

14. Deleuze, *The Fold*, 14.

15. Ibid., 41.

16. Ibid., 15.

17. Gilles Deleuze, *Foucault*, trans. Sean Hand (Minneapolis: University of Minnesota Press, 1988), 105.

18. Mark C. Taylor, "Betting on Vegas," in *God, the Gift, and Postmodernism*, ed. John D. Caputo and Michael Scanlon (Indianapolis: Indiana University Press, 1999), 240–41.

19. Nancy, "Corpus," in *The Birth to Presence*, 194.

20. My thanks to Prof. Mary Ann Donnelly for bringing this to my attention. The liturgy may be found at http://people.enternet.com.au/~beswick/rclresources/GFABC956799.htm.

21. Cf. Psalms 102:1. In the King James version, this reads: "(A Prayer of the afflicted, when he is overwhelmed, and poureth out his complaint before the LORD.) Hear my prayer, O LORD, and let my cry come unto thee."

22. Kierkegaard, 125f.

23. One commentator on the *Protevangelium* takes this parallel still further, remarking that "The 'gynaecological test' as a proof of faith has reminiscences of John 20:25" (W. S. Vorster, "The Protevangelium of James and Intertextuality," in *Text and Testimony: Essays on New Testament and Apocryphal Literature in Honour of A. F. J. Klijn*, ed. T. Baarda, A. Hilhorst, G. P. Luttikhuizen, and A. S. van der Woude [Kampen: Kok], 269). My thanks to Jennifer Glancy on this one too.

24. E. M. Cioran, *Tears and Saints,* trans. Ilenca Zarifopol-Johnston (Chicago: University of Chicago Press, 1996), 115.

25. According to the *Catholic Encyclopedia*, "This well-known prayer dates its origin from the first half of the fourteenth century and was enriched with indulgences by Pope John XXII in the year 1330. All the manuscripts practically agree as to these two facts so there can be no doubt of their exactness. In regard to its authorship all we can say is that it was, perhaps, written by John XXII. Of this we are not certain, as this Pope has been falsely accredited with similar pious compositions, and a mistake could easily be made of confounding the one who gave the indulgence with the real author. The Anima Christi was and is still generally believed to have been composed by St. Ignatius Loyola, as he puts it at the beginning of his 'Spiritual Exercises' and often refers to it. This is a mistake, as has been pointed out by many writers, since the prayer has been found in a number of prayer books printed during the youth of the saint and is in manuscripts which were written a hundred years before his birth (1491)" (http://www.newadvent.org/cathen/01515a.htm).

Fold

1. Irigaray, *The Way of Love*, 18.

2. Ibid., 133.

3. Georges Bataille, *Inner Experience*, trans. Leslie Ann Boldt (Albany: State University of New York Press, 1988), 83.

4. See Michel Foucault, "The Concern for Truth," in *Foucault Live*, ed. Sylvère Lotringer, trans. Lysa Hochroth and John Johnston (New York: Semiotext[e], 1996), 455.

5. Deleuze, *The Fold*, 22.

6. Gilles Deleuze, *Negotiations 1972–1990* (New York: Columbia University Press, 1997), 87.

7. Deleuze, *The Fold*, 7.

8. See Deleuze, *Foucault*, 47.

9. Ibid., 58–59.

10. Ibid., 60. Note the echoes of the Kantian language of the first *Critique*.

11. Hollier, *Against Architecture*, x.

12. Foucault, *Madness and Civilization*, 100.

13. Deleuze, *Foucault*, 73.

14. Foucault, *The Order of Things*, 93.

15. Nancy, "Corpus," in *The Birth to Presence*, 191.

16. Carol Siegel, personal communication.

17. Deleuze, *The Fold*, 137.

18. See Nietzsche, *Beyond Good and Evil*, § 188, p. 100.

19. Deleuze, *The Fold*, 77.

20. Ibid., 98.

21. Wittgenstein, 203.

22. Carol Siegel, personal correspondence.

23. Acker, "Bodies of Work," in *Bodies of Work*, 143–44.

24. Ibid., 150.

25. I resist the temptation here to develop this observation into a critique of well-intentioned "positive consent" policies such as those known as the Antioch Rules.

26. Deleuze, *The Fold*, 18.

27. Acker, "The City," in *Bodies of Work*, 122.

28. Cf. Deleuze: "Subjectification thus appears as a middle term between knowledge and power, a perpetual 'dislocation,' a sort of fold, a folding or enfolding" ("Life as a Work of Art," in *Negotiations*, 151).

29. Jacques Derrida, "From a Restricted to a General Economy," in *Writing and Difference*, trans. Alan Bass (Chicago: University of Chicago Press, 1980), 272.

30. Deleuze, *The Fold*, 35.

31. Jane Arthurs and Jean Grimshaw, introduction to *Women's Bodies: Discipline and Transgression*, ed. Jane Arthurs and Jean Grimshaw (New York: Cassell, 1999), 3–4.

32. Deleuze, *The Fold*, 137.

33. Deleuze, "Life as a Work of Art," in *Negotiations*, 97.

34. Bynum, *The Resurrection of the Body*, 253.

35. Ibid., 248–49.

36. Nancy, "Corpus," in *The Birth to Presence*, 205.

37. Michelle Henning, "Doing Looks," in Arthurs and Grimshaw, 132.

38. Tamsin Wilton, "Temporality, Materiality: Towards a Body in Time," in Arthurs and Grimshaw, 51.

39. Bataille, *Inner Experience*, 82.

40. Deleuze, *The Fold*, 6.

41. Ibid., 3.

42. Ibid., 26.

Sacred Hearts

1. Marche Noir, http://www.marchenoir.com/homea.html.

2. Fuzzy, student at Maryland Institute College of Art, personal correspondence. "New school" tattooing, characterized by the use of bold black outlines and bright colors, often takes up the images of "old school" or traditional American tattooing, usually in a self-conscious manner.

3. Generally this visibility is rather mysterious, given that the wound in the side, devotion to which precedes the Sacred Heart devotions, is, curiously, seldom in evidence.

4. See references to St. Ambrose and St. John Chrysostom, at the Monks of Adoration, http://www.monksofadoration.org/earlyhrt.html. See also http://www.newadvent.org/cathen/07163a.htm#II. This is the online site of *Catholic Encyclopedia* (New York: Robert Appleton Company, 1912; online edition, 1999, by Kevin Knight).

5. *Catholic Encyclopedia*, http://www.newadvent.org/cathen/07168a.htm

6. Ibid.

7. Ibid.

8. Ibid., no specific reference from Augustine given.

9. *Catholic Encyclopedia*, http://www.newadvent.org/cathen/07168a.htm.

10. Traditionally, these are: the prophecy of Simeon; the flight into Egypt; the loss of the Holy Child at Jerusalem; the meeting with Jesus on his way to Calvary; the wait at the foot of the Cross; Jesus being taken from the Cross; the burial of Christ.

11. The devotion can be found "in a sermon by St. Bernard (De duodecim stellis), from which an extract has been taken by the Church and used in the Offices of the Compassion and of the Seven Dolours" ("The Immaculate Heart," http://www.angelfire.com/sd2/mendelhouse/immaculate.html).

12. "As a sequens-melody the earliest printed form of the Stabat Mater can be found in the Graduale Romanum Antwerpiae of 1712. . . . Technically, the sequens was the addition of text to the final melisma of the Alleluia, as a means of facilitating its memorization. In the twelfth century the sequens established itself as an independent piece in which music and text were closely related, and as such it became one of the most influential of all the literary and musical forms of the Middle Ages. During the sixteenth century the number of sequenses (more than 4,500!) had grown in such a way that normal liturgical practice was put under pressure. Another development was that composers in the Renaissance increasingly began to make use of exceedingly complicated polyphony, which certainly did not help listening to the text. This, and the fact that the texts were not taken from the Bible, were the reason that all sequenses, with the exception of four (Victimae paschalis laudes, Veni sancte spiritus, Lauda Sion, and Dies Iriae), were banned by the Council of Trent (1545–1563), the Stabat Mater included. It was not allowed to be sung during services anymore, but only at other religious manifestations. However, in 1727 it returned definitely in the liturgy by the initiative of Pope Benedict XIII, as fifth sequens in the missal, sung on the third Sunday in September on the Feast of the Seven Sorrows of our Lady (de Compassione Mariae). In the official liturgy nowadays a nineteenth century version by Dom Fonteinnes is used" (http://www.stabatmater.dds.nl/).

13. "History of Devotion to the Sacred Heart, Part One: The Early Church" (http://www.monksofadoration.org/earlyhrt.html).

14. *Catholic Encyclopedia*, http://www.newadvent.org/cathen/07163a.htm.

15. Ibid., http://www.newadvent.org/cathen/07168a.htm.

16. Ibid.

17. *Catholic Encyclopedia*, http://www.newadvent.org/cathen/07163a.htm.

18. Ibid.

19. Michael Carroll, *The Cult of the Virgin Mary* (Princeton: Princeton University Press, 1986), 175–77.

20. Ibid. 166.

21. Bynum, *The Resurrection of the Body*, 224.

22. *Catholic Encyclopedia*, http://www.newadvent.org/cathen/07168a.htm.

23. Ibid., http://www.newadvent.org/cathen/07163a.htm#II. Citing: *Legatus Divinae Pietatis*, 4, 305, and *Revelationes Gertrudianae* (Paris, 1877). *Legatus Divinae Pietatis* is available in the Latin online at http://www.peregrina.com/matrologia/gertrud1.html (Part 1) and http://www.peregrina.com/matrologia/gertrud2.html (Part 2).

24. Johannes Tauler (authorship debated), *Meditations on the Life and Passion of Our Lord Jesus Christ*, trans. A. Cruikshank (New York: Benzinger Bros., 1925), 326.

Cited in Margaret Williams, R.S.C.J., *The Sacred Heart in the Life of the Church* (New York: Sheed and Ward, 1957), 58.

25. Thomas Merton, *What Are These Wounds? The Life of a Cistercian Mystic, Saint Lutgarde of Aywières* (Milwaukee: Bruce Publishing Co., 1950), 75.

26. *Catholic Encyclopedia,* http://www.newadvent.org/cathen/07163a.htm.

27. "Thus His Heart is eternally open, eternally torn; His glory does not take away His wound, for it is the wound of love; this rent made by the lance is but a mark of the true interior rending of His Heart. This rent side is peculiarly His; it is not shared with others who bore the same torment, or who bore crucifixion; it is an eternal wounding. It is a pain and a wound unto death, but lasting unto eternity; a wound begun in death but to last on into life. This is not the way of other wounds, for they will not endure through the resurrection" (Cardinal Bérulle, ca. 1611, quoted in Henri Bremond, *Historie Littéraire du Sentiment Religieux en France* [Paris, 1929], 65f; cited in Williams, 103).

28. Monks of Adoration, http://www.monksofadoration.org/earlyhrt.html.

29. Monks of Adoration, http://www.monksofadoration.org/margmary.html.

30. "It is the authentic mark of the Devotion to the Sacred Heart thus to see the physical and not merely the metaphorical heart of Christ as the symbol of His love for men" (Williams, 66).

31. Gilbert of Hoyland, Sermon 22, in *Sermons on the Song of Songs,* trans. Lawrence C. Braceland, S.J. (Kalamazoo, Mich.: Cistercian Publications, 1979). Adapted from citation in Williams, 236.

32. St. Lutgarde (1182–1246), *Acte Sanctorum* for June 11. Cited in Williams, 47.

33. Angele of Foligno, *Memorial,* chaps. 1 and 7, in *Complete Works,* trans. Paul Lachance, O.F.M. Classics of Western Spirituality (New York: Paulist Press, 1993), 128, 181–82. Cited in McIntosh, *Mystical Theology* (Oxford: Blackwell, 1998), 80.

34. Nancy, "The Intruder," 4.

35. Ibid., 3.

36. Mechtild of Magdeburg, *Flowing Light of Divinity,* book E.22, trans. Christiane Mesche Calvani, Garland Library of Medieval Literature vol. 72, series B (New York: Garland Publishing, 1991), 15. Cited in McIntosh, 80.

37. Julian of Norwich, *Revelations of Divine Love,* http://www.ccel.org/j/julian/revelations/.

38. Carolyn Walker Bynum, *Fragmentation and Redemption: Essays on Gender and the Human Body in Medieval Religion* (New York: Zone Books, 1992), 206.

39. Poems in Couplets, 16, in Hadewijch, *The Complete Works,* trans. Mother Columba Hart, O.S.B., Classics of Western Spirituality (New York: Paulist Press, 1980), 353. Cited in McIntosh, 79.

40. Merton, vii.

41. *Catholic Encyclopedia*, http://www.newadvent.org/cathen/07163a.htm.

42. Ibid.

43. Ibid.

44. Cited in Williams, 81.

45. Angele of Foligno, *Le Livre de l'expérience des rais fidèles: Texte Latine publié de l'après le manuscrit d'Assisse*, ed. and trans. M. J. Ferré and L. Baudry (Paris: Droz, 1927), par. 151, p. 326. Cited in Bynum, *Fragmentation and Redemption*, 194.

46. Merton, 15.

47. St. Catherine of Siena, *I, Catherine: Selected Writings of St. Catherine of Siena*, ed. and trans. Keneim Foster and Mary John Ronayne (London: Collins, 1980), 120. Cited in Richard Kieckhefer, *Unquiet Souls: Fourteenth Century Saints and Their Religious Milieu* (Chicago: University of Chicago Press, 1984), 109.

48. Monks of Adoration, http://www.monksofadoration.org/earlyhrt.html.

49. Bynum, *Fragmentation and Redemption*, 215f.

50. Nancy, "Corpus," in *The Birth to Presence*, 198.

51. Steven Webb, *Blessed Excess: Religion and the Hyperbolic Imagination* (Albany: State University of New York Press, 1993), 39.

52. Ibid., 23.

53. Ibid., 164.

54. *The American Heritage Dictionary of the English Language*, 4th ed., 2000; http://www.bartleby.com/61/81/T0318100.html.

55. *The Catholic Study Bible*, 152. note to John 3:15.

56. Jean-Luc Nancy, "Abandoned Being," in *The Birth to Presence*, 36–37.

57. Nancy, "The Intruder," 13.

58. Bynum, *Fragmentation and Redemption*, 25.

59. Ibid. Her note cites "Bergson, *Laughter*, 1900, 77." Though this point is certainly present throughout the first half of Bergson's text, I was not able to locate this citation on page 77 of either the English or the French edition (Henri Bergson, *Laughter: An Essay on the Meaning of the Comic*, trans. Cloudesley Brereton and Fred Rothwell [London: Macmillan, 1911], and Henri Bergson, *Le Rire: Essai sur la signification du comique* [Paris: Presses Universitaires de France, 1950]). It may, however, be in another edition.

60. Fuzzy, personal communication.

61. Jesse, artist, personal communication.

62. Henry Ferguson and Lynn Procter, *The Art of the Tattoo* (Philadelphia: Courage Books, 1998), 20. See also Albert Parry, *Tattoo: Secrets of a Strange Art as Practiced by Natives of the United States* (New York: Collier Books, 1933): "It was, and still is, customary for a Christian pilgrim, shortly after his arrival in Jerusalem, to have a religious

symbol, or a whole series of them, tattooed on his chest or arms. The custom is said to have been introduced by Armenians. . . . There was a certain element of sacrificial masochism in the tattooing of these holy Christians" (122–23).

63. *Body Modification Ezine*, http://www.bme.freeq.com/qod/index.html. Inquiry from Lindsay, response from Gary. Surnames and further information are not provided in these postings.

64. See Michael McCabe, *New York City Tattoo: The Oral History of an Urban Art* (Honolulu: Hardy Marks Publications, 1997).

65. Margo DeMello, *Bodies of Inscription: A Cultural History of the Modern Tattoo Community* (Durham, N.C.: Duke University Press, 2000), 68.

66. Jerry Collins, *Sailor Jerry Collins*, ed. Don Ed Hardy (Honolulu: Hardy Marks Publications, 1994), 60.

67. "Good God Almighty," *Tattoo World* I, no. I (1994): 8.

68. Personal conversation.

69. See online glossary for *Body Modification Ezine*, http://www.bmezine.com/glossary/.

70. *Tattoo Energy*, Verve Press, no. 2, 2000; and *International Tattoo Art*, January 2000.

71. Both, Guido, Sacred Tattoo, 2000. Flash sheet in the archives of Matty Jankowski and Lisa Marie Bell Jankowski, New York Body Archive.

72. Flash by Clay Decker 1994, includes other variants as well. Flash sheet in the New York Body Archive.

73. Webb, 146.

74. Ibid., xiv.

75. Nancy, "Hyperion's Joy," in *The Birth to Presence*, 73.

76. Mark C. Taylor, *Hiding* (Chicago: University of Chicago Press, 1997), 123.

Cut

1. Taylor, *Hiding*, 167.

2. Maurice Blanchot, *The Infinite Conversation*, trans. Susan Hanson (Minneapolis: University of Minnesota Press, 1993), 28.

3. In its most literal form, this dermal scratching would be the "hysterical" phenomenon of dermographism. Mariel Henning describes the phenomenon in her essay "Don't Touch Me (I'm Electric)": "Usually, hysteria was associated with hypersensitivity. Perhaps the most interesting instance of this is dermographism, in which a condition of the skin makes it so sensitive that touching or scratching produces welts which may last for up to forty-eight hours. . . . To demonstrate the condition doctors would write on the anaesthetized skin of the patient and then

photograph it. As Janet Beizer points out, this hypersensitive skin and the practice of writing on it reinforced the idea of the hysteric's body as 'expressive' . . . yet what it 'expresses' are merely the whims of the doctor" (in Arthurs and Grimshaw, 22).

4. Maurice Blanchot, *The Writing of the Disaster,* trans. Ann Smock (Lincoln: University of Nebraska Press, 1986), 6–7.

5. Taylor, *Hiding,* 13.

6. Anne Tomiche, "Writing the Body," in MacCannell and Zakarin, 124–25. The quotation is from Jacques Derrida, *Dissemination,* trans. Barbara Johnson (Chicago: University of Chicago Press, 1981), 301, see also his *Glas,* trans. John P. Leavey, Jr., and Richard Rand (Lincoln: University of Nebraska Press, 1986).

7. Gary Shapiro, "Jean-Luc Nancy and the Corpus of Philosophy," in MacCannell and Zakarin, 54.

8. Georges Bataille, *Guilty,* trans. Bruce Boone (Venice, Calif.: Lapis Press, 1988), 27.

9. Ibid., 65.

10. I avoid going on and on about this matter here only because I have done so elsewhere. See my *Immemorial Silence* (Albany: State University of New York Press, 2001), chap. 2.

11. Nancy, "Corpus," in *The Birth to Presence,* 202.

12. Maurice Blanchot, "Interruptions," trans. Rosmarie Waldrop and Paul Auster, in Gould, 43.

13. Bynum, *The Resurrection of the Body,* 313.

14. Ibid., 199. (Bynum quotes Peter of Celle, *Tractatus de disciplina claustrali,* chap. 23, *Patrologia Latinae* 202, cols. 1132–33, trans. Hugh Feiss, *Peter of Cella,* 112–13.)

15. MacKendrick, *Immemorial Silence,* esp. chap. 2.

16. Jacques Derrida, "From a Restricted to a General Economy," in *Writing and Difference,* 277.

17. Taylor, *Hiding,* 54.

18. Acker, "Bodies of Work," in *Bodies of Work,* 145.

19. Barthes, *A Lover's Discourse,* 44.

20. Nancy, "The Intruder," 6.

21. Ibid., 1.

22. Antonin Artaud, *The Artaud Anthology,* ed. Jack Hirschman, (San Francisco: City Lights Books, 1965), 45.

23. Ibid., 131.

24. Ibid., 30.

25. Derrida, "La Parole soufflée," in *Writing and Difference,* 187.

26. Ibid., 188.

27. Celan, untitled, in *Poems of Paul Celan,* 337.

28. Nancy, "The Intruder," 10.

29. Paul Auster, "Book of the Dead: An Interview with Edmond Jabès," in Gould, 23.

30. Ibid.

31. Salvaggio, "Skin Deep," in *Cross Purposes*, ed. Dana Heller, 52.

32. Susan Bordo, "The Body and the Reproduction of Femininity: A Feminist Appropriation of Foucault," in *Gender/Body/Knowledge: Feminist Reconstructions of Being and Knowing*, ed. Alison M. Jaggar and Susan R. Bordo (New Brunswick, N.J.: Rutgers University Press, 1989), 16. Later in the article Bordo reiterates this theme: "We begin with the painfully literal inscription, on the anorexic's body, of the rules governing the construction of contemporary femininity." She adds emphatically, "On the body of the anorexic woman such rules are deeply etched" (18).

33. Arthurs and Grimshaw, introduction, 6.

34. Tamsin Wilton, "Temporality, Materiality: Towards a Body in Time," in Arthurs and Grimshaw, 57–58.

35. Ibid., 60.

36. Arthurs and Grimshaw, 7.

37. Derrida, *Dissemination*, 310.

38. Ibid., 300.

39. Edmond Jabès, in Paul Auster, "An Interview with Edmond Jabès," in Gould, 13–14.

40. It is my understanding that some trace of any act performed with a computer leaves some lingering mnemonic mark, but of this I know so little that I consider it unwise to try to say more. I feel safe, however, in speaking of the screen as I see it: disappeared text, fingerprints, cat hair, and all.

41. Nancy, "Corpus," in *The Birth to Presence*, 197.

42. Dennis Patrick Slattery, *The Wounded Body: Remembering the Markings of Flesh* (Albany: State University of New York Press, 2000), 24.

43. Ibid., 36.

44. Ibid., 40.

45. Ibid., 41.

46. Bynum, *The Resurrection of the Body*, 77.

47. Ibid., 86.

48. Burrus, 74.

49. Bynum, *The Resurrection of the Body*, 29. See Paul, Corinthians 3.

50. St. Augustine, *City of God*, book 22, chap. 19, in *Basic Writings of St. Augustine*, ed. Whitney J. Oates (New York: Random House, 1948), 2:639ff.

51. Bynum, *The Resurrection of the Body*, 313.

52. Ibid., 223, n. 81. From Caesarius of Heisterbach, *Dialogus Miraculorum*, ed. Joseph Strange (Cologne: Heberle, 1851), distinctio 12, chap. 50, 2:355–56.

53. Nancy, "The Intruder," 11.

54. Slattery, 43.

55. Maurice Blanchot, *The Step Not Beyond*, trans. Lycette Nelson (Albany: State University of New York Press, 1992), 31.

56. Cf. Slattery: "When the wound becomes a scar, there is always present the 'afterthought' of the original violation" (54).

57. Bataille, *Guilty*, 27.

58. Barthes, *A Lover's Discourse*, 68.

59. Slattery, 160.

60. Barthes, *A Lover's Discourse*, 152.

61. Nancy, "The Intruder," 9.

62. Ibid., 10.

63. Acker, "The City," in *Bodies of Work*, 123.

64. Burrus, 76.

65. Slattery, 53–54.

66. In Derrida, *Dissemination*, 300.

67. Ibid., 302.

68. Ibid., 337.

69. Stephen Moore, *God's Gym: Divine Male Bodies of the Bible* (New York: Routledge, 1996), 40.

70. Webb, 71.

71. Hélène Cixous, preface to *The Cixous Reader*, ed. Susan Sellers (New York: Routledge, 1996), xv.

72. Nancy, "Corpus," in *The Birth to Presence*, 198.

73. "I can't imagine a *spiritual* way of life that isn't impersonal, dependent on chance" (Bataille, *Guilty*, 74).

Conclusion: Figures of Desire

1. See Ferdinand de Saussure, *Course in General Linguistics*, trans. Roy Harris (Chicago: Open Court Publishing, 1988).

2. Nancy, "Corpus," in *The Birth to Presence*, 195.

3. Cixous, "The Art of Innocence," in *The Cixous Reader*, 96.

4. Jeanette Winterson, *The Powerbook* (New York: Vintage Books, 2001), 40.

5. Friedrich Hölderlin, "To the Fates," in *Selected Poems and Fragments*, trans. Michael Hamburger (Ann Arbor: University of Michigan Press, 1968), 7.

6. Blanchot, *The Step Not Beyond*, 67.

7. Augustine, *Confessions*, 8.12 (29) for "Take and read"; bk. 8 for loss in desire; 10.27 (38), e.g., for surrender to God.

8. The idea of resistance in words was prompted for me by Nancy's "Of Divine Places," in *The Inoperative Community*, § 36, p. 144.

9. Nancy, "Abandoned Being," in *The Birth to Presence*, 36–37.

10. Ibid., 37.

11. Acker, "The City," in *Bodies of Work*, 122.

12. Barthes, *A Lover's Discourse*, 14.

13. Cixous, preface to *The Cixous Reader*, xv.

14. Cixous, "Inside," in *The Cixous Reader*, 21.

15. Cixous, preface to *The Cixous Reader*, xxii.

16. Cixous, "Three Steps on the Ladder of Writing," in *The Cixous Reader*, 202.

17. Moore, *God's Gym*, 38.

18. Kojève, 3.

Works Cited

He does not pile up bibliographical references in the traditional habit of scholars convinced that the one who has the most footnotes when he dies wins.

Richard Marius, *Martin Luther: The Christian between God and Death*

Acker, Kathy. *Bodies of Work*. New York: Serpent's Tail Press, 1997.

The American Heritage Dictionary of the English Language. 4th ed., 2000. Online edition: http://www.bartleby.com/61/81/T0318100.html.

Aristotle. *Metaphysics*. Trans. Richard Hope. Ann Arbor: University of Michigan Press, 1952.

———. *Nicomachean Ethics*. Trans. Terence Irwin. Indianapolis: Hackett, 1985.

Artaud, Antonin. *The Artaud Anthology*. Ed. Jack Hirschman. San Francisco: City Lights Books, 1965.

Arthurs, Jane, and Jean Grimshaw, eds. *Women's Bodies: Discipline and Transgression*. New York: Cassell, 1999.

Augustine. *City of God*. In *Basic Writings of St. Augustine*. Ed. Whitney J. Oates. New York: Random House, 1948.

———. *Confessions*. Trans. Henry Chadwick. New York: Oxford University Press, 1991.

Barthes, Roland. *A Lover's Discourse: Fragments*. Trans. Richard Howard. New York: Hill and Wang, 1978.

————. *The Pleasure of the Text.* Trans. Richard Miller. New York: Noonday Press, 1980.

Bataille, Georges. *Erotism: Death and Sensuality.* Trans. Mary Dalwood. San Francisco: City Lights Books, 1986.

————. *Guilty.* Trans. Bruce Boone. Venice, Calif.: Lapis Press, 1988.

————. *Inner Experience.* Trans. Leslie Ann Boldt. Albany: State University of New York Press, 1988.

————. *On Nietzsche.* Trans. Bruce Boone. New York: Paragon House, 1994.

Baudelaire, Charles. *Flowers of Evil.* Ed. James McGowan. New York: Oxford University Press, 1998.

Baudrillard, Jean. *Seduction.* Trans. Brian Singer. New York: St. Martin's Press, 1990.

Blanchot, Maurice. *The Infinite Conversation.* Trans. Susan Hanson. Minneapolis: University of Minnesota Press, 1993.

————. *The Step Not Beyond.* Trans. Lycette Nelson. Albany: State University of New York Press, 1992.

————. *The Writing of the Disaster.* Trans. Ann Smock. Lincoln: University of Nebraska Press, 1986.

Body Modification Ezine: http://www.bme.freeq.com/.

Burrus, Virginia. *The Sex Lives of Saints: An Erotics of Ancient Hagiography.* Philadelphia: University of Pennsylvania Press, 2003.

Bynum, Carolyn Walker. *Fragmentation and Redemption: Essays on Gender and the Human Body in Medieval Religion.* New York: Zone Books, 1992.

————. *The Resurrection of the Body in Western Christianity, 200–1336.* New York: Columbia University Press, 1995.

Caputo, John D., and Michael Scanlon, eds. *God, the Gift, and Postmodernism.* Indianapolis: Indiana University Press, 1999.

Carroll, Michael. *The Cult of the Virgin Mary.* Princeton: Princeton University Press, 1986.

Catholic Encyclopedia. Online version: http://www.newadvent.org/cathen/.

The Catholic Study Bible. New York: Oxford University Press, 1990.

Celan, Paul. *Collected Prose.* Trans. Rosmarie Waldrop. Riverdale-on-Hudson, N.Y.: Sheep Meadow Press, 1986.

————. *Poems of Paul Celan.* Trans. Michael Hamburger. New York: Persea Books, 1988.

Cioran, E. M. *Tears and Saints.* Trans. Ilenca Zarifopol-Johnston. Chicago: University of Chicago Press, 1996.

Cixous, Hélène. *The Cixous Reader.* Ed. Susan Sellers. New York: Routledge, 1996.

Classen, Constance. *Worlds of Sense.* New York: Routlege, 1993.

Collins, Jerry. *Sailor Jerry Collins.* Ed. Don Ed Hardy. Honolulu: Hardy Marks Publications, 1994.

Deleuze, Gilles. *The Fold: Leibniz and the Baroque.* Trans. Tom Conley. Minneapolis: University of Minnesota Press, 1993.

———. *Foucault.* Trans. Sean Hand. Minneapolis: University of Minnesota Press, 1988.

———. *Kant's Critical Philosophy.* Trans. Hugh Tomlinson and Barbara Habberjam. Minneapolis: University of Minnesota Press, 1993.

———. *Negotiations 1972–1990.* New York: Columbia University Press, 1997.

———. *Nietzsche and Philosophy.* Trans. Hugh Tomlinson. New York: Columbia University Press, 1983.

Deleuze, Gilles, and Felix Guattari. *Anti-Oedipus.* Trans. Helen R. Lane and Robert Hurley. Minneapolis: University of Minnesota Press, 1985.

Deleuze, Gilles and Claire Parnet. *Dialogues.* Trans. Hugh Tomlinson and Barbara Habberjam. New York: Columbia University Press, 1987.

DeMello, Margo. *Bodies of Inscription: A Cultural History of the Modern Tattoo Community.* Durham, N.C.: Duke University Press, 2000.

Derrida, Jacques. *Dissemination.* Trans. Barbara Johnson. Chicago: University of Chicago Press, 1981.

———. "Economimesis." *Diacritics* 11 (June 1981): 3–25.

———. *Glas.* Trans. John P. Leavey, Jr., and Richard Rand. Lincoln: University of Nebraska Press, 1986.

———. "Le toucher: Touch / To Touch Him." Trans. Peggy Kamuf. *Paragraph* 16, no. 2 (July 1993): 122–57.

———. *Writing and Difference.* Trans. Alan Bass. Chicago: University of Chicago Press, 1980.

Descartes, René. *Meditations on First Philosophy.* Trans. Donald A. Cress Indianapolis: Hackett, 1993.

Eckhart, Meister Johannes. *The Best of Meister Eckhart.* Ed. Halcyon Backhouse. New York: Crossroad Publishing, 1995.

———. *Meister Eckhart: Teacher and Preacher.* Ed. Bernard McGinn. New York: Paulist Press, 1986.

Eliot, T. S. *Four Quartets.* New York: Harvest Books. 1974.

———. *Selected Poems.* New York: Harcourt Brace Jovanovich. 1988.

Ferguson, Henry, and Lynn Procter. *The Art of the Tattoo.* Philadelphia: Courage Books, 1998.

Foucault, Michel. *Archaeology of Knowledge.* Trans. A. M. Sheridan Smith. New York: Pantheon, 1972.

―――. *Discipline and Punish.* Trans. Alan Sheridan. New York: Vintage Books, 1995.

―――. *Foucault Live.* Ed. Sylvère Lotringer. Trans. Lysa Hochroth and John Johnston. New York: Semiotext(e), 1996.

―――. "Langage è l'infini." *Tel Quel* 15 (1963): 44–53.

―――. *Madness and Civilization.* New York: Vintage Books, 1988.

―――. *The Order of Things.* New York: Random House. 1970.

―――. "Preface à transgression." *Critique* 195–96 (1963): 751–70.

Freud, Sigmund. *Civilization and Its Discontents.* Trans. James Strachey. New York: W. W. Norton, 1961.

―――. *The Ego and the Id.* Trans. Joan Riviere. New York: W. W. Norton, 1960.

Gemerchak, Christopher. *The Sunday of the Negative.* Albany: State University of New York Press, 2003.

"Good God Almighty." *Tattoo World* I, no. I (1994): 8.

Gould, Eric, ed. *The Sin of the Book: Edmond Jabès.* Lincoln: University of Nebraska Press, 1985.

Gregory of Nyssa. *Commentary on the Song of Songs* and *Gregory the Wonderworker.* At http://www.bhsu.edu/dsalomon/nyssa/epekt.html.

Heidegger, Martin. *Basic Writings.* Ed. David Farrell Krell. New York: Harper and Row, 1977.

Heller, Dana, ed. *Cross Purposes: Lesbians, Feminists and the Limits of Alliance.* Bloomington: Indiana University Press, 1997.

Hölderlin, Friedrich. *Selected Poems and Fragments.* Trans. Michael Hamburger. Ann Arbor: University of Michigan Press, 1968.

Hollier, Denis. *Against Architecture.* Boston: MIT Press, 1992.

International Tattoo Art. January 2000.

Irigaray, Luce. *The Irigaray Reader.* Ed. Margaret Whitford. Oxford: Blackwell, 1991.

―――. *The Way of Love.* Trans. Heidi Bostic and Stephen Pluhácek. New York: Continuum, 2002.

Jaggar, Alison M., and Susan R. Bordo, eds. *Gender/Body/Knowledge: Feminist Reconstructions of Being and Knowing.* New Brunswick, N.J.: Rutgers University Press, 1989.

Josipovici, Gabriel. *Touch.* New Haven: Yale University Press, 1996.

Julian of Norwich, *Revelations of Divine Love.* At http://www.ccel.org/j/julian/revelations/.

Kandinsky, Wasily. "The Spiritual in Art." In Robert Herbert, ed., *Modern Artists on Art: Ten Unabridged Essays.* Garden City, N.J.: Prentice-Hall, 1965: 19–44.

Kant, Immanuel. *Grounding for the Metaphysics of Morals.* Trans. James W. Ellington. Indianapolis: Hackett, 1981.

Kieckhefer, Richard. *Unquiet Souls: Fourteenth Century Saints and Their Religious Milieu.* Chicago: University of Chicago Press, 1984.

Kierkegaard, Søren. *A Kierkegaard Anthology.* Ed. Robert Bretall. Princeton: Princeton University Press, 1946.

Kojève, Alexandre. *Introduction to the Reading of Hegel: Lectures on the Phenomenology of Spirit.* Trans. James H. Nichols, Jr. Ithaca: Cornell University Press, 1980.

Lacan, Jacques. *Écrits: A Selection.* Trans. Alan Sheridan. New York: W. W. Norton, 1977.

Lectionary for Good Friday: http://people.enternet.com.au/~beswick/rclresources/GFABC956799.htm.

Leslie, John. *Fifty Key Contemporary Thinkers.* New York: Routledge, 1994.

Levinas, Emmanuel. *Totality and Infinity: An Essay on Exteriority.* Trans. Alphonso Lingis. Pittsburgh: Duquesne University Press, 1979.

Lovric, Michelle. *How to Write Love Letters.* New York: Shooting Star Press, 1995.

McCabe, Michael. *New York City Tattoo: The Oral History of an Urban Art.* Honolulu: Hardy Marks Publications, 1997.

MacCannell, Juliet Flower, and Laura Zakarin, eds. *Thinking Bodies.* Stanford: Stanford University Press, 1994.

McIntosh, Mark. *Mystical Theology.* Oxford: Blackwell, 1998.

MacKendrick, Karmen. *Immemorial Silence.* Albany: State University of New York Press, 2001.

Marche Noir: http://www.marchenoir.com/homea.html.

Merleau-Ponty, Maurice. *The Visible and the Invisible.* Trans. Alphonso Lingis. Evanston: Northwestern University Press, 1968.

Merton, Thomas. *What Are These Wounds? The Life of a Cistercian Mystic, Saint Lutgarde of Aywières.* Milwaukee: Bruce Publishing Co., 1950.

Mirandola, Pico della. *Oration on the Dignity of Man.* Washington, D.C.: Regnery Gateway, 1956.

Monks of Adoration. History of the Sacred Heart. At http://www.monksofadoration.org/.

Moore, Stephen. *God's Gym: Divine Male Bodies of the Bible.* New York: Routledge, 1996.

———. *Post Structuralism and the New Testament: Derrida and Foucault at the Foot of the Cross.* Minneapolis: Fortress Press, 1994.

Nancy, Jean-Luc. *Being Singular Plural.* Trans. Robert D. Richardson and Anne E. O'Byrne. Stanford: Stanford University Press, 2000.

———. *The Birth to Presence.* Trans. Brian Holmes et al. Stanford: Stanford University Press, 1993.

———. *The Inoperative Community.* Ed. Peter Connor. Minneapolis: University of Minnesota Press, 1991.

———. "The Intruder." Trans. Anne E. O'Byrne. Manuscript.

Nietzsche, Friedrich. *Beyond Good and Evil.* Trans. Walter Kaufman. New York: Vintage Books, 1989.

———. *The Birth of Tragedy.* In *The Birth of Tragedy and the Genealogy of Morals.* Trans. Francis Golffing. New York: Anchor Books, 1956.

———. *Ecce Homo.* Trans. R. J. Hollingdale. New York: Penguin Books, 1993.

———. *The Gay Science.* Trans. Walter Kaufmann. New York: Vintage Books, 1974.

———. *Twilight of the Idols and The Anti-Christ.* Trans. R. J. Hollingdale, New York: Penguin Books, 1968.

———. *Will to Power.* Trans. Walter Kaufmann and R. J. Hollingdale. New York: Vintage Books, 1968.

Ockham, William of. *Quodlibita.* In *Ockham: Philosophical Writings, a Selection.* Ed. and trans. Philotheus Boehner, O.F.M. New York: Thomas Nelson and Sons, 1957.

Origen. *First Principles.* Trans. G. W. Butterworth. Gloucester, Mass.: Peter Smith, 1973.

Parry, Albert. *Tattoo: Secrets of a Strange Art as Practiced by Natives of the United States.* New York: Collier Books, 1933.

Plato. *The Collected Dialogues of Plato.* Ed. Edith Hamilton and Huntington Cairns. Princeton: Princeton University Press, 1961.

Plotinus. *Enneads.* Trans. Stephen MacKenna. New York: Penguin Books, 1991.

———. *Plotinus VII: Ennead VI Books 6–9.* Trans. A. H. Armstrong. Cambridge: Harvard University Press, 1989.

Proust, Marcel. *Remembrance of Things Past.* Trans. C. K. Scott Moncrieff and Terence Kilmartin. New York: Vintage Books, 1982.

Rilke, Rainer Maria. *The Selected Poetry of Rainer Maria Rilke.* Trans. Stephen Mitchell. New York: Vintage Books, 1989.

Saussure, Ferdinand de. *Course in General Linguistics.* Trans. Roy Harris. Chicago: Open Court Publishing, 1988.

Slattery, Dennis Patrick. *The Wounded Body: Remembering the Markings of Flesh.* Albany: State University of New York Press, 2000.

Stabat Mater: Religious Background. http://www.stabatmater.dds.nl/.

Tattoo Energy, no. 2. Verve Press, 2000.

Taylor, Mark C. *Hiding.* Chicago: University of Chicago Press, 1997.

Vasseleu, Catherine. *Textures of Light: Vision and Touch in Irigaray, Levinas and Merleau-Ponty.* New York: Routledge, 1998.

Webb, Stephen. *Blessed Excess: Religion and the Hyperbolic Imagination.* Albany: State University of New York Press, 1993.

Williams, Margaret, R.S.C.J. *The Sacred Heart in the Life of the Church.* New York: Sheed and Ward, 1957.

Winterson, Jeanette. *The Powerbook.* New York: Vintage Books, 2001.

———. *Written on the Body.* New York: Vintage Books, 1994.

Wittgenstein, Ludwig. *The Wittgenstein Reader.* Ed. Anthony Kenny. Oxford: Blackwell, 1994.

Index

Color, 80–81

Comic element, 130

Communication, 3–4, 23, 150, 159, 166–68, 172; articulation and, 142; Bataille on, 155–56; and the cut, 140; desire and, 164; memory and, 157; and touch, 50, 62, 63–70

Completion, 69

Comprehension, 7

Computer screens, 152

Confessions (Augustine), 55–56

Congregation of Rites, 120

Constantine, Emperor, 131

Consumption, 66, 109

Conversation, 94, 100, 142, 151, 164, 165

"Conversation about Dante" (Mandelstam), 171

"Corona" (Celan), 55

"Corpus" (Nancy), 24, 49, 127, 141, 162

Council of Trent, 120

Creation, 42, 46

"Critical Languages" (Acker), 170–71

Crucifixion, 30, 45, 46, 74, 118, 119

Culture: and biology, 111; and nature, 149

Cut, 2, 7, 9, 11, 23, 137–60, 170; and disruption, 141–46; and fold, 142; and fragmentation, 141–46; and inscription, 146–52; and language, 138, 141, 151, 157; and sacred hearts, 115–36; and scars, 152–60; and silence, 142–43; and wounds, 152–60. *See also* Scars; Wounds

Daedalus, 108

Damnation, 77, 89

Dance, 10, 99, 101, 171

Dante, 171

Darkness, 27, 28, 79, 81

Death, 11, 17, 30, 32, 44, 81, 83, 139, 142, 143. *See also* Crucifixion; Resurrection

Deleuze, Gilles, 5, 6, 10, 11, 38, 77; on articulation, 96, 101, 102; on desire, 12, 13, 19–20, 23–24, 40–42; on fold, 23, 72–74, 78–79, 80, 82–83, 89;

94–95, 104–9, 112, 113; on Foucault, 97, 98; on power, 98, 99; and psychoanalysis, 21; quoted, 9, 85, 91, 161

DeMello, Margo, 132

Dermographism, 192*n*3

Derrida, Jacques, 162; on Bataille, 107, 142–43; and cut, 139, 144, 158; on Nancy, 23; quoted, 116; on touch, 59, 62, 64, 66; on writing, 139, 150

Descartes, René, 37

Desire, 1, 2, 9, 53, 62, 104, 109, 168, 169, 172; aim of, 17; as annihilation, 66, 107; in "Ash Wednesday," 76, 78, 87, 89; Augustine and, 167; Christ and, 27; and consumption, 109; divine, 57, 123; and excess, 113, 163; figures of, 161–73; and fold, 91, 106; in John (Gospel), 16, 26, 35–40, 41–42, 51, 52, 78; as lack, 13, 14, 17, 18, 19–20, 22, 40–41, 164; and language, 146; and limits, 2, 4, 6, 11, 12–24, 50, 57, 162, 166; object of, 17, 18, 20, 66; and power, 10, 164; sacred character of, 163; and self, 164–65, 173; theories of, 9–12, 14; and touch, 58, 65, 106, 112; and truth, 30; wrapture and, 110, 112

Despair, 79

Destruction, 168

Devotion, 78, 124; ascetic, 128; to the Passion, 119; to sacred hearts, 116–20, 120–21, 122–23; and tattooing, 134; to wounds of Christ, 117

Difference, 162

Dionysus, 6, 41, 42, 45, 170

Diotima, 13

Disciples, 117

Discontinuity, 64–65

Discourse, 10, 11, 96, 97, 100, 141, 147; amorous, 53; doubleness of, 63; erotic, 51, 59; religious, 128

Disruption, 137, 138, 139, 141–46, 147, 156, 159

Dissemination (Derrida), 158

Distance, 60, 106, 107, 142, 168

Fragmentation, 6, 7, 105, 123, 138, 140, 141–46, 159; as evil, 142, 147; of Sacred Heart, 130
Fragmentation and Redemption (Bynum), 125
Freedom, 35–40, 85, 101–2
Freud, Sigmund, 15–18, 20, 21, 64, 66, 166, 167

Gallop, Jane, 168
"The Garden of Forking Paths" (Borges), 71, 92–93
The Gay Science (Nietzsche), 4, 54
Gender, 72, 88, 89, 111, 116, 126, 127, 148, 149; and sacred hearts, 124–25
Genealogy, 7, 10, 95, 98
Gertrude the Great, Saint, 122, 125
Gilbert of Hoyland, 123–24
God, 16, 67–68, 106, 167, 168, 170, 177n50; in "Ash Wednesday," 77, 81, 84–85, 87; Cixous and, 162–63; and creation, 113; flesh of, 159; in John (Gospel), 25–47; Nancy and, 24, 69, 100, 129, 162, 166; Nietzsche and, 22; and St. Augustine, 55–56; will of, 37
Gods, 13, 23, 53
God's Gym (Moore), 115, 171–72
Goethe, Johann, 96
Good Friday, 85, 119
Goodness, 28
Gospels, 172. *See also* John (Gospel); Luke (Gospel)
Grace, 41, 88, 135, 160
Graham, Martha, 99
Graphosomatology, 127, 159
Grasp, 7, 165; and desire, 11; and faith, 40; and fold, 92; and love, 53; and sacred, 160; and touch, 3, 31, 47, 52, 58, 65, 67–68, 106, 167, 170
Gratification, 19
Gregory of Nyssa, 41, 42, 153
Grishaw, Jane, 148, 149
Grosz, Elisabeth, 69
Guadalupe, Our Lady of, 121, 132
Guattari, Felix, 12, 13, 19–20, 21, 23, 161

Hadewijch, 125
"Hail Holy Queen," 81, 84
"Hail Mary," 76
Happiness, 38
Healing, 33, 34, 35, 36, 44, 112, 139, 153, 155
Hearing, 29, 32, 40, 57, 64, 68, 70, 109; and truth, 29–30
Heart of Mary. *See* Heart of Sorrows; Immaculate Heart; Sacred hearts
Heart of Sorrows, 116–17, 119. *See also* Sacred hearts
Hearts: exchange of, 125–26, 128. *See also* Sacred hearts
Hegel, Georg, 14, 15, 17, 18, 61, 169, 177n50
Heidegger, Martin, 8, 77, 151
Henning, Michelle, 111
Heraclitus, 5
Heresy, 26
Heterosexuality, 147
Hiding (Taylor), 126, 130
Hold: and touch, 31
Holiness, 46
Hollier, Denis, 97
Holy Spirit, 29, 32, 46
Holy Week, 74
Hope, 76, 79, 81, 85, 87, 88
How to Write Love Letters, 51
Human: and divine, 68
Humans, 13
Hussites, 119
Hyperbole, 128, 134, 135, 172
Hysteria, 148, 192n3

Id, 178n51
Identity, 143, 154, 155, 157, 159
Idolatry, 117–18, 123, 138
If on a Winter's Night a Traveler (Calvino), 1
Ignatius Loyola, Saint, 186n25
Illumination, 28
Imitation, 118
Immaculate Heart, 116–17, 120, 142. *See also* Sacred hearts

Quiddity, 5

Rationality, 38
Raymond of Capua, 126
Reading, 2, 3, 68, 109, 143, 164, 171; and
    cut, 139, 149–50; and libraries, 93–94;
    and touch, 51, 68
Reason, 37, 38, 97
Receptivity, 96–97, 165
Recollection, 185n12
Redemption, 46, 77, 147; in "Ash
    Wednesday," 85–89
"Refiguring Lesbian Desire" (Grosz), 69
Religion, 43, 51, 67, 135, 167, 178n52
Religious expression, 128
Religious symbols, 131, 135
REM, 96
Rembrandt, 8
Remembrance of Things Past (Proust), 57–58
Renunciation, 76
Repetition, 50, 52–55, 62, 68, 69, 81, 89,
    161; and fold, 92, 112–14; in language,
    58; and prayer, 53, 59; and touch,
    52–55, 93, 112
Resignation, 76, 79, 87–88
Response, 62, 100, 101
Resurrection, 26, 30, 31, 32, 34, 35, 36,
    40, 43, 87, 165
*The Resurrection of the Body in Western
    Christianity* (Bynum), 35
Rhythm, 9–10, 53–54, 58, 69
Rilke, Rainer Maria, 17, 168
Rolland, Romain, 178n52

Sacred, 57, 59, 88, 128; and desire, 163;
    and profane, 45, 51, 68, 79, 83, 87, 89,
    92, 129, 135, 160, 168; and tattooing,
    134
Sacred Heart (Christ's), 2, 115–36, 159,
    160
Sacred hearts, 115–36, 137, 142, 156;
    excess and, 128–30; history of,
    116–21; and inside outness, 126–28;
    and tattooing, 130–36
Salvaggio, Ruth, 147
Sarkic desire, 38

Satisfaction, 16, 19, 41, 164–65
Saussure, Ferdinand de, 162
Scars, 7, 11, 129, 136, 137, 138, 142,
    144, 149; and cut, 152–60
"The Scission" (Derrida), 158
Scriptures, 128. *See also* John (Gospel)
Sculpture, 73
Seduction, 112
Seeing, 28, 36
Segmentarity, 99
Self, 2, 13, 16, 17, 21, 23, 60, 63, 77,
    107, 166, 172; and body, 153, 156;
    boundaries of, 146; communication
    and, 140; and cut, 142, 144, 145; and
    desire, 20, 163, 164–65, 173;
    displacement of, 159; and Lacan,
    18–19; limits of, 135; and world, 14,
    101, 113, 139, 156
Self-abandonment, 169
Self-completion, 13
Self-containment, 154, 172
Self-exceeding, 129–30
Self-expression, 101
Selfhood, 15, 17, 19, 124, 167
Self-possession, 164
Self-sufficiency, 107, 111
Senses, 111, 162; in "Ash Wednesday," 87;
    Augustine and, 56; and desire, 53; in
    John (Gospel), 29, 43, 44, 45, 46; light
    and, 96; touch and, 54, 60–62
Sequentiality, 44
Sex, 111, 127, 128
The Sex Lives of Saints (Burrus), 75
Sexuality, 11
Sexual politics, 148
Shapiro, Gary, 25, 139, 140
Shiffermacher, Henk, 133
Sight, 27, 28–29, 31, 32, 33, 40, 54, 57
Silence, 97, 99, 104, 106, 142–43, 145,
    151, 157
Simeon, 118, 119
Simon Peter, 30–31, 32, 39–40
Sin, 89, 135; communication as, 140; and
    cut, 158
Skin, 8, 23, 24, 66, 165, 170; and cut,
    150; and fold, 95, 110; language as, 64;

Nancy and, 46–47; sacred hearts and, 135, 136; and touch, 57, 68. *See also* Tattooing

"Skin Deep: Lesbian Interventions in Language" (Salvaggio), 147

Slattery, Dennis Patrick, 153, 155, 156, 157

Smoothness, 100

Socrates, 5, 6, 13, 15

Sollers, Philippe, 139, 158

"A Song for Simeon" (Eliot), 121–22

Sorrows, 119, 120

Soul, 14, 42, 80, 85, 113, 126, 144; and body, 27, 34, 45, 109, 118; and desire, 109; and wounds, 157

Sound, 27, 31, 57

Speaking, 64, 67, 69, 170; and cut, 139–42, 144, 150–51, 156; and divine, 128; and fold, 99, 100–103, 105, 109; Foucault and, 10; in John (Gospel), 32, 36, 40; of love, 51, 55; and touch, 57, 68, 164

Speech, 8, 10, 14, 44, 51, 97, 99, 138, 156, 172

Spirit, 27; and body, 32

"Spiritual Exercises" (Ignatius Loyola), 186*n*25

Spontaneity, 96–97

Stabat Mater, 120

Stairs, 78–79

Stations of the Cross, 119

Stein, Gertrude, 52

Stigmata, 135, 145

Structuralism, 9

Style, 151

Subjectivity, 18, 20, 22, 23, 63, 83, 111

Suffering, 135, 153, 154

Superego, 178*n*51

Superficial, 7

Surfaces, 4, 7–8, 9, 75, 127, 163, 172; communication and, 140; and cut, 138, 146, 152; and discourse, 11; and fold, 73, 93, 95, 98, 103, 108; and inflection, 82, 83; in John (Gospel), 27, 31; limits and, 24; and tattooing, 134;

and touch, 11, 58, 61, 63, 68, 91–92, 112

Suso, Henry, 125

Symposium (Plato), 13, 66

Synaesthesia, 29, 50, 54, 56–58

Taste, 58

Tattooing, 115–16, 130–36, 144, 145, 149; Christian imagery in, 130, 131, 132, 133; Latino, 132, 133; New School, 133

Tattoo Museum, 132

Taylor, Mark, 83, 126, 130, 136, 138, 139, 143, 169

Textuality, 158

Thanatos, 17

Theology, 5, 14, 66, 67, 76

Thomas (apostle), 33, 34, 35, 36, 39, 40, 42, 44, 101

Thought from the Outside (Foucault), 59

"Thunder, Perfect Mind," 79

Time, 54, 55, 63, 69; in "Ash Wednesday," 75–79, 83, 84; and cut, 157, 158; and fold, 113; in John (Gospel), 35–36, 39, 43, 44; and touch, 58

Tomiche, Anne, 139

"To Touch" (Derrida), 116

Touch, 2, 3, 7, 49–70, 129, 137, 164, 170, 171; and articulation, 103; and communication, 50, 62, 63–70; and desire, 58, 65, 106, 112; and flesh, 27, 153; and fold, 91–92, 106, 107, 110, 113; and fragmentation, 123; and grasp, 3, 31, 47, 52, 58, 65, 67–68, 106, 167, 170; and hold, 31; in John (Gospel), 27, 29, 30–32, 33–34, 36, 40, 44–45, 46, 47, 160; and language, 50, 51, 54, 62, 65, 104–5; and limits, 59–63, 67, 68; Nancy and, 23, 44–45, 51, 57, 60, 66, 68, 110; and repetition, 52–55, 93, 112; surfaces and, 11, 58, 61, 63, 68, 91–92, 112; and synaesthesia, 56–58

"Le Toucher" (Derrida), 23

Transcendence, 168

Transfigurations, 22, 42; of faith, 40–47; and tattooing, 134

Transformation, 6, 22, 27, 40, 41, 47, 82; of body, 148–49

Transgression, 21, 128, 129, 135, 148; and tattooing, 134

Transversal, 87

Trinity, 29, 39, 46, 84, 185n6

Truth, 5, 6, 7, 46, 67, 77–78, 95, 163; and desire, 30; and goodness, 28; and hearing, 29–30; in John (Gospel), 30; and light, 28, 29

Tuttle, Lyle, 132

Twilight of the Idols (Nietzsche), 21–22

Union, 64, 66, 68, 110

Unity, 6, 17, 78, 136

Universals, 5, 6

Vagina, 185n13

Violence, 139, 140, 142, 144, 146, 152, 154, 158

Virginity, 83, 185n13

Virtue, 37–38, 76, 154; scars as, 142

Visibility, 96, 98

The Visible and the Invisible (Merleau-Ponty), 9, 56

Vision, 33, 40, 46, 47, 56

Visions, 120, 121; of Christ's wounds, 122; of the Sacred Heart, 121–25; of wounds, 127

Voluntarism, 38

Vulnerability, 157, 164

Water, 117, 127, 159

Webb, Steven, 128, 135, 159

Wholeness, 19

Will, 35–40, 46, 167

William of Ockham, 36–37, 39

Will to power, 21, 41, 45

Wilton, Tamsin, 111, 148, 149

Wine, 125

Winterson, Jeanette, 53–54, 56, 63, 165

Wisdom, 4–5, 6, 7, 11, 14–15

Wittgenstein, Ludwig, 7–8, 9, 67, 104

Women, 108, 111, 120

Word, 83, 84, 128, 129; in John (Gospel), 25–47; made Flesh, 24, 25–47, 73, 97, 121, 159

Words, 2, 3–4, 94, 135, 139, 146, 167, 170; and articulation, 102, 103, 113, 164; in "Ash Wednesday," 83, 84, 85, 87, 88, 89; and blood, 145; and body, 2, 7, 70, 111, 139, 143, 165–66; and cut, 112, 142, 152; and desire, 10; and flesh, 8–9, 12, 15, 50, 95, 127; and fold, 94, 100, 106, 110, 111, 113, 114; Freud on, 16; inadequacy of, 105; and memory, 16; and repetition, 10, 68; and touch, 51, 64, 66, 69; and wounds, 155; and writing, 149, 151

"The Words to Say It" (Acker), 75

World: self and, 14, 101, 113, 139, 156; words and, 170

The Wounded Body (Slattery), 153

Wounds, 22, 164, 170; Christ's, 33–34, 36, 40, 45–46, 117, 123–24, 124–25; cut and, 137, 138, 142, 145, 152–60; sacred hearts and, 116, 118, 126, 128–29; tattooing and, 134; visions of, 122, 127. *See also* Cut; Scars

Wrapture, 92, 106–12, 137

Writing, 2–3, 59, 67, 105, 109, 135, 150, 164, 170, 171; and articulation, 102–3; on body, 127, 128, 148, 149, 151, 158; and cut, 138–39, 141–42, 144, 146, 150–51, 155, 157; and fold, 94; and love, 53, 59; and movement, 57, 58, 101; Nancy and, 2, 127, 159; and touch, 51, 53, 63–64, 68

The Writing of the Disaster (Blanchot), 168

Written on the Body (Winterson), 53–54

Zechariah, 119

Zeno, 107, 162

Zizek, Slavoj, 62–63

DATE DUE